The Black Newspaper and the Chosen Nation

The Black Newspaper and the Chosen Nation

# The Black Newspaper and the Chosen Nation

BENJAMIN FAGAN

The University of Georgia Press   Athens

A Sarah Mills Hodge Fund Publication
This publication is made possible in part through a grant
from the Hodge Foundation in memory of its founder,
Sarah Mills Hodge, who devoted her life to the relief and
education of African Americans in Savannah, Georgia.

Paperback edition, 2018
© 2016 by the University of Georgia Press
Athens, Georgia 30602
www.ugapress.org
All rights reserved
Set in Minion Pro by Graphic Composition, Inc., Bogart, GA

Most University of Georgia Press titles are
available from popular e-book vendors.

Printed digitally

The Library of Congress has cataloged the
hardcover edition of this book as follows:

Names: Fagan, Benjamin author.
Title: The black newspaper and the chosen nation / Benjamin Fagan.
Description: Athens : The University of Georgia Press, 2016. | Includes
    bibliographical references and index.
Identifiers: LCCN 2015037495 | ISBN 9780820349404 (hardcover : alk. paper) |
    ISBN 9780820349398 (e-book)
Subjects: LCSH: African American press—History—19th century. | African
    American newspapers—History—19th century. | Press and politics—
    United States—History—19th century.
Classification: LCC PN4882.5 .F35 2016 | DDC 071.3089/96073—dc23 LC record
    available at http://lccn.loc.gov/2015037495

Paperback ISBN 978-0-8203-5469-9

For my parents. All of them.

# Contents

Acknowledgments  ix

*Introduction.* The Records of Black Chosenness  1

*Chapter 1.* Acting Chosen  20

*Chapter 2.* Prophecies for a Chosen Nation  42

*Chapter 3.* Revolutionary Chosenness  71

*Chapter 4.* The Limits of Black Chosenness  95

*Chapter 5.* Joining the Chosen Army  119

*Conclusion.* The Ends of Black Chosenness  142

Notes  149
Index  179

## Acknowledgments

This book has been inspired and supported by numerous individuals and institutions, and I am grateful for the opportunity to name and thank them here. Deborah McDowell not only first suggested that I explore the archive of early black newspapers and guided this project from its inception but also taught me through her example what it means to be an ethical scholar. For that lesson, especially, I will always be grateful. Eric Lott, Anna Brickhouse, and Matthew Hedstrom all helped shape this project from its beginnings, and I continue to rely upon their guidance and support. Kathleen Diffley first introduced me to periodicals when I was a student in her undergraduate seminar, and I am grateful to now be able to count her as a dear friend. A community of scholars working in and around black print culture studies has inspired and encouraged me throughout this project. For their example and support I would like to thank John Ernest, P. Gabrielle Foreman, Eric Gardner, Joycelyn Moody, and Carla Peterson. And while I know her only through her scholarship, I owe a profound debt of gratitude to Frances Smith Foster for her pathbreaking work.

A number of institutions have provided crucial support for this project. A fellowship at the Carter G. Woodson Institute for African American and African Studies at the University of Virginia allowed me to finish my dissertation, and the Visiting Scholars program at the American Academy of Arts and Sciences provided me with invaluable resources as I began the book manuscript. A Joyce Tracy Fellowship from the American Antiquarian Society allowed me to conduct essential research for this project, and a Robert C. and Sandra Connor Fellowship from the University of Arkansas assisted with important travel. I am deeply grateful to the National Endowment for the Humanities for giving me the opportunity to spend a semester at the Library Company of Philadelphia, where I completed this project. In visiting a variety of institutions, I have acquired debts to a long list of incredible people. For their friendship and support, I want to especially thank Paul Erickson at the American Antiquarian Society; Marlon Ross and Cheryll Lewis at the Carter G. Woodson Institute; James Green, Krystal Appiah, Linda August, Connie King, and Charlene Knight at the Library Company of Philadelphia; and Patricia Meyer Spacks, Mary Maples Dunn, and John Tessitore at the American Academy of Arts and Sciences.

A much earlier version of chapter 2 appeared first as an article in *American Periodicals* 21, no. 2 (Fall 2011): 97–119; and a section of chapter 4 first appeared in *African American Review* 47, no. 1 (Spring 2014): 51–67 (copyright © 2014 St. Louis University and The Johns Hopkins University Press). I would like to thank the Ohio State University Press and the Johns Hopkins University Press, respectively, for permission to include revised versions of those articles in this book. I would also like to thank the New York Public Library, the Library Company of Philadelphia, and the Library and Archives Canada for permission to include images from their holdings.

Feedback from numerous friends and colleagues has made this a vastly better book. I am especially grateful to Patricia Meyer Spacks for her careful attention to this manuscript in its early stages and also for her encouragement that I write a very different kind of book than I had originally intended. A Mellon-Sawyer workshop at the Robert Penn Warren Center for the Humanities at Vanderbilt University provided an invaluable opportunity for me to share my work, and I am grateful to Richard Blackett, Teresa Goddu, and Jane Landers for organizing this workshop. I would also like to thank the fellows at the Woodson Institute, American Antiquarian Society, American Academy of Arts and Sciences, and Library Company of Philadelphia for their attention to my work in progress. At the University of Arkansas, the English faculty writing group, organized by Vivian Davis, provided invaluable suggestions; and conversations with Calvin White and James Gigantino, friends and colleagues in African and African American Studies, helped me better understand the stakes of my project. Robin Bernstein, whom I first met while I was just beginning this work, always took the time to answer questions big and small and provided me with key insights at a critical late stage of the manuscript. I am grateful to Heike Paul and Nicole Waller for inviting me to share my work with audiences at the University of Nurnberg-Erlangen and the University of Potsdam. For graciously agreeing to read sections of my manuscript I would like to thank John Barnard, Kathleen Diffley, Eric Gardner, Teresa Goddu, Matthew Hedstrom, Brian Roberts, Matthew Rubery, Martha Schoolman, Jolie Sheffer, Janice Simon, and Derrick Spires. I would also like to thank Walter Biggins, Jon Davies, and Beth Snead at the University of Georgia Press for shepherding this project to publication, and Kay Kodner for her meticulous copyediting. I am deeply indebted to Trish Loughran and an anonymous reader for the press, both of whom offered invaluable feedback on my proposal and sample chapters as well as the completed manuscript.

I could not have completed this project without my family. To my father Jack and stepmother Sharon, sister Kara and brother Derek, late mother Elaine and her partner Roberta, I owe a debt of love and gratitude that can never be repaid. But I'll keep trying. Finally, I would like to thank Juliane Braun, my partner in all things, without whom none of this would be possible.

# The Black Newspaper and the Chosen Nation

"The Black Newspaper and the Chosen Nation

## Introduction

### THE RECORDS OF BLACK CHOSENNESS

We lead the forlorn hope of Human Equality, let us tell of its onslaught on the battlements of hate and caste, let us record its triumphs in a Press of our own.
—"Report of the Committee on a National Press," 1847

On October 6, 1847, nearly seventy black men gathered in Troy, New York, for the National Convention of Colored People. While most hailed from the northeastern states, delegates arrived from as far west as Michigan and as far south as Kentucky. For four days, attendees discussed issues of education, commerce, agriculture, and, of course, the "Best means to Abolish Slavery and Caste in the United States."[1] But before taking up any of these crucial questions, delegates engaged in a fierce debate over the report from the Committee on a National Press. The committee, led by James McCune Smith, called for the creation of a "national" newspaper "through which," McCune Smith imagined, "at any and all times the voice of the Colored People may be heard."[2] Some in attendance, though, worried that a designated national newspaper could not be sustained. Thomas Van Rensselaer, for example, feared "that the undertaking was too great to be carried into successful operation."[3] Others expressed concerns that, if successful, such an organ would make it appear that the opinions of a few constituted a national consensus. Arguing this point, Frederick Douglass contended that a "Paper started as a National organ, would soon dwindle down to the organ of a clique."[4] Despite such objections, though, the convention voted overwhelmingly in support of the committee's report.

The fact that the delegates to the 1847 convention chose to tackle the question of a national newspaper first, and spent nearly one-quarter of the convention passionately debating the subject, underscores the pride of place that the black press occupied in antebellum black activism. Indeed, many of the men who argued over a national newspaper were intimately connected to black newspapers. Thomas Van Rensselaer, for example, edited the *Ram's Horn*, and Frederick Douglass had already begun laying the groundwork for his *North Star*, which he would launch before the end of the year. Recognizing such connections, Henry Highland Garnet, who warmly supported a national organ, coyly expressed surprise that the strongest objections to the new paper came from "editors, who are, or are to be," and sarcastically concluded that "[o]f course there was nothing of selfishness in all this."[5] Van Rensselaer and Douglass may very well have worried that a national paper would draw support away from their own publications, but many of those arguing for the proposal had similarly strong connections to the black press. Charles B. Ray, one of the strongest proponents for a national paper, had edited the *Colored American* earlier in the decade, while Garnet himself was a regular contributor to a number of black newspapers. And James McCune Smith, chairman of the Committee on a National Press, served in a variety of roles during a nearly thirty-year engagement with the black press. Exemplary rather than exceptional, such connections illustrate the central role that black newspapers played in antebellum black activism.

The report, produced by the Committee on a National Press, offers a powerful explanation for why antebellum black activists invested so much time and energy in black newspapers. Repeatedly invoking martial metaphors, the report's authors cast the black press as a key weapon in the war against tyranny and oppression. Black Americans needed a newspaper, they wrote, "that shall keep us steadily alive to our responsibilities, which shall constantly point out the principles which should guide our conduct and our labors, which shall cheer us from one end of the land to the other, by recording our acts, our sufferings, our temporary defeats and our steadily approaching triumph—or rather the triumph of the glorious truth 'Human Equality,' whose servants and soldiers we are."[6] Such an account painted the fight for black liberation in the United States as one front in this war for human equality. By providing a record of the "steadily approaching triumph" of black freedom in the United States, then, black newspapers could offer hope and inspiration to all those engaged in this larger cause. For, as the report made clear, black Americans were not merely foot soldiers but indeed stood at the vanguard of the fight for universal freedom. "We lead the forlorn hope of Human Equality," the authors of the report proclaimed, "let us tell of its onslaught on the battlements of hate and caste, let us record its triumphs in a Press of our own."[7] Newspapers produced by and directed toward black Americans engendered such passionate support, then, because they were the medium that could most effectively speak to and for those who led the fight for freedom and equality.

The report produced by the 1847 Committee on a National Press reflects the fact that many black Americans in the antebellum era connected their commitment to establishing and maintaining black newspapers to their belief that black Americans would lead the world to universal emancipation. Such a claim rested on the belief that God had selected black Americans as his chosen people on Earth. *The Black Newspaper and the Chosen Nation* tells the story of how a handful of early black newspapers took up, explored, and shaped this faith in black chosenness. The community of black intellectuals and activists who led and contributed to these publications includes the familiar faces of Frederick Douglass and Mary Ann Shadd, as well those of the less-well-known Samuel Cornish, Charles Ray, and Robert and Thomas Hamilton. In addition to their work as abolitionist agitators, doctors, clergymen, and schoolteachers, these individuals each served as an editor of at least one newspaper. Many edited multiple journals. And in the pages of their papers, these editors applied their faith in black chosenness to specific sites of struggle.

But the journals did more than simply act as containers for the ideas of their editors. Rather, the newspapers' institutional and material forms transformed black chosenness in specific ways, shaping the manner in which editors translated their faith into plans for black liberation. The business of the press brought editors into close contact with printers, publishers, agents, business managers, and correspondents, all of whom had their own visions of chosenness and its relationship to the fight for black freedom and equality. In an issue of a newspaper, an editor collected and arranged the particular voices and viewpoints of the contributors. This chorus provided each newspaper with a distinct personality that transcended the individual ideas of its editor. *The Black Newspaper and the Chosen Nation* examines the interplay of a black newspaper's multiple parts, the ways that the voices of its many makers combined and collided, and how the relationship between black chosenness and black freedom evolved through this process.

In exploring and shaping the contours of black chosenness, black newspapers built on and engaged with a project that had begun decades before the birth of the black press in the United States. In an addendum to their 1794 pamphlet defending the conduct of black Philadelphians during an outbreak of yellow fever, for example, Richard Allen and Absalom Jones subtly asserted black chosenness by drawing a typological association between black Americans and God's original chosen nation, the Israelites. Addressing "Those Who Keep Slaves and Uphold the Practice," the two religious leaders reminded proslavery whites "that God himself was the first pleader of the cause of slaves," urging them, "[w]hen you are pleaded with, do not you reply as Pharaoh did."[8] In his 1810 "Dialogue between a Virginian and an African Minister," the Reverend Daniel Coker made a more explicit claim to black Americans' divine favor. Toward the conclusion of his pamphlet Coker quoted from the First Epistle of Peter: "But ye are a chosen generation, a royal priesthood, and an holy nation."[9] For Jones, Allen, and Coker, black Americans' special status could be used to help convince whites to abandon their support of slavery.

Chosenness was not simply a status to be enjoyed and proclaimed; black religious leaders consistently reminded their brethren that chosenness carried with it a particular set of responsibilities. William Miller built his 1810 sermon celebrating the anniversary of the abolition of the slave trade around a passage from the book of Joel: "PRAISE THE NAME OF THE LORD YOUR GOD THAT HATH DEALT WONDERFULLY WITH YOU; AND MY PEOPLE SHALL NEVER BE ASHAMED."[10] At the conclusion of his remarks, Miller drew the familiar parallel between black Americans and the Israelites as he explained that "the words [']my people['] is as applicable to those of us that fear God, as it was to the children of Israel in their most favorable standing with God." But like that earlier covenanted community, he concluded, "in order to be numbered among the people of God, it behoves [sic] you to be implicit in his commands."[11] Two years earlier, during a sermon delivered to celebrate the same occasion, Absalom Jones enumerated some of these commands. "Let our conduct be regulated by the precepts of the gospel," he preached, "let us be sober minded, humble, peaceable, temperate in our meats and drinks, frugal in our apparel and in the furniture of our houses, industrious in our occupations, just in all our dealings, and ever ready to honour all men."[12] Linking such behavior to the fight for black liberation, Jones argued that black Americans had a responsibility to "conduct ourselves in such a manner as to furnish no cause of regret to the deliverers of our nation, for their kindness to us." Acting according to divine precepts, then, was not only a way of giving thanks to God, but also in this case to "our benefactors, who, by enlightening the minds of the rulers of the earth, by means of their publications and remonstrances against the trade in our countrymen, have produced the great event we are this day celebrating."[13] To be chosen, for men like Miller and Jones, was to act a certain way. And as Jones especially illustrates, many understood acting chosen as a pathway to black liberation.

Appeals to the special mission and attendant responsibilities of black Americans dovetailed with similar claims to chosenness that white colonists had been making since the seventeenth century. Chosenness became, for white Americans, the foundation of American exceptionalism. In 1630, for example, John Winthrop famously reminded his fellow New England colonists that they had "entered into covenant" with God to create a new holy civilization, a "city upon a hill," that would inspire the world. A century later, Jonathan Edwards saw the First Great Awakening as "the dawning, or at least a prelude of that glorious work of God, so often foretold in scripture, which, in the progress and issue of it, shall renew the world of mankind," and surmised that "there are many things that make it probable that this work will begin in America."[14] Indeed, he concluded, "[t]his new world is probably now discovered, that the new and most glorious state of God's church on earth might commence there; that God might in it begin a new world in a spiritual respect, when he creates the *new heavens* and *new earth*."[15] In the early national period, preachers and politicians transferred claims of American chosenness onto the United States. Casting U.S. Americans as akin to the biblical Israelites, one New England clergyman christened the new nation "God's American Israel," while another imagined that "God hath graciously patronized our cause and taken us under his special care, as he did his ancient covenant people."[16] And in his first inaugural address, Thomas Jefferson assured his fellow citizens that they lived in a "chosen country."[17] American preachers and politicians thus developed their arguments for an exceptionalism limited to the United States, one that cast the nation-state as the "city on a hill" for the rest of the world to aspire to and admire through an existing tradition of American chosenness. And in the early nineteenth century alone, this state-specific American exceptionalism was invoked to justify a range of policies including westward expansion, Indian removal, and racial slavery.[18]

Black chosenness could also appeal to American exceptionalism. But, especially in the antebellum period, black activists rarely accepted the United States as an extension of the American chosen nation. In 1854, for instance, the black activist, author, and newspaper editor Martin Delany proclaimed that "the continent of America was designed by Providence as a reserved asylum for the various oppressed people of the earth, of all races."[19] Delany made this claim in the course of advocating for black emigration from the United States to Central and South America. His "continent of America," then, extended beyond the boundaries of the United States. Moreover, Delany set up an opposition between an "America" providentially designed for the oppressed "of all races" and a U.S. American identity rooted in slavery and white supremacy.

In casting God's chosen people as oppressed Americans, and the United States as their oppressor, Delany picked up on a central theme of black chosenness. As black activists would argue throughout the antebellum era, the suffering that black Americans endured in the United States solidified their connection to the biblical Israelites and thus confirmed their status as God's new chosen nation. Rather than "God's American Israel," black Americans often recognized the United States as an American Egypt.[20] And many, as the activist and religious leader Maria Stewart articulated in an 1833 address, detected a powerful resemblance between the United States, "a seller of slaves and the souls of men," and "the great city of Babylon."[21] Through a variety of biblical typologies, then, theories of black chosenness upended the dominant reading of the United States as the New Jerusalem and, in the process, transformed the very notion of a chosen American nation.

Black chosenness also at times involved a distinctly black exceptionalism that offered an alternative to exceptionalist understandings of the United States or even America more broadly conceived. Being chosen, for some black writers and orators, meant that black people possessed superior gifts and talents that they were destined to share with the world. In his 1854 remarks, for example, Delany contended that "in the true principles of morals, correctness of thought, religion, and law or civil government, there is no doubt but the black race will yet instruct the world."[22] Eight years later, in a speech on "Negro Self-Respect and Pride of Race," T. Morris Chester assured his listeners that black Americans "will eventually radiate this continent with our moral and intellectual grandeur."[23] The mark of chosenness, in these readings, was not primarily residence in a certain location or participation in a particular political entity, but rather membership in the "black race." Being black, more than any other factor, qualified one to be a part of God's chosen nation. This form of black exceptionalism claimed blackness as the marker of chosenness and, by extension, of a special destiny to lead the world to holy perfection.

As the 1847 committee report suggests, black newspapers had a special role to play in the development and transmission of black chosenness. For, while black men and women continued to produce a variety of printed materials throughout the antebellum period, from 1827 on black newspapers became, as Eric Gardner writes, "*the* central publication outlet for many black writers."[24] Beyond providing a space for black writing, the black newspaper offered antebellum black Americans an outlet in the most important medium of their era. Noting the ubiquity of the newspaper in the United States, a British visitor in the mid-1840s remarked that "[o]n board the steamer and on the rail, in the counting-house and the hotel, in the street and in the private dwelling, in the crowded thoroughfare and in the remotest rural district, he is ever sure of finding the newspaper."[25] Recognizing the power that this potential reach endowed upon a newspaper, the leaders of Pennsylvania's 1841 Colored Convention declared that newspapers "tend to impart the same sentiments and the same views to all who read them," and as a result "bring as it were into the society of each other, the most distant places and kingdoms of the earth."[26] Scholars have typically read the newspaper's ability to unite distant peoples as a tool of nation-state formation.[27] But as the Pennsylvania convention minutes reveal, black Americans expected newspapers to create communities that transcended national boundaries. "We imagine the day not far distant," proclaimed attendees at that convention, "when, by the influence of the press, shall be united in one, the whole family of man."[28]

Black editors defined the communities created in and through the pages of their newspapers in a variety of often-contested ways. Membership in a certain race or class, or adherence to a particular revolutionary ideology, could (dis)qualify one as a member of a particular newspaper's community. But early black newspapers never considered allegiance to the government of the United States of America to be something that connected their readers. Indeed, as conditions for nominally free black Americans deteriorated in the decades leading up to the Civil War, black newspapers increasingly worked to bring black Americans into chosen nations that existed independently of, and at times in direct opposition to, the United States. Looking closely at the kinds of communities black newspapers imagined, then, forces us to reconsider the relationship between newspapers and formation of the U.S. nation-state.

As the men and women who would edit, contribute to, and read black newspapers well understood, the newspaper was designed not only to connect readers to a community but also to inspire members of that community to act in a certain way. In 1837 Samuel Cornish argued in the *Colored American* that a weekly newspaper would not only unite black Americans but also "rouse them up"; and in the late 1850s Thomas Hamilton contended in an early number of the *Weekly Anglo-African* that every people required "an especial *organ* of their own, through which to direct the minds, efforts, and actions of their class."[29] Black newspapers could instruct readers in general terms, but the direction they provided would also necessarily relate and respond to current events. As David Ruggles wrote in the first issue of his *Mirror of Liberty*, readers could expect his periodical to "contain facts and arguments, strictures and animadversions upon things as they are; strictures and disquisitions shall be applicable to existing persons and events."[30] Black newspapers taught readers how to act in the world as members of a chosen nation, and these lessons changed and evolved in response to conditions on the ground. So rather than transmitting a singular, static theory, black newspapers shaped and recorded the many practices of a dynamic black chosenness.

Black newspapers also recorded the disagreements within and among black communities that accompanied attempts to define and enforce particular versions of black chosenness. For example, some readers of *Freedom's Journal* roundly rejected that paper's equation of acting chosen with a class-based propriety, while the *Provincial Freeman* considered black chosenness itself to be a barrier to freedom because of the essentialisms (black, American) that could accompany it. But despite their differences, the black newspapers in this study consistently separated being chosen from being a citizen of the United States. This is a crucial and striking feature of the black chosenness that emerges in and through black newspapers, especially since chosenness and the newspaper have traditionally been considered pillars of U.S. nation-state formation. Black newspapers fundamentally upset this narrative by connecting black Americans to chosen communities. These were defined by behavior, condition of oppression, revolutionary ideology, and race but not, until the Emancipation Proclamation, by U.S. citizenship. Papers like the *Colored American* and the *North Star* did at times envision black chosenness saving the United States, but the antebellum black newspapers in this study never saw U.S. citizenship as a requirement for membership in the chosen nation. By placing the early black press at the center of its story, *The Black Newspaper and the Chosen Nation* reveals the sophisticated and nuanced ways in which black men and women used the most powerful medium of their day to imagine and enact a chosen nation that existed in relation to, but ultimately transcended, the United States.

The pages of early black newspapers, then, provide us with a tantalizing record of how black Americans used print to explore pathways for liberation that traveled beyond acceptance into the United States' national community. But newspapers in general, and early black newspapers in particular, can be hard to read. With originals scattered across the country, and digital copies guarded by prohibitive paywalls, the antebellum black press remains a largely inaccessible archive. And even once such barriers have been overcome, the nineteenth-century newspaper page confronts readers with a chaotic mix of shipping tables, political speeches, local reporting, editorials, letters, fiction, and poetry, to say nothing of the various and sundry pieces relegated to a paper's "miscellaneous" column. As Benedict Anderson sighs in *Imagined Communities*, in an exasperated footnote, "[r]eading a newspaper is like reading a novel whose author has abandoned any thought of a coherent plot."[31] The challenges of obtaining and analyzing newspapers may in part explain why many scholars, even when attending to early black cultures of print, tend to sidestep black newspapers.[32] I want to suggest, though, that the lack of attention paid to black newspapers in such work reflects not only the difficulty of researching the early black press but also one unfortunate consequence of mapping the priorities of book history onto the study of African American literature and culture. Early black newspapers are almost entirely absent from dominant histories of the book in the United States. The two volumes of *A History of the Book in America* that cover the antebellum era, for example, make only cursory mention of black newspapers in their sections on periodicals.[33] In her chapter "African American Cultures of Print" in *The Industrial Book 1840–1880*, by contrast, Jeannine DeLombard admirably underscores the importance of black newspapers. However, in a piece charged with covering the entirety of black print culture between 1840 and 1880, DeLombard necessarily moves quickly through her treatment of the early black press.[34] Book historians' tendency to overlook the black press helps explain why black newspapers remain neglected despite a renewed attention to early African American cultures of print.

Unlike book historians, though, experts in African American literature and culture have long devoted a considerable amount of attention to black print in general and black newspapers in particular. Scholars such as Frances Smith Foster, John Ernest, and Elizabeth McHenry have explored a range of subjects, but all emphasize the critical importance of the black press to early African American print culture.[35] Indeed, recognizing the religious dimension of early black newspapers, Foster argues that "[e]arly African-American print culture ... is virtually synonymous with the Afro-Protestant press."[36] This statement, and the tradition from which it emerges, has inspired my decision to write a book focused on the reciprocal relationship between early black newspapers and certain strains of American Christianity. My approach to reading black newspapers has also been shaped by the priorities of African Americanist scholars. For, while deeply interested in print, scholars such as Joycelyn Moody, P. Gabrielle Foreman, and Carla Peterson remind us that books, newspapers, and pamphlets emerge from communities of black writers, orators, editors, and readers, and that the people in these communities understood and engaged with the print that surrounded them in highly sophisticated ways.[37]

In other words, African American literary studies insists not only that we remember the people along with the print but also that our own approaches be shaped by the theories and practices developed by the black men and women who lived with the print we study. The minutes of Colored Conventions, for example, offer revealing accounts of why and how black northerners expected someone to read a newspaper. In 1841 the attendees at Pennsylvania's state convention resolved that, "as newspapers contain, besides the ordinary news of the day, much useful knowledge, which tends to enlighten the understanding and improve the character, we therefore recommend that every family, who can possibly afford it, take one or more well conducted newspapers."[38] This resolution shows how newspapers were understood not simply as carriers of information but, more crucially, as educational instruments. Through reading a newspaper one could grow morally as well as intellectually, thus developing the proper behaviors that, according to men like Absalom Jones, a chosen people needed to maintain. The 1841 resolution also hints at communal reading practices. Each family is advised to take a newspaper, with the understanding that a single paper can be shared among adults and read to children. Black northerners recognized the social nature of newspapers—how they could connect not only individuals across the country but also those that lived under the same roof. My own readings of black newspapers attend to these multiple scales of community formation, showing how newspaper editors and their audiences understood the medium as a way to create connections between readers and listeners at local, national, and international levels.

Black northerners recognized newspaper reading as a public, as well as social, endeavor. In addition to reading newspapers at home with their families, those living in northern cities could find the news in reading rooms designed for quickly perusing a newspaper. An Englishman visiting New York City in the 1830s described a reading room "furnished with papers from every part of the Union, together with those of the Canadas," which were "fastened to high sloping desks, to which the reader is obliged to stand."[39] Such spaces may have welcomed a variety of newspapers, but they did not necessarily offer the same courtesy to black American newspaper readers. Understanding the importance of such public reading spaces for black men and women, David Ruggles established a reading room in 1838 in New York City where, as he wrote in the *Mirror of Liberty*, "those of our citizens who are despised for their complexion and refused admission to public reading rooms generally, may enjoy the rich benefits which such an establishment furnishes."[40] These benefits presumably included the educational content of the papers as well as entry into a physically present community of black newspaper readers. Ruggles's reading room illustrates, then, not only the importance of the public reading of black newspapers but also how such publications could produce communities of men and women who met face to face.

Convention minutes and articles in black newspapers point to how black leaders expected their brethren to obtain and read newspapers. But firsthand accounts of newspaper reading reveal the unexpected ways in which black men and women received and engaged with newspapers. Unfortunately, few diaries and journals from free black northerners (where we might hope to find such accounts) have survived and been archived, a silence that makes it especially difficult to recover the readership of black newspapers.[41] However, numerous descriptions of newspaper reading appear in slave narratives. The experiences of enslaved men and women in the South should not be conflated with those of nominally free black northerners, but the descriptions of newspaper reading in slave narratives help us better understand how unintended readers took up and used newspapers in unexpected ways.

For example, the narratives of Frederick Douglass, Mattie Jackson, and Harriet Jacobs contain detailed passages involving newspaper reading. In their narratives, Douglass, Jackson, and Jacobs are all readers who live outside of the communities imagined by most early American newspapers, and they have limited if any access to the networks that we normally associate with print cultures (spaces like roads and post offices). But nevertheless they understand print and its pathways as necessarily open to revision and manipulation. In each narrative, a newspaper slips the yoke of formal (white) distribution networks and finds its way into the hands of enslaved readers, who read the paper against its intentions. More than just serving as interesting anecdotes, the ways in which these readers obtained, understood, and engaged with newspapers can guide our own readings of the early black press.

Each of these accounts reveals how the very nature of the newspaper invites unintended audiences and counterreadings. As Benedict Anderson has famously observed, one of the defining features of the newspaper is its "ephemeral popularity," the fact that the information on its pages becomes obsolete as soon as the next issue of the paper is printed.[42] This obsolescence makes the newspaper disposable, and this disposability in turn makes it particularly apt to be laid aside and picked up by an unintended reader. In his 1845 *Narrative*, Frederick Douglass recounts how, after adopting her husband's attitude of horror at literate slaves, Sophia Auld flew into a rage whenever she found Douglass with printed matter and "nothing," he writes, "seemed to make her more angry than to see me with a newspaper."[43] Douglass does not mention just how he came into possession of a newspaper, but most likely he simply picked up an outdated issue set aside by the Aulds. Or, perhaps, he borrowed a paper from a neighbor's stoop. After all, the ephemeral nature of the newspaper made it cheap, and thus not particularly well guarded by those in charge of its delivery. Remarking upon the system of newspaper distribution in 1830s New York City, one visitor described how "the papers are either thrust under the doors, or thrown into the areas, or even left upon the step, should the newsman's knock not be immediately attended to."[44] The habit of leaving a paper unattended on a subscriber's stoop invited passersby to glance at, read, or even "borrow" the neglected journal, leading the author to wryly observe that "[n]one are so poor as not to have a newspaper."[45]

The newspapers that Douglass found left behind by the Aulds or a Baltimore newsboy would likely have had little sympathy for the antislavery cause. But Douglass read these papers against their intentions. For example, Douglass used a local newspaper to help him understand the connection between the word "abolition" and his enslavement. The dictionary definition afforded little help, but one of the "city papers" contained "an account of the number of petitions from the north, praying for the abolition of slavery in the District of Columbia, and of the slave trade between the States."[46] In the *Narrative*, this episode of newspaper reading serves as Douglass's introduction to the abolitionist community. And Douglass learned of these allies by reading articles in proslavery papers denouncing the abolitionists precisely because their petitions for the end of slavery might, if slaves became aware of them, disturb the imagined tranquility of the southern plantation. Douglass thus used the southern newspaper to achieve precisely what it most feared: knowledge of abolitionist allies.

Nearly two decades after Douglass's experience with Baltimore newspapers, an enslaved mother and daughter in St. Louis transformed cast-off newspapers into agents of liberation. In her account of slavery during the early years of the Civil War, Mattie Jackson writes that she and her mother, Ellen Turner, could "read enough to make out the news in the papers." The two women could not simply subscribe to a paper, so they obtained their papers through the informal networks endemic to newspaper distribution. Like Douglass, Jackson and Turner may have done some of their newspaper reading in pro-slavery journals set aside by enslavers, but the two women also received papers from "Union soldiers" who, Jackson writes, "took much delight in tossing a paper over the fence to us."[47] Such "delight" was well founded, as Jackson and Turner used the newspapers to disturb the tranquility of their captors. As Jackson explains, the knowledge of their newspaper reading "aggravated my mistress very much," as Turner especially used what she learned from the northern papers to contradict the misinformation her "mistress" provided regarding the war's progress. And in a bold pronouncement of her loyalties, Turner cut a picture of Abraham Lincoln out of a newspaper and hung it on the wall of her room. Beyond providing a particularly effective illustration of the newspaper's material malleability, the appearance of the Lincoln picture on Turner's wall underscores how newspaper readers creatively connected all types of newspaper items to their local circumstances. For the cutout picture of Lincoln in Turner's bedroom not only offered hope and support to an enslaved woman but also reminded her would-be master (who was certain to see the picture) that his way of life was coming to a violent end, and that those he claimed as his slaves understood that fact. Turner's captor apparently recognized the devastating significance of the Lincoln portrait, as in response to its presence he "knocked her down three times, and sent her to the trader's yard for a month as punishment."[48] Through the story of Ellen Turner, Mattie Jackson's narrative not only offers another powerful example of a black reader using newspapers in her struggles against slavery but also reveals the risks that such readings potentially involved.

These examples from Douglass and Jackson focus on how literate black men and women read newspapers. An episode of newspaper reading in Harriet Jacobs's *Incident in the Life of a Slave Girl*, though, reveals how oral recitation routinely carried the pages of a paper to audiences who understood newspapers as something to be heard, rather than read. As Jacobs relates, her fellow slaves "knew that I could read; and I was often asked if I had seen anything in the newspapers about white folks over in the big north, who were trying to get their freedom for them."[49] "One woman," she continued, "begged me to get a newspaper and read it over" in order to verify rumors that emancipation had already been declared in the North, but was being refused by southern slaveholders.[50] This account of newspaper reading not only establishes the paper as an authority, even among those who could not read, but also illustrates the common practice of a single literate person transmitting the news to a larger community. Rather than an account of an isolated incident, Jacobs tells how she was "often" asked to share the fruits of her newspaper reading with other enslaved women and men. By remembering and reciting what she had read, Jacobs could carry the content of a paper to people unable themselves to read the pages of newspapers, but who were nevertheless desperate for news related to their liberation. Such oral performances should remind us, again, that newspapers reached readers, and listeners, whose names would never appear on a subscription roll.

As the accounts of Frederick Douglass, Mattie Jackson, Ellen Turner, and Harriet Jacobs reveal, antebellum black readers obtained and used newspapers in multiple ways. These examples do not offer a concrete method for reading early American newspapers, but they do suggest a set of principles that inform and inspire my approach to study of the early black press. For instance, all of these accounts point out how readers can connect the content of a newspaper to unexpected concerns and contexts. In each of the following chapters I connect a black newspaper to specific local, national, and international contexts; tease out the ways in which these contexts created new relationships between and among various items in the newspaper; and explore how these relationships in turn shaped the notion of black chosenness. Moreover, Turner especially underscores how the materiality of the newspaper invites readers to creatively engage with its pages. My readings attempt to work through the relationship between a paper's physical presence and the content of its pages. Finally, the very appearance of newspapers in the narratives of formerly enslaved men and women highlights how the formal and informal networks of newspaper distribution made them particularly available to unexpected readers. Newspapers, black and white alike, imagined communities composed of particular kinds of readers who would perform certain kinds of readings. But the material malleability of the newspaper invited unintended readings. Throughout this book I not only attempt to reconstruct the intended readership and their readings of a newspaper but also account as much as possible for the inevitable presence of unexpected readers. For, despite the claims of many black editors that their particular publication represented the uncontested voice of a monolithic black America, the early black press reveals how a chorus of voices, some of whom struggled for a presence in the pages of black newspapers, combined and collided in their attempts to define, shape, and direct the chosen nation.

Chapter 1 begins with the founding of *Freedom's Journal*, the first black newspaper in the United States. Believing that proper black behavior could convince whites across the United States to abolish slavery, the paper's editors capitalized upon the particular features of the newspaper to craft an organ that could quicken the pace of black liberation. The *Journal* was filled with articles teaching black men and women how to behave. These didactic pieces attempted to close the perceived gap between *being* chosen and *acting* chosen. God may have anointed black Americans as members of a chosen nation, but it was then their responsibility to perform the mission of black chosenness. *Freedom's Journal* could help its black readers transform their chosen status into action. Reflecting the specific conditions and concerns of New York City's black elites, the paper imagined acting chosen as acting middle class. Happenings during the summer of 1827 prompted the newspaper to put this theory into practice. That year's Fourth of July marked not only the anniversary of the independence of the United States but also the date when the state's gradual emancipation law would free most of New York's remaining slaves. *Freedom's Journal* urged its readers to celebrate the occasion in a way that would have made Absalom Jones proud, instructing its readers to conduct themselves with decorum and give thanks to their white benefactors. But many black New Yorkers defied the paper's editors and the class they represented, making *Freedom's Journal* a record of the local struggles that shaped black chosenness.

Chapter 2 follows the New York City–based *Colored American* from its founding in 1837 up to the end of its run in 1841, and explores in particular the ways in which the paper used millennialism to instruct its readers how to respond to an increasingly hostile United States. Invoking a particular kind of American exceptionalism, the *Colored American* saw black Americans as part of a distinctly American chosen nation, but the newspaper increasingly uncoupled American chosenness from the U.S. nation-state. The paper initially imagined that political entity as an imperfect but redeemable institution that could become the legitimate earthly representative of the chosen American nation, but in its final years began to present readers with parallels between the

United States and Babylon, an empire that had held God's chosen nation in bondage and was destroyed as a result. The *Colored American* thus offered its readers multiple paths to freedom, but the ultimate outcome of such efforts was never in doubt. Through reform or the divine destruction of their enemies, black Americans would be free. Whether or not the United States survived their liberation, though, remained an open question.

The book's next two chapters step away from the confines of black Manhattan and focus on black newspapers in other locales. Chapter 3 travels to Rochester, New York, where Frederick Douglass launched the *North Star* in 1847. Drawing support and readers from both sides of the ocean, the newspaper possessed a decidedly transatlantic character. As a result, in its first year of operation the *North Star* worked to link the revolutions rocking the Atlantic world in 1848 to the fight for black freedom in the United States. In doing so, the newspaper took up and revised some of the central tenets of black chosenness. Like the *Colored American*, the *North Star* promised its black American readers that they would achieve freedom from slavery and racial oppression. But whereas the earlier paper had filtered its vision of black liberation through American millennialism, the *North Star* saw black Americans as one part of a global army of liberation that was scoring repeated victories. By routing black chosenness through a transnational community of the oppressed rather than rooting it in a particularly American identity, the *North Star* upended the American exceptionalism that anchored the *Colored American*'s vision of a chosen nation.

Chapter 4 moves across the border to the free black communities in the area commonly known as Canada West, where Mary Ann Shadd founded the *Provincial Freeman* in 1854. As a newspaper designed by and for women and men who existed at the margins of U.S. black activism, the *Provincial Freeman* took aim at the two exceptionalisms that anchored the black chosenness developed by earlier black newspapers: American and black. Similar to the *North Star*, the *Provincial Freeman* uncoupled the promise of black liberation from its claim to an American identity. In the mid-1850s British soil seemed to offer the only sanctuary for black freedom, and so the *Provincial Freeman* urged its black readers to move to Canada, abandon all claims to American identity, and embrace their status as subjects of the British Crown. In privileging Britishness over all other markers of identity, the *Provincial Freeman* upended black exceptionalism. Having experienced firsthand how self-appointed black leaders used the idea of racial unity to silence dissenting voices, Shadd remained deeply suspicious of any talk of race-based communal identity. Emerging as a challenge to the patriarchy of black activism, at a moment when British soil seemed to offer the only sanctuary for black freedom, the *Provincial Freeman* tried to convince its readers that being British was more important than being black. In doing so, the newspaper revealed the limits of black chosenness.

Chapter 5 returns to New York City and looks closely at the *Weekly Anglo-African*, a black newspaper whose run encompassed the entire Civil War. As a wartime newspaper, the *Weekly Anglo-African* not only covered but also helped shape the black response to the Civil War. While endorsing the view that God had sent the war to finally free his chosen nation, the paper explored the appropriate worldly ways in which northern black men, in particular, should respond to the conflict. Ultimately, the newspaper counseled black men to prepare for battle. But, in order to remind would-be soldiers that they fought for their enslaved brethren rather than for any government, the paper cast black military preparations as akin to a slave conspiracy. After the January 1, 1863 Emancipation Proclamation, the *Weekly Anglo-African* reasoned that the United States had become the best hope for black liberation. With the Union Army now admitting black soldiers, the newspaper urged northern black men to formally join the fight. But despite the fact that these volunteers would now be Union soldiers, the newspaper reminded them that their loyalties ultimately lay with the still enslaved. As the paper began imagining life after emancipation, and after the war, it called upon its black readers in the North to go south and help educate the newly free. But a part of their mission, according to the paper, would be to instruct former slaves how to be citizens. In the wake of emancipation, then, the *Weekly Anglo-African* turned away from earlier visions of black chosenness and began to equate being chosen with support for the United States. In the book's conclusion I look closely at a series of letters from black soldiers, published in black newspapers, debating whether or not the United States could be trusted to keep its promises to black Americans. During the antebellum era, black newspapers had consistently imagined a chosen nation that transcended the United States. This vision seemed out of place, though, if the United States would indeed welcome its black inhabitants as free and equal citizens. But as the war came to a close, some black Americans understood that the United States had already broken faith with its black citizens, and turned again to black chosenness as a pathway to liberation.

By exploring how five black newspapers, over the course of nearly four decades, shaped and were shaped by black chosenness, *The Black Newspaper and the Chosen Nation* tells one kind of story about early black newspapers. But the early black press remains an immense and vastly understudied archive and there are, of course, other stories to tell.[51] Even during the antebellum era, for example, black communities beyond the northeastern United States and Canada produced newspapers.[52] But by telling the story of a group of newspapers located in a small region, whose editors, printers, and contributors often knew and influenced one another, this book reveals how interconnected yet distinct local communities shaped and were shaped by nominally "national" black newspapers. New York City especially emerges as an important site for this study, and chapters 1 and 2 in particular underscore the ways in which changing conditions in that metropolis affected how black newspapers envisioned the chosen nation. This book thus adds to a growing body of scholarship that explores antebellum New York City's vibrant black print culture, but far more work remains to be done connecting New York's black press to the city's other formal and informal black institutions.[53]

Despite the importance of institutions like the black church to the production of black print, this book focuses primarily on black newspapers unaffiliated with particular churches. This might seem an odd choice for a book so invested in exploring the relationship between religious concepts and black print culture. In my early chapters this is a choice dictated by the archive, since the most prominent church-based newspaper, the African Methodist Episcopal (A.M.E.) Church's *Christian Recorder*, did not emerge until the 1850s. But even in the chapters covering this later period I have chosen to focus on unaffiliated newspapers in order to underscore the impossibility of clearly separating the religious and the worldly in early black print culture. Many of the newspapers in this study were edited by ministers, and even those that were not made liberal use of religious rhetorics and concepts. I want to suggest, in other words, that in order to understand the language and logic of early black print culture, even in its most seemingly secular forms, we must account for the importance of religion in general, and evangelical Christianity in particular.[54] At the same time, the deeply religious nature of unaffiliated black newspapers potentially expands the boundaries of what we typically consider to count as religious print culture.[55] This is not to discount the potential for important differences between official church organs like the *Christian Recorder* and its unaffiliated contemporary the *Weekly Anglo-African*, and work comparing these papers and others like them would help us to better understand the different strains of a rich and varied black print culture. But drawing too clear a line between the sacred and the secular in black newspapers would establish a distinction that had little meaning for the makers and readers of those papers.

Most importantly, my logic of selection for *The Black Newspaper and the Chosen Nation* is guided by the relationships between and among the people who produced the papers. To give just a quick sketch, Samuel Cornish not only coedited *Freedom's Journal* but also served as the first editor of the *Colored American*; and, along with other members of that paper's staff, he was one of the first men to greet Frederick Douglass upon his arrival in New York City days after escaping from slavery. Less than ten years later Douglass enlisted the aid of Martin Delany and John Dick when he began his *North Star*, both of whom would later join Mary Ann Shadd in Canada and make important contributions to the *Provincial Freeman*. And at the beginning of the Civil War the *Weekly Anglo-African* newspaper would serialize Delany's novel *Blake*. That paper's editors, Robert and Thomas Hamilton, had both worked for the *Colored American*, and their father, William, had been a leading member of the community that founded *Freedom's Journal*. These kinds of human relationships knit the newspapers in this study together, and make this book as much about people as it is about print.

CHAPTER 1

# Acting Chosen

Righteousness Exalteth a Nation.
—Motto, *Freedom's Journal*, 1827

Samuel Cornish did not come to New York City to start a newspaper. Rather, having been recruited by the members of a local evangelical society, the recently ordained Presbyterian minister came to carry God's word to the city's poorest black residents (see fig. 1.1). His training had prepared him for exactly this kind of work. Born free in 1795 in Delaware, Cornish had begun his studies at a small Methodist school before being invited to teach and continue his own education at the school affiliated with Philadelphia's First African Presbyterian Church. Excelling as a teacher and a student, Cornish began his formal ministerial training in 1817 and received his orders two years later. The new minister served as an interim pastor until, in 1820, he traveled first to Maryland's eastern shore and then to New York City, ministering to the impoverished black men and women living in those places. The New York Evangelical Missionary Society of Young Men provided Cornish with a small room in Lower Manhattan that he used as a school and place of worship for the neighborhood's black residents. In 1822, with the support of the New York Presbytery, he founded the First Colored Presbyterian Church of New York. By 1824 the church boasted nearly one hundred members, and Cornish raised thousands of dollars for a new building.[1] By 1827, Cornish had attracted the attention of a small but influential group of black New Yorkers who shared his values and concerns. Indeed, the minister's education, religious convictions, and fundraising acumen made him the perfect leader for their newest and most important endeavor: a newspaper.

And so, early in 1827, the successful black businessman Boston Crummel invited Cornish to a gathering at his home. A number of Crummel's neighbors joined the meeting, and together the group formally founded *Freedom's*

Figure 1.1. *Rev'd Samuel Cornish, Pastor of the First African Presbyterian Church in the City of N. York.* Photographs and Prints Division, Schomburg Center for Research in Black Culture, New York Public Library, Astor, Lenox and Tilden Foundations.

*Journal*, the nation's first black newspaper, and installed Cornish as "senior" editor. John Brown Russwurm, only recently arrived in the city, also attended the meeting (see fig. 1.2). Originally from Jamaica, Russwurm had received a formal education in Montreal and taught school in a number of northeastern cities. He spent the majority of his time in Boston, where he befriended many of that city's black luminaries including the Reverend Thomas Paul (whom he likely lived with) and a clothing store proprietor named David Walker. In 1824 Russwurm enrolled in Bowdoin College, where, two years later, he delivered his class's commencement address on "The Condition and Prospects of Hayti." After graduation, Russwurm returned to Boston briefly before moving on to New York City. Like Cornish, Russwurm possessed an excellent education as well as important connections to black communities in other cities. Perhaps because of these qualifications, Crummel and his associates named the new arrival as *Freedom's Journal*'s "junior" editor.[2]

Together, Cornish and Russwurm began to make a newspaper. Neither man

Figure 1.2. *John B. Russwurm*. In Irvine Garland Penn, *The Afro-American Press and Its Editors* (Springfield, Mass.: Willey & Co., 1891), 24. Courtesy of the Library Company of Philadelphia.

had any experience, but within weeks of the Crummel meeting they had established an office and equipped it with a printing press, type, paper, and ink. On March 16, 1827, *Freedom's Journal*'s first issue appeared, and the black press in the United States was born. The new paper had a clear mission. Through editorials, letters from correspondents, and news coverage, *Freedom's Journal* consistently focused on the relationship between black liberation and black behavior. Believing that proper black behavior could convince whites across the United States to abolish slavery, Cornish and Russwurm capitalized upon the particular features of the newspaper form to craft an organ that could quicken the pace of black liberation. Addressing their black readers, the two editors filled *Freedom's Journal* with articles teaching black men and women how to act right. Applying the precept that being a member of a chosen nation brought with it certain responsibilities in everyday life, these didactic articles attempted to teach readers how to act chosen. God may have anointed black Americans as his new chosen people, but it was then their responsibility to perform the mission of black chosenness. *Freedom's Journal* could help its black readers transform their chosen status into action. In reflecting the specific conditions and concerns of New York City's black elites, *Freedom's Journal* imagined acting chosen as acting middle class. Indeed, the paper's columns on proper black behavior anticipated the many conduct manuals that the black middle classes would produce and consume during the antebellum era.[3] But unlike those later books and pamphlets, a black newspaper would likely find its way into the hands of white readers. For this potential audience, Cornish and Russwurm included numerous accounts of upright black behavior, with the hope that such examples would counter negative depictions of black Americans and help convince white Americans to support emancipation. The expansiveness of the newspaper form allowed *Freedom's Journal* to simultaneously create and advertise black propriety.

The regular appearance of the newspaper also meant that *Freedom's Journal* could apply the principles of acting chosen to current events. On the Fourth of July in 1827, New York's gradual emancipation law would effectively free the vast majority of the state's remaining slaves, and black communities across the state planned a variety of events to commemorate the occasion. Throughout the summer of 1827 Cornish and Russwurm spent a great deal of ink sanctioning speeches and dinners that displayed black propriety and decorum, while condemning potentially unruly parades. Such commentary applied the idea of acting chosen to the plans and practices of black New Yorkers, and created substantial resentment among the many targets of the paper's relentless criticism. The presence of these dissenting voices slipped into the pages of the newspaper. *Freedom's Journal* exemplifies, then, the ways in which black chosenness emerged out of the contests and concerns of local black communities.

## Making a Middle-Class Newspaper

*Freedom's Journal* was published weekly from March 16, 1827, until March 28, 1829. In its first year the paper was a four-page publication, with four columns per page. The second volume was expanded to eight pages per issue, with three columns on each page. Throughout its run, the paper cost three dollars for a yearly subscription. The men who met in Boston Crummel's home wanted to create more than just a local newspaper. Rather, they hoped that *Freedom's Journal* would reach and unite black readers scattered across the United States. "It is our earnest wish," wrote Cornish and Russwurm in their opening editorial, "to make our Journal a medium of intercourse between our brethren in the different states of this great confederacy."[4] Toward this end, the editors engaged prominent black men in other northern cities as subscription agents. Ideally, these agents could convince their friends, neighbors, or parishioners to subscribe to *Freedom's Journal*. Initially, this network reflected the editors' own personal connections. For example, John Brown Russwurm's friends David Walker and the Reverend Thomas Paul served as the paper's Boston agents, and Thomas's brother Nathaniel took up a similar position in Albany. By the time the paper ceased operations, it listed agents across New England and the mid-Atlantic; in the southern states of Louisiana, Virginia, and North Carolina; and in international locales such as Canada, England, and Haiti. Together, these agents enlisted roughly seven hundred subscribers for *Freedom's Journal*. By comparison, white newspapers during the same period averaged around one thousand subscribers.[5]

Circulation figures, though, only begin to tell the story of a newspaper's readership, as they fail to account for common practices of papers being read aloud or shared between and among families and institutions. As an 1831 letter to the abolitionist *Liberator* illustrates, informal distribution networks could carry *Freedom's Journal* to readers and listeners who would never appear on its subscription roll:

> A few years since, being in a slave state, I chanced one morning, very early, to look through the curtains of my chamber window, which opened upon a back yard. I saw a mulatto with a newspaper in his hand, surrounded by a score of colored men, who were listening, open mouthed, to a very inflammatory article the yellow man was reading. Sometimes the reader dwelt emphatically on particular passages, and I could see his auditors stamp and clench their hands. I afterwards learned that the paper was published in New-York, and addressed to the blacks.[6]

The fact that this episode occurred a "few years" before 1831 clearly marks the newspaper being read as *Freedom's Journal*. Not only, then, was it possible that *Freedom's Journal* reached enslaved readers, but this scene illustrates how the communal and oratorical nature of newspaper reading allowed a single "reader" to spread the news to an entire community. So while *Freedom's Journal*'s subscriber list was relatively small, and its readership concentrated in northern cities, there is a distinct possibility that the newspaper found its way into the hands of enslaved men and women. How exactly a newspaper designed by and for black Americans affected such readers remains largely undocumented, but the letter to the *Liberator* offers a glimpse at how the newspaper could be used to inspire and educate those still in bondage.

Cornish and Russwurm crafted an ostensibly national organ, and their newspaper did indeed reach readers in a variety of locations. But *Freedom's Journal* nevertheless spoke with a distinct New York accent. In particular, the newspaper reflected the attitudes and anxieties of its founders, leaders of the city's emerging black middle class. By the late 1820s, stark class divisions divided New York City. The opening of the Erie Canal in 1825 had brought with it the possibility of local prosperity and expansion, as farmers from the western countryside sent their goods more easily to an urban market, and the city became the primary gateway through which European goods passed into the rest of the United States. For some residents, the increased flows of goods brought the promise of increased wealth. While older divisions among the city's white elites—such as the ethnically inflected Yankee/Knickerbocker distinction—remained relevant, shared wealth helped soften such differences.[7] Yet not all New Yorkers reaped such economic benefits. Between the canal's opening in 1825 and the decade's end, the gap between the city's upper and lower classes widened, with less than 5 percent of New Yorkers controlling half the city's wealth. Class tensions rose, while fissures also began to emerge within the working classes. Those ignored by established artisan organizations (such as unskilled workers and women) eschewed traditional negotiation practices in favor of more direct action. A series of often-violent strikes punctuated the second half of the decade, as "tailoresses," weavers, and dockworkers publicly demanded better wages and working conditions.[8]

Most black New Yorkers lived in spaces increasingly associated with the city's working classes. For the men who founded *Freedom's Journal*, this association presented a problem. In the first two decades of the nineteenth century, these men purchased or leased lots on Collect Street (shortly renamed "Centre Street"). They owned property, ran businesses, and accumulated capital. Part of the city's burgeoning middle class, this group cherished religious faith and formal education. They clustered their homes around St. Philip's Episcopal Church and sent their children to be educated together at the nearby African Free School. But an integrated working-class neighborhood surrounded their small stretch of Centre Street, and the already infamous Five Points lay just a few blocks away. In the late 1820s wealthy white New Yorkers escaped the city's laboring masses by carving out elite enclaves around St. John's Park and City Hall. Black elites could not hope to follow suit, but they could stand apart from their neighbors in other ways. In contrast to the rowdy, rambunctious style increasingly adopted by the city's black and white working classes, those on Centre Street privileged piety and decorum. By putting these principles into practice, members of New York's black middle class hoped to distinguish themselves from their working-class brethren, who lived right next door.[9]

But white onlookers made no distinction between the different pieces of New York City's black community. Instead, those who commented upon the city's black residents invariably focused only on their vices, as the noise of the Five Points overwhelmed the quiet reserve of Centre Street. In justifying the need for their newspaper, *Freedom's Journal*'s editors directly addressed this problem. "From the press and the pulpit," wrote Cornish and Russwurm, "we have suffered much by being incorrectly represented." "The virtuous part of our people," they continued, "feel themselves sorely aggrieved under the existing state of things—they are not appreciated."[10] While speaking in general terms, the editors expressed the specific anxieties of New York's black middle class. Such concerns may have resonated with readers across the country, but they emerged from the local conditions of New York City, the Five Points, and Centre Street.

The men who founded and edited *Freedom's Journal* expected the paper to lift the voice of the city's black middle class above the common din. Every element of the paper, down to the location of its offices, supported this goal. After the initial meeting at Crummel's home, the newspaper's editors and backers established an office only a short walk away, at No. 5 Varick Street. Though close, this location physically situated the journal outside of the working-class Five Points area. *Freedom's Journal*'s first office sat only a block from St. John's Park, the center of one of the city's wealthy white neighborhoods. By May 1827, the paper had relocated to 152 Church Street, a building closer to Centre Street but still squarely within an upper-class area, situated only a few blocks from the Broadway homes of the wealthiest white New Yorkers. To be sure, the close quarters of Lower Manhattan made the boundaries of its neighborhoods fluid and permeable. Nevertheless, there was a stark difference between the manicured gardens of St. John's and the muddy streets of the Five Points.

*Educating a Chosen Nation*

With the voice of the black middle class amplified through their newspaper, Cornish and Russwurm set out to educate their readers. *Freedom's Journal* would show white readers a complete picture of black life, countering the distortions that cast all blacks as ignorant and vicious. The paper would, promised its editors, offer a "simple representation of facts" concerning black conduct and conditions, "with a view to arrest the progress of prejudice, and to shield ourselves against the consequent evils."[11] For misrepresentations had consequences, feeding antiblack racism and undermining the struggle for black freedom and equality. To counter such effects, the paper included a variety of pieces that highlighted black accomplishments, such as histories of African civilizations, sermons from black preachers, and portraits of impressive black individuals. The editors began this effort immediately, printing a selection from the "Memoirs of Capt. Paul Cuffee" just below their opening editorial.[12]

While conscious of *Freedom's Journal*'s effect on white readers, Cornish and Russwurm mainly addressed a black audience. The newspaper, they insisted, would instruct black readers in a variety of subjects. The two men carried their earlier experiences as schoolteachers into their editorial work. They promised to include "many practical pieces, having for their basis, the improvement of our brethren." Alongside these selections, the editors themselves would "dwell occasionally upon the general principles and rules of economy," embracing the "task of admonishing our brethren on these points."[13] Cornish and Russwurm had both received a formal education, but they realized that many of their readers did not share that training. By taking a subscription to *Freedom's Journal*, black readers (or listeners) could receive an education otherwise unavailable. The editors imagined *Freedom's Journal* as an educational institution, though they hoped that the next generation of black Americans could attend actual schools.

*Freedom's Journal*'s first issue contained a single advertisement, urging black parents to enroll their children "of both Sexes" in a new school established by one of the paper's agents, located in the basement of St. Philip's Church on Centre Street.[14] While not appealing directly to the promise of black chosenness, Cornish and Russwurm explained their emphasis on education in terms of black liberation. By correcting white misperceptions and educating black readers, *Freedom's Journal*'s editors set about "raising our community into respectability."[15] Rather than serving as separate agendas, changing white minds and shaping black behavior represented the two parts of a single mission. Samuel Cornish gave *Freedom's Journal* a motto that elegantly expressed its two-pronged strategy for black liberation: "Righteousness Exalteth a Nation." Drawn from the book of Proverbs, this phrase sat just below the paper's title, reminding readers that obedience to God's will would lift them out of bondage and oppression.[16] The newspaper, for its part, could carry accounts of this righteous behavior to readers across the country. "It is for us to convince the world by uniform propriety of conduct, industry and economy," wrote Cornish and Russwurm, "that we are worthy of esteem and patronage."[17] In theory, *Freedom's Journal* would bring positive black examples to the attention of white America, lessening antiblack prejudice and hopefully loosening restrictions on black freedom. At the same time the paper would, through educational articles, increase the number of respectable black people across the country. These men and women would then provide more evidence of upright behavior for the paper to present to its white readers, who would consequently view black Americans as equals and treat them accordingly. In other words, Cornish and Russwurm hoped to establish a venue where respectable black behavior and positive white attitudes reinforced one another, creating something akin to a feedback loop that would ultimately result in black freedom and equality.

These were very high stakes. Cornish and Russwurm fervently believed that proper black behavior was the key to achieving black freedom in the United States, as it would convince white Americans to support emancipation and end discrimination. "It is our duty and privilege, by the faithful improvement of all the advantages which we possess," proclaimed the editors, "to convince a Religious and Republican nation, of the importance and policy of raising us in the scale of being."[18] In order to be free, black Americans had to learn how to act right. Hence, *Freedom's Journal*'s educational articles returned again and again to the question of conduct. For example, in a three-part series titled simply "Education," one correspondent lamented the "incalculable" damage done to all black Americans by the "loose and depraved habits of many of the rising generation." Black parents in the city, the writer complained, allowed their children "to wander from street to street, to indulge in every species of juvenile dissipation, and to imbibe habits the most pernicious to their future interests, and destructive of every moral and social obligation." Ending up in prisons and poorhouses, these youths provided "the enemies of our race arguments, to prove the futility of amelioration of our political existence!" To avert this disaster, the author urged black parents to send their children to school, where they would not only avoid disgrace but also become "glorious to our race."[19]

The author of the "Education" series also suggested that uneducated adults attend Sabbath schools or "schools of *mutual instruction*," and engage in appropriate "*Reading and Reflection*."[20] *Freedom's Journal* proved particularly helpful in this last area, offering a variety of pieces to help adults conduct themselves properly. The paper's editors included articles that answered the most basic of questions. One selection counseled readers to eat "sound and wholesome food, three times a day," drink only "pure water, the best of all drinks," and dress in "crisp and neat" clothing.[21] Short stories, written specifically for *Freedom's Journal*, offered lessons in humility and temperance.[22] Advertisements helped readers find shops where they could buy respectable clothes, businesses that would keep their coats and dresses clean, and even a "Mead Garden" (if they had to imbibe) that catered to "genteel and respectable persons of colour" and turned away "unprotected females."[23] These pieces not only instructed black readers in respectable conduct but also displayed the values and institutions of the black middle class to white readers. Each selection furthered *Freedom's Journal* mission by helping to create a respectable black community and showing that community to white America.

## A Day of Thanksgiving

In the summer of 1827, *Freedom's Journal*'s editors applied their general lessons to a specific, monumental occasion. In 1817, New York's state legislature had passed a gradual emancipation law that set the Fourth of July in 1827 as the date when most of the state's slaves would be free.[24] Despite the fact that some black New Yorkers would remain in bondage for another two decades, black leaders across the state marked the Fourth of July as the date of emancipation and began planning celebrations. For *Freedom's Journal*, the Fourth of July celebration in New York City represented a tremendous opportunity as well as a moment of great danger. If conducted properly, the day's activities could convince white audiences that black Americans deserved and could handle freedom. But any misstep could gravely damage the cause of black liberation, reinforcing existing prejudices and discouraging future acts of emancipation. All black behavior could help or harm the struggle for freedom and equality, but the stakes surrounding the Fourth of July were particularly high, for on this special occasion whites would certainly be watching. Sensitive to this increased scrutiny, *Freedom's Journal* took up the issue of public celebrations with a vengeance.

Cornish and Russwurm began covering the Fourth of July plans in late April. Their early reports seem peaceful enough but hint at the issue that would, in the months ahead, deeply divide the city's black communities: whether or not the celebration would include a parade. The first planning meeting that appears in the paper's pages occurred not in New York City but in Albany. There, the Reverend Nathaniel Paul led a discussion about that city's proposed celebration. For *Freedom's Journal*'s editors, Paul exemplified black propriety. They held him up to their readers as "a highly respectable and pious man of colour" who had sought to instill in his brethren "a just sense of their own rights and the duties which they owe to the community." At Paul's direction, Albany's black community designed an event where they could "express our gratitude to Almighty God, and our public benefactors."[25] In this spirit, and wary of interfering with white Fourth of July celebrations, the gathering decided to wait one day and hold their commemoration on the fifth. *Freedom's Journal* reprinted these resolutions without comment, its editors unfazed by the date change. A week later the paper printed a similar notice of a planning meeting in New York City. Conducted by men who may very well have been present at *Freedom's Journal*'s founding, the meeting chose the Fourth of July as the day when black New Yorkers would "express our gratitude for the benefits conferred on us by the honourable Legislature of the State of New-York." Perhaps concerned, like their friends in Albany, that their own plans might interfere with the day's white celebrations, the meeting resolved to "abstain from all processions in the public streets on that day."[26]

While this decision to keep the celebration indoors seemed to relate to the specific concerns of the Fourth of July, it actually reflected a growing hostility among some black elites toward parades of any sort in their city. This stance marked a decided shift in policy, as parades had been an integral part of black life in New York City for generations. Black slaves had participated in Pinkster parades when the Dutch still controlled the island, and in the early nineteenth century public processions announced anniversaries, funerals, and the formations of new societies.[27] This tradition continued into the 1820s, with mutual aid societies (pillars of the black middle class) holding annual parades. In 1826, a European visitor to the city witnessed a parade put on by the Wilberforce Society, whose members donned "ribands of several colours, and badges like the officers of free masons," and marched down Broadway.[28] A year later, the African Association for Mutual Relief celebrated its seventeenth anniversary with a parade, and a number of other societies joined in the festivities. *Freedom's Journal* covered the event. The editors lauded the efforts of such societies, but "as guardians for the public welfare" lodged a "protest against all public processions." Parades, declared the editors, only invited scorn from white onlookers. "The rules of propriety, prudence and economy certainly require that we do nothing which may be displeasing to the community at large," they wrote, and public processions led only to drunkenness and chaos.[29]

Parades like the one put on by the African Association for Mutual Relief had been a cornerstone of black civic life in New York City, bringing black New Yorkers together and proclaiming the vitality of their institutions. But when *Freedom's Journal*'s editors and supporters watched a parade, they saw only the vices and degradations of their working-class neighbors. The specific class struggles of 1820s New York City supported this reading. As workers increasingly engaged in strikes, parades became a primary way for them to demonstrate unity while coercing support from their fellow laborers. Though formal labor organizations often excluded black workers, strikes and processions involved both black and white workers. In the spring of 1825, for example, the city's docks ground to a halt. As one newspaper reported, nearly one thousand dockworkers, including "both white and colored persons," walked out of work and paraded up and down the wharves, demanding higher wages. The march was rowdy and violent, as angry workers "forced many quiet persons to join them, and committed some other excesses."[30] Only police intervention dispersed the marchers.

*Freedom's Journal*'s editors saw the parade as a distinctly working-class activity and worried that white observers would share their feelings. Parading on the Fourth of July would especially encourage this reading. From its inception in the eighteenth century, the Fourth of July had been a contested holiday, with Federalists and Democratic Republicans holding separate celebrations. Elites, moreover, routinely excluded those they perceived as lower classes from participating fully in their marches, sparking sometimes-violent countercelebrations.[31] A British visitor witnessed one such occasion in New York City in 1830. "Although the more intellectual part of the population, as the members of literary and scientific institutions, and the ministers of religion," the Englishman wrote, "might be content to celebrate the occasion by delivering patriotic odes and addresses, the joyful feeling of the bulk were expressed in a manner more congenial to their tastes." The city's workers staged "a review of some thousand militia, cavalry, infantry, and artillery, with marchings and counter-marchings in close order, open order, and, perchance, disorder."[32] In *Freedom's Journal*, Cornish and Russwurm worked hard to convince white readers that black New Yorkers resembled "the more intellectual part of the population" far more than the "bulk," but a parade on the Fourth of July would invite an opposite interpretation.

But the legacy of striking workers and rowdy revelers only partially explains *Freedom's Journal*'s incredible disdain for public processions of any sort. After all, the city's black parades had traditionally been solid middle-class affairs. Instead, the paper's stance reflected the high stakes of acting chosen. By teaching black New Yorkers how to act properly and then displaying that behavior to skeptical whites, Cornish and Russwurm believed that their newspaper could accelerate the pace of emancipation. Acting chosen in public spaces, like the pages of a newspaper or streets of a city, would, they hoped, erase white racism and pave the way for black freedom and equality in the United States. By contrast, though, the paper's editors worried that any instance of black disorder would be used by white Americans to condemn the entire race. *Freedom's Journal* could direct white eyes toward black virtues and accomplishments. But despite their best intentions, black elites could not hope to control the thousands of marchers joining a parade, and if even one participant stepped out of line, the entire community would suffer. At the very moment when freedom and equality seemed imminent, this danger could not be tolerated. Cornish and Russwurm sincerely believed that properly conducted emancipation celebrations could inspire nationwide abolition. A parade was simply too great a risk to take.

Many black New Yorkers disagreed. As discussions surrounding the Fourth of July celebration progressed, plans for an alternative event emerged. Less than two weeks before the Fourth, Cornish and Russwurm revealed this disagreement in a brief notice. "For the information of our friends," they wrote, "we feel it our duty to state, that there will be two CELEBRATIONS in this City, in honour of the Abolition of Slavery in this State. One party will celebrate the Fourth of July, without any public procession; and the other, the Fifth, with a Grand Procession, Oration and Public Dinner."[33] The editors' reluctance to even acknowledge the second celebration immediately emerges, as "duty" alone compelled their comment. Perhaps the two men hoped that their brethren would change their mind, or that the day's events would be small enough to escape attention. Always conscious of a white audience, Cornish and Russwurm tried not to shine too bright a light upon the planned procession.

But if the editors hoped that plans for a Fifth of July parade would slip by unnoticed, they were sorely disappointed. Mordechai Noah, the editor of the *Morning Chronicle*, a prominent white newspaper that routinely attacked black New Yorkers, had learned of the parade and written a scathing editorial in response. Noah related the plans for a parade to his readers and complained that such a display would likely devolve into "excess, extravagance, and riot of every sort."³⁴ With the plans now in plain view, and with less than a week to go before the celebrations, Cornish and Russwurm abandoned their earlier caution and devoted four of the paper's columns to the question of a parade. The editors walked a fine line in their approach to Noah's outburst. On the one hand, the man had a history of racist tirades and had to be condemned.³⁵ Through his editorial, wrote Cornish and Russwurm, Noah hoped only to "create hostile feelings towards our community" and "excite the lower class of the population to riotous conduct." By trying to incite violence against black New Yorkers, Noah had revealed himself as "an enemy to his country, and a leader of the rabble." But the white editor had placed Cornish and Russwurm in the awkward position of having to defend the planned procession. For though his motives had been sinister, Noah had voiced an opinion shared by *Freedom's Journal*'s supporters. *Freedom's Journal*'s editors defended their brethren's "right to indulge" in a procession but reminded readers that they themselves were "no friends to public parades, and have long since entered our *protest against them*."³⁶ After their commentary on the matter, Cornish and Russwurm reprinted Noah's editorial in its entirety. The piece had already appeared in the *Morning Chronicle*, so there was no real danger of bringing more white attention to the issue. But Noah's article showed black readers exactly how whites would react to their parade. Indeed, the very idea of a public procession brought charges of ingratitude and indolence against the city's black community. If they insisted upon going through with their plans, black marchers risked bodily injury from whites who had been stirred up by Noah's fear mongering. Cornish and Russwurm undoubtedly hoped that Noah's editorial, while reprehensible, might convince their readers to abandon the plans for a parade.

Lest readers miss the significance of Noah's attack, in reprinting his editorial Cornish and Russwurm surrounded it with articles from black authors condemning the planned parade. If white threats made little impact, perhaps this chorus from within the city's black communities could persuade the Fifth of July planners to stay indoors. Two correspondents wrote in to plead their case. The first reminded black readers that the "eyes of the world are upon us, our enemies watch us narrowly, to catch each little failing." If readers doubted these words, they only needed to glance a few inches to the right to read Noah's editorial. During this time of increased visibility, the correspondent argued, black New Yorkers should show white onlookers "that we are men, as well as they" by expressing their thanks to God and "those, who have spent their lives and their fortunes in the promotion of our welfare." Black celebrants could best display this gratitude "by abstaining from all riotous indulgence."[37] The second letter took up the issue of the parade in particular. "Can we not," its author asked, "manifest the joy of our hearts and our gratitude to God, and our earthly benefactors without making a parade in the streets?" Rather than express thanks, he argued, a parade would only insult the white allies who had ushered in emancipation, men who "heartily disapprove of our making a street parade." In conclusion, the correspondent hoped that the parade's planners would "give over the idea of parading the streets on the occasion" and "join with their brethren in celebrating the proper day in a proper manner."[38]

Alongside the two correspondents' individual appeals, Cornish and Russwurm printed a collective denunciation of the planned parade. Just below Noah's editorial, *Freedom's Journal*'s editors placed a report of a "large and respectable Meeting of the People of Colour." This illustrious gathering resolved that, in planning emancipation celebrations, black New Yorkers should focus their attention on "express[ing] our gratitude for the benefits conferred on us by the honorable Legislature of the state of New-York." In that spirit, those in attendance committed to "abstain from all processions in the public streets" and firmly denounced "any public Procession whatever in the streets on the fifth of July."[39] Like the individual correspondents, this group of black New Yorkers framed the emancipation celebrations as occasions for thanksgiving. Moreover, the object of thanks would not only be God but also white allies in the statehouse.

Cornish and Russwurm thus put an earthly spin on the idea that a chosen nation must act the part. In order to be free, black Americans had to prove their fitness for freedom to white Americans. By teaching black readers how to act properly and displaying that behavior to white America, *Freedom's Journal* could act as a midwife of emancipation and thus help God fulfill the promise of black chosenness. In retrospect, such a notion appears at once grandiose and naive, but in the summer of 1827 this strategy seemed to be working. For example, a white lawyer speaking at Albany's regular Fourth of July festivities cheered emancipation. He pointed to black educational institutions such as schools, churches, and, in particular, *Freedom's Journal* as venues where the "Negro mind, long supposed to be incapable of expansion, has given evidence of powers no less capacious and tractable than those of the white man." With such evidence in hand, the speaker confidently imagined the moment when Americans could "proclaim to the world with all the truth of glorious reality, that slavery in this *country* is extinct forever."⁴⁰ Black New Yorkers had gained their freedom without bloodshed, and without the direct intervention of God. Instead, he had helped them change the minds of white men who could change laws. For *Freedom's Journal*, a parade would throw the gift of freedom back in the faces of the white men who had procured it and the Almighty God who had softened their hearts.

## Parades and Propriety

When the day of emancipation finally arrived, black Americans across the country rejoiced. Black communities across the northeast held grand public celebrations, and free blacks in the South proudly (if privately) toasted New York's accomplishment.⁴¹ In the weeks following the Fourth of July, Cornish and Russwurm commended their brethren for their proper conduct and documented the positive impression such celebrations had made on white audiences. As proof that whites were watching, the editors reprinted numerous accounts from white newspapers. The celebration in Albany was, according to one such report, "conducted with a degree of order and propriety highly creditable," and the observer concluded that the "very becoming spirit which seems to prevail among the coloured people at this period of their history, promises well for the future."⁴² A similar notice from a Cooperstown paper commended that city's black inhabitants for conducting their celebration in a manner that "gratified" the "large assemblage of white citizens" in attendance.⁴³ Through these reports, *Freedom's Journal* showed its readers how properly conducted celebrations had accomplished the desired effect by elevating the status of the state's black population in the minds of white Americans.

For *Freedom's Journal*, New York City's Fourth of July celebration exemplified a proper emancipation commemoration. Cornish and Russwurm, having undoubtedly attended the day's festivities, described the event in loving detail. The editors painted a picture of a celebration perfectly designed to give thanks to white benefactors. A "large and respectable" group of black New Yorkers gathered in a church decorated with "discriminating taste." Portraits of the white politicians who had fought for abolition hung on the walls, and banners emblazoned with words like "*unity, charity, temperance*, &c." hung from the rafters. These decorations "reminded us very forcibly of the daily need we have of all of these, in our relations to the world." William Hamilton, a leading member of the Mutual Aid Society, addressed the gathering in a "plain and sensible" manner, delivering a "highly creditable" performance. A white audience observed the celebration, and among their number sat the former governor who had introduced the emancipation bill a decade earlier. The event was a great success, and the editors downplayed the debates leading up to its execution, seeing "no sufficient reasons, why matters of a trifling nature, should cause so much excitement and division among us." They did, though, take particular pleasure in the fact that "no public parade added to the confusion of the day."[44]

With emancipation celebrations across the state going off without a hitch, and white onlookers expressing so much approval, *Freedom's Journal*'s editors at first appeared unwilling to wade back into the fight over public processions. Just as they had only reluctantly mentioned the plans for the Fifth of July event, they now seemed eager to pretend like the parade never happened. But their initial silence could not erase the fact that, on the morning of the fifth, nearly two thousand black New Yorkers gathered near St. John's Park to begin their march. The parade's organizers picked a particularly bold starting point, as St. John's anchored one of New York's richest white neighborhoods. Some of the city's wealthiest white residents thus awoke to find thousands of black men massing in front of their homes. Several bands joined the fray, and the noise of their instruments may have jolted sleeping men, women, and children from their beds. Peeking out of windows, these startled whites could have seen the parade's marshal, a physically imposing black man named Samuel Hardenburgh, surveying his troops from atop the large horse he normally rode on such occasions, perhaps directing the marchers with his sword. The audacity of this scene speaks to the mood among some black New Yorkers that, with the arrival of emancipation, their time had come. At noon the parade set out, eventually arriving at the Zion Church. Its massive columns almost certainly wove down the streets around Broadway, passing by City Hall and, one block further on, *Freedom's Journal*'s office.[45]

The newspaper could not ignore this spectacle. Nearly 10 percent of New York City's black population had joined in the parade. *Freedom's Journal* had less than half that number of subscribers. A few days after the parade, Russwurm traveled away from the city, leaving Cornish to decide how to handle the situation. The parade itself had not produced a white backlash, and the senior editor tried not to bring any more attention to the event. Instead, he used the paper's layout to minimize the parade's impact and level an indirect attack on its participants. Cornish provided his readers with a curt summary of the Fifth of July celebration, offering no title and burying the report in the corner of the paper's third page. After describing the parade's general makeup and route, Cornish concluded that "not having been present, we can say nothing of its merits." He simply gave thanks that "the day passed off without disturbance."[46] Cornish wrapped a lengthy editorial titled "Propriety of Conduct" around the unassuming notice. The editor named a set of "imperative duties" that, in his view, should govern the conduct of black Americans. Among these, Cornish included "honouring those unto whom honour is due," a general maxim that took on a specific significance when placed alongside the report of the Fifth of July parade. For months, *Freedom's Journal* had insisted that emancipation celebrations perform this duty by offering black thanksgiving to white allies. Moreover, Cornish reminded readers of the stakes involved in an event like a public parade. If white onlookers considered even one black man "guilty of some indecorous conduct in the streets" all black Americans would be found "wanting in decorum."[47] Without ever mentioning the Fifth of July parade, the editor lodged a final complaint against its potentially disastrous impact.

*Freedom's Journal*'s black readers in New York City recognized the link between "Propriety of Conduct" and the Fifth of July parade, and some deeply resented Cornish's claims. Though the newspaper offered no specific space for these dissenting voices, their position snuck into its pages through the second installment of "Propriety of Conduct." In the weeks following the Fifth of July festivities, the parade's organizers had evidently gotten tired of *Freedom's Journal*'s harangues and begun publicly denouncing its editors, forcing Cornish to respond. "What few remarks we have hitherto made," explained the senior editor, "have always been for the public good; but how disheartened have we been, to hear our motives questioned by some who are apparently leading men, among certain *classes* of our brethren." Though Cornish seemed annoyed at having to answer charges made by "apparent" leaders of "certain *classes*," two thousand black New Yorkers could not be ignored. Indeed, the parade had garnered far more support from black New Yorkers than *Freedom's Journal* ever would. Reluctantly, Cornish admitted that it "becomes us not to tell our brethren what should or should not be done on particular days of the year, in a dictatorial manner." However, the editor knew that "the judicious part of our community" expected the paper to weigh in on such issues and promised to continue his efforts "to render us more respectable to the world at large." Ultimately, Cornish just wanted to get beyond the whole issue. "It is really astonishing," he concluded, "that we should waste so much time upon the frivolous amusements of the hour."[48]

Cornish downplayed the parade's significance, and *Freedom's Journal* soldiered on in its efforts to shape its black readers into respectability. But the Fifth of July parade was a symptom of the problem that fundamentally undercut the paper's goal of cultivating and enforcing a particular version of black chosenness rooted in the class aspirations of a small group of black elites. The editors and their supporters claimed to speak for black Americans across the country, but the parade's massive popularity shattered this illusion. Instead, it became clear that even within Manhattan the authority of the newspaper carried very little weight, as the thousands of black New Yorkers marching down Broadway refused to conform to *Freedom's Journal*'s specific vision of acting chosen. To make matters worse for the newspaper, schisms began to appear within its founding cadre. Samuel Cornish left *Freedom's Journal* in September, only six months after its inception. The senior editor cited poor health as the reason for leaving, but increasing disagreements with Russwurm likely influenced his decision to depart.[49] The two men most famously parted ways over the issue of colonization, but their different attitudes toward religion may have been just as significant. Russwurm never shared Cornish's evangelical zeal, and after assuming full control of *Freedom's Journal* he changed its motto from "Righteousness Exalteth a Nation" to the less biblical "Devoted to the Improvement of the Coloured Population." But despite Russwurm's continued efforts, the paper's lessons in respectability increasingly fell upon deaf ears. Upon his own departure in 1829, the junior editor saw "no probability, that we as a community, will ever make it our earnest endeavour to rise from our ignorance and degradation."[50]

By the time *Freedom's Journal* ceased its operations in 1829, the optimism of two years earlier had vanished. While the recalcitrance of black readers infuriated Russwurm, the fact that emancipation in New York had failed to inspire a wave of similar moves across the United States proved far more devastating. Completely discouraged by this failure, Russwurm took the drastic step of endorsing colonization and personally emigrating to Africa. A month before the paper folded, Russwurm explained that he had come to consider it a "mere waste of words to talk of ever enjoying citizenship in this country" and advised readers yearning for freedom and equality to "cast their eyes elsewhere."[51] Indeed, in the years following emancipation, life for free black New Yorkers would become far more difficult and dangerous, and the once-imminent fulfillment of the promise of black chosenness receded into the distance. Convinced that black men and women would never be welcome on American soil, Russwurm set sail for Liberia.

This was not the ending that Crummel and his associates had in mind when they met two years earlier. *Freedom's Journal* was supposed to change black behavior and white perceptions, but it had failed on both accounts. However, while Cornish and Russwurm may have lost some faith in their brethren and even their country, their belief in the necessity of a black newspaper remained unshaken. Cornish returned to the business of making a newspaper in New York City as soon as Russwurm left, founding a new journal titled the *Rights of All*. That paper lasted only six issues, but Cornish seemed determined to succeed. In 1837 he signed on as the editor of the *Colored American*, a post he retained for two years. For his part, Russwurm brought his editorial experience with him to his new Liberian home and founded a newspaper for the colony shortly after his arrival.[52] In the United States, black newspapers began to appear in small towns and big cities across the North. While a failure in terms of its founders' local ambitions, *Freedom's Journal* succeeded in a far more important sense by proving that a newspaper conducted by and for black Americans could survive under even the most trying of conditions.

## *The Legacy of Acting Chosen*

Beyond laying the foundation for a tradition of black newspapers, *Freedom's Journal*'s legacy extended into other venues of black activism. Delegates to the 1832 "[Convention] for the Improvement of the Free People of Color In These United States," for example, shared the newspaper's anxiety about parades. The convention recommended "to the people of color throughout the United States, the discontinuance of public processions on any day." Such exhibitions, the resolution concluded, would be "highly prejudicial to our interests as a people."[53] This opposition to parades expressed a specific application of the convention's larger belief in acting chosen. The "Conventional Address to Free Coloured Inhabitants of the United States" concluded by urging black men and women to "[b]e righteous, be honest, be just, be economical, be prudent, offend not the laws of your country—in a word, live in that purity of life, by both precept and example—live in the constant pursuit of that moral and intellectual strength, which will invigorate your understandings, and render you illustrious in the eyes of civilized nations, when they will assert, that all that illustrious worth, which was once possessed by the Egyptians, and slept for ages, has now arisen in their descendants, the inhabitants of the new world."[54] Like *Freedom's Journal*, this address urged black Americans to adopt the middle-class norms of economy and prudence in order to not only "invigorate your understandings" but also, and as importantly, demonstrate their "illustrious worth" to observers. Convention delegates, then, powerfully echoed the newspaper's emphasis on acting chosen.

*Freedom's Journal*'s legacy also extended into other areas of black print culture. Less than a year after *Freedom's Journal* ceased its operations, for example, David Walker released his *Appeal to the Coloured Citizens of the World*. As he wrote and revised his manifesto of black chosenness, the paper's former subscription agent kept copies of *Freedom's Journal* close at hand, and the newspaper's language and lessons made their way into his pamphlet. Walker directly quoted *Freedom's Journal* and its senior editor, Samuel Cornish. Moreover, the *Appeal*'s focus on education dovetailed with the priorities of the newspaper. Walker urged his educated readers "to cast your eyes upon the wretchedness of your brethren, and to do your utmost to enlighten them."[55] Such work, Walker argued, would prepare black Americans for the moment when God lifted them out of bondage. "God will not suffer us, always to be oppressed," Walker promised, and once liberated "we will want all the learning and talents among ourselves, and perhaps more, to govern ourselves."[56] But even more than equipping black Americans for their eventual freedom, black educators laid the groundwork for liberation by proving their worth in the eyes of God and man. By educating their brethren, black educators would shine a positive light on themselves and their charges, proving "to the Americans and the world, that we are MEN, and not *brutes*, as we have been represented, and by millions treated."[57] In a similar spirit, *Freedom's Journal* had constantly worried over the consequences of misrepresentation and specifically urged black New Yorkers to celebrate emancipation in a way that would convince white onlookers "that we are men, as well as they."[58]

More so than any particular theme, though, *Freedom's Journal*'s very existence may have inspired Walker to put his idea of black chosenness into print. Black writers had been producing pamphlets for decades, but *Freedom's Journal* proved that a local production could have a national impact. Cornish and Russwurm believed that their publication could reach black readers scattered across the country, change their behavior, and as a result bring about black liberation. Walker brought these same ambitions to the *Appeal*. He was especially keen to reach black readers in the South and mailed copies of his pamphlet to free southern blacks that he believed would help him distribute the work. *Freedom's Journal* had successfully reached southern readers, and it makes sense that as a former subscription agent Walker would have drawn upon the newspaper's network of subscribers as well as his own personal connections when selecting these potential allies.

But Walker learned from *Freedom's Journal*'s failures as well as its successes. Like Russwurm in his bitter farewell, Walker doubted that white Americans could ever be convinced to voluntarily enact nationwide emancipation. Both *Freedom's Journal* and the *Appeal* urged black Americans to prove their fitness for freedom. However, while the paper's editors focused on impressing white benefactors, for Walker only God's opinion mattered. When and how he would fulfill the promise of black chosenness had nothing to do with white Americans. Throughout the *Appeal*, Walker assured his readers that they would be liberated with or without white support. At the close of the 1820s, with the optimism of *Freedom's Journal*'s first six months shattered, liberation through God's direct intervention seemed far more likely than freedom through voluntary emancipation.

*Freedom's Journal* had begun with a vision of black chosenness grounded in a perceived relationship between proper black behavior and white acceptance into the national body. That theory emerged from the particular values and anxieties of the paper's founders and editors, who applied it to the events surrounding New York's emancipation celebrations. Despite their sincere attempts to display black propriety to white America, racism and oppression increased and freedom and equality seemed more distant than ever. In the next decade, black writers and activists bravely fought worsening conditions with an increasing faith, and urged their brethren to follow suit. Unsurprisingly, they turned to the newspaper to spread a more explicit and aggressive black chosenness across the country.

CHAPTER 2

# Prophecies for a Chosen Nation

Who is unwilling to be a coworker with Jesus Christ, in purifying the
world, in bringing in the millennium glory?
—Samuel Cornish, "Age of Reform," *Colored American*, March 11, 1837

On the Fourth of July in 1834, a group of black and white New Yorkers gathered in a New York City church to mark the anniversary of the state's abolition of slavery. Such commemorations had become an annual event, with celebrants reminding one another of the optimism that had accompanied emancipation seven years earlier. The city's black residents in particular needed such reminders, as black life in New York City had become an increasingly dangerous affair. Incidents of white-on-black violence occurred with alarming frequency. Rather than protect their black constituents, local authorities codified racial discrimination by banning black riders from public transportation and, as a sign of things to come, marking black men and women for arrest and incarceration. With the implicit endorsement of city officials, white thugs began targeting meetings like the 1834 emancipation commemoration. In the weeks leading up to the Fourth of July, the city's white press condemned the celebration's organizers as proponents of racial mixing. Stirred up by such accusations, and confident that the police would not intervene, a white mob attacked the gathering, transforming an event held to celebrate interracial harmony into the beginning of a devastating antiblack riot. For four days, well-coordinated packs of white New Yorkers roamed the streets, stalking and beating their black neighbors and destroying black homes and businesses. Rather than an isolated incident, the 1834 riot exemplified the increasingly dire situation for "free" black Americans living in the North.[1]

Philip Bell was twenty-six years old when the riots erupted in his native city (see fig. 2.1). A scion of the city's black elite, Bell had been formally educated at the African Free School, where his classmates included James McCune Smith,

Figure 2.1. *Phillip A. Bell*. In Irvine Garland Penn, *The Afro-American Press and Its Editors* (Springfield, Mass.: Willey & Co., 1891), 93. Courtesy of the Library Company of Philadelphia.

Henry Highland Garnet, and Alexander Crummel. In the early 1830s Bell joined with Alexander Crummel's father, Boston, and Samuel Cornish in an attempt to establish a college for black Americans in New Haven, Connecticut. White opposition scuttled the plan, but the project brought Bell into close contact with the men who had founded *Freedom's Journal*. That paper may have inspired Bell's interest in journalism, or perhaps the absence of any black voice in the city's press during the 1834 riots convinced him of the need for a black newspaper. Regardless, by the mid-1830s Bell had moved to Boston to work on the abolitionist *Liberator* and learn the newspaper trade from its fiery editor, William Lloyd Garrison.[2] Upon his return home Bell worked quickly to reestablish New York City's black press, which had lain dormant since 1830. He gained the support of Manhattan's black elders and courted the city's white abolitionists, who quickly threw their support behind his paper. These white allies may very well have steered Bell toward Robert Sears, a white Canadian printer. Sears arrived in New York City sometime in the early 1830s, and by 1836 had set up a printing office across the street from Tammany Hall. With Bell acting as editor and proprietor, Sears signed on to print the city's newest black newspaper. The two men named their new journal the *Weekly Advocate* and wasted no time getting out its first issue. On January 7, 1837, New York City's black press came back from its seven-year hiatus.

Bell and Sears guided the *Advocate* for a few months, but two other prominent voices quickly joined the paper's staff. In March 1837 Samuel Cornish took over as editor. Having previously edited *Freedom's Journal* and the short-lived *Rights of All*, Cornish brought a wealth of experience to his new post, along with an increasingly passionate evangelicalism. Cornish immediately transformed the look and feel of the newspaper, including changing its name from the *Weekly Advocate* to the *Colored American*. Throughout its run, the *Colored American* was a four-page affair, with four or five columns per page.

In April, the Congregationalist minister Charles B. Ray became the paper's "general agent," supervising its subscription efforts and traveling throughout the North promoting the paper (see fig. 2.2). Originally from Massachusetts, Ray was a leader among New York City's black activist community. As a member of the city's Vigilance Committee, he helped protect black New Yorkers against would-be kidnappers and frequently sheltered runaway slaves in his home.[3] Ray coordinated subscription agents who were, by the early 1840s, located across the northeast and mid-Atlantic, as well as in the "western" states of Ohio and Indiana. Unlike *Freedom's Journal*, the *Colored American* did not claim agents in England, but the paper did list international agents in Jamaica, Bermuda, and Toronto.[4] At the start of its second year the *Colored American* boasted a subscriber list of "at least eighteen hundred" and estimated its actual readership at "more than ten thousand."[5] These subscribers were charged one dollar and fifty cents per year for the paper until 1839, when the price was raised to two dollars annually. In June 1839 Cornish left the paper, and Ray began to assume increasing control over its operations.[6] By March 1840 the *Colored American*'s masthead listed Ray as its sole editor and proprietor, and he would remain at the paper's helm until its final extant issue on December 25, 1841.[7]

The *Colored American* ran for nearly five years, and its tone and subject matter cannot be easily summarized. However, one theme especially unites much of the paper's coverage: millennialism. The *Colored American* emerged during the heyday of American millennialism, as Protestants in the United States increasingly debated how and when Christ would return to Earth. Some believed that Christ would arrive in a blaze of glory, destroying the works of man and cleansing the world of its sins. The question of when this apocalypse might

Figure 2.2. *Portrait of Charles B. Ray.* In Charlotte Augusta Burrough Ray, *Sketch of the Life of Rev. Charles B. Ray* (New York: J. J. Little & Co., 1887), n.p. Manuscripts, Archives and Rare Books Division, Schomburg Center for Research in Black Culture, New York Public Library, Astor, Lenox and Tilden Foundations.

arrive took on a special urgency. A mild-mannered preacher named William Miller, for example, believed he had cracked the code of biblical prophecy and, through newspapers, pamphlets, and posters, began warning his countrymen that Christ would return in the early 1840s. Others thought that the millennium would arrive gradually and without bloodshed, as mankind perfected the world through reform. Many advocates of causes such as temperance and abolitionism thus believed that their efforts paved the way for the Second Coming. Both strains of this distinctly American millennialism cast Americans as God's chosen people, who would either help create his kingdom on Earth or who had betrayed his trust and would suffer as a result. In 1835, for example, the white evangelical minister and reformer Lyman Beecher conceded that, while he had first greeted Jonathan Edwards's claim "that the millennium would commence in America" with profound skepticism, "all providential developments since, and all the existing signs of the times, lend corroboration to it." "There is not a nation upon earth," Beecher concluded, "which, in fifty years, can by all possible reforms place itself in circumstances so favorable as our own for the free, unembarrassed applications of the physical effort and pecuniary and moral power to evangelize the world."[8] American millennialists could disagree about the how and when of the millennium, but the where was never in doubt. Whether achieved through catastrophe or reform, the millennium would begin on American soil.

The language and logic of American millennialism deeply inflected the *Colored American*'s coverage in general and its discussion of black chosenness in particular. Millennial messages covered the paper's pages, as the paper's editors used millennialism as a way to help define who belonged to God's chosen nation and to instruct the members of that nation how to act. Throughout its run, the *Colored American* consistently envisioned black Americans as members of a distinctly American chosen nation. But the broader outlines of this nation remained uncertain. Ultimately, the status of the United States would determine who else had been chosen. Reflecting millennialism's reformist impulse, the *Colored American* at times saw the United States as an imperfect but not irredeemable institution. Once perfected through reform, the United States would embrace all Americans and become the legitimate earthly representative of the chosen American nation. The paper thus urged its readers, as a chosen people, to help reform the United States and usher in the millennium. But as 1840 arrived, conditions for black Americans in the United States continued to deteriorate. Increasingly, the *Colored American* began imagining the United States not as the representative of the chosen American nation but as its oppressor. Invoking millennial visions of an American apocalypse, the paper promised its readers that God would destroy their captors, as he had destroyed those who enslaved the Israelites. In its final years, the paper defined the members of the chosen American nation as those oppressed by the United States, and it explicitly brought American Indians into the fold. In so doing, the *Colored American* redefined American national identity in a way that erased the United States from a perfected American future.

*Making a Prophetic Newspaper*

Like *Freedom's Journal*, the *Colored American* had strong roots in New York City's black communities. Bell, Cornish, and Ray were all connected to the city's black elites, and at the end of its first year the newspaper announced that nearly half of its subscribers lived in New York City.[9] While still attentive to the class-based concerns of New York's black elites, though, the *Colored American*'s broader tone and coverage extended beyond its local constituency. Reflecting the religious priorities of its minister-editors Cornish and Ray, the *Colored American* routinely relied upon the language of evangelical millennialism. In the paper's early years, Cornish tried to convince his black readers to keep working for freedom and equality despite repeated setbacks, and consistently invoked evangelical faith in the coming millennium for support. "Who," he asked in an early editorial, "is unwilling to be a coworker with Jesus Christ, in purifying the world, in bringing in the millennium glory?"[10] Cornish expected the arrival of a millennium brought about by the reformation of earthly institutions, and cast the fight for black freedom and equality as part of this larger effort. Since there could be no doubt that the millennium *would* arrive, such work would inevitably succeed. Through the medium of the *Colored American*, Cornish used this certainty as a way to inspire those discouraged by increasingly powerful foes and seemingly insurmountable odds.

Cornish's millennial expectations expressed a central tenet of faith among evangelical Protestants. As itinerant preachers and tent revivalists carried the Second Great Awakening across the United States in the 1820s and 1830s, millennialism moved into the mainstream. Scholars typically divide American millennialists into two overlapping camps. Premillennialists took a pessimistic view of human progress, seeing a world riddled with sin and debauchery. Only through direct (and likely cataclysmic) intervention could God redeem mankind. Christ's arrival would accompany such a catastrophe, worldly institutions would be destroyed, and the millennium would begin on a blank canvas. The more optimistic postmillennialists believed that mankind would achieve perfection on Earth without any direct divine intervention. Guided by God, reformers would purify human institutions without destroying them, ushering in a thousand years of harmony. For postmillennialists, the Second Coming would signal the end of the millennium rather than its beginning.[11]

Samuel Cornish swung toward the optimistic end of the millennial spectrum. He believed that reformers would create a perfect world, but realized that much work remained to be done before Christ's arrival. For his part, the minister concentrated on purifying the church by ridding it of support for slavery and racial prejudice. As soon as he took over as the *Colored American*'s editor, Cornish set out to use the newspaper as a weapon in that fight. In his first editorial, Cornish explained that black Americans needed a newspaper in order to combat slavery and prejudice, two evils that "have their strong hold in the Church of Jesus Christ, where they abide and act themselves out, contrary to all its holy precepts." Through the press, black Americans could "speak out in THUNDER TONES, until the nation repent and render to every man that which is just and equal—and until the church possess herself of the mind which was in Christ Jesus, and cease to oppress her poor brother, because God hath dyed him a darker hue." As Cornish explained, in its tolerance of slavery and prejudice the church had moved away from Christ's teachings. The *Colored American* could help bring this fact to light by telling "tales of woe, both in the church and out of the church; such as are calculated to make the heart bleed and the ear burn."[12] In a running column titled "Prejudice in the Church," Cornish chronicled instances of discrimination in Christian houses of worship, relating stories of black ministers being barred entry, or black children being relegated to the "negro pews."[13] Such discrimination, he argued, kept the millennium at bay. "Can the promises of God be fulfilled, or the world be converted," the editor asked his readers, "while the church bosoms this sin[?]"[14] By printing stories of prejudice, Cornish hoped to shame the paper's white Christian readers into rooting out such practices in their own churches. The *Colored American* could thus shepherd American Christians back to God and help inaugurate the millennium.

By using its pages to spread a millennial message, Cornish situated the *Colored American* within a rapidly emerging evangelical culture of print. Throughout the 1830s, evangelical organizations produced books, pamphlets, posters, and newspapers, all designed to carry their message to potential converts at home and abroad. Biblicism, or the belief that the text of the Bible infallibly recorded the will of God, provided the ideological foundation for this practice. Regardless of the medium, biblical passages carried the Word of God, and it was the duty of all evangelicals to spread this message through whatever means they could manage. Groups like the American Tract Society and the American Bible Society formed for the precise purpose of disseminating printed matter, and in the late 1830s the abolitionist activist Joshua Himes encouraged William Miller to embrace the printed word. Himes founded and edited a number of Millerite newspapers, warning Americans of Christ's imminent arrival through journals with suggestive titles such as *Signs of the Times* and *Midnight Cry*.[15]

Anticipating Himes's efforts, Cornish crafted the *Colored American* into a prophetic publication. Just as biblical prophets had urged their countrymen to repent and return to God, the *Colored American* pleaded with white Christians to abandon the prejudicial practices that had carried them away from Christ. Cornish explained to his readers that "God hath assigned to his ambassadors, different departments in his Church, and we feel that ours is, to warn the people of *this sin*, lest the sword come, and they fall by the hand of the sword, and their blood be required at our hands. We will, therefore, *cry aloud, and spare not*. We will lift our voice as a trumpet, 'and show the people their sins, and the house of Israel their transgressions.'"[16] Cornish here paraphrases the prophet Isaiah, who, like his successor Jeremiah, preached during a time when the Israelites faced grave threats from powerful enemies. Isaiah saw Israel fall to the Assyrians, while Jeremiah witnessed Jerusalem's destruction at the hands of the Babylonians. Convinced that his people had turned away from God, Jeremiah in particular had warned his brethren that such a fate awaited them unless they repented and restored the covenant. In his attempts to reform the American church, Cornish made the *Colored American* into a modern-day Jeremiah. The Bible records numerous prophets working from the margins of the Israelite nation to bring God's chosen people back into alignment with his will. By casting the *Colored American* as a prophetic medium working in this tradition, Cornish suggested that black Americans possessed a special ability and responsibility to bring the chosen American nation, which included black and white members, back to God before it was too late. Toward this end, the newspaper revealed the church's "transgressions," and hinted at the violence that awaited white Americans if they refused to change course.

By casting the *Colored American* as a prophet in the tradition of Jeremiah, Cornish also tapped into an already well-established rhetoric for proclaiming American chosenness. Beginning with the Puritans, American preachers and politicians addressed their congregants and constituencies as God's chosen people. This special status brought with it certain responsibilities, and a string of American Jeremiahs warned their countrymen of the dire consequences that awaited them if they abandoned their covenant with God. Yet despite its visions of impending destruction, the American jeremiad carried an essentially optimistic message. Divine punishment took the form of war, famine, and economic collapse, but such tribulations only confirmed American chosenness. After all, the thinking went, God would not bother to wreak such havoc upon a lesser people. Moreover, the jeremiad promised Americans that, despite their sins, they could avert total disaster by returning to God.[17] The *Colored American* repeated this refrain. The newspaper warned white Americans that a violent end awaited them unless they eradicated racial prejudice from their churches. But white Christians still had time to change their ways and embrace their black brethren. The paper promised that such a reform would not only prevent divine retribution but also bring Americans one step closer to millennial perfection.

## The Perfection of Israel

The *Colored American*'s millennial vision embraced the idea that Americans represented God's chosen people. The question of who qualified as an American thus took on a spiritual significance, since membership in an American nation acted as a passport into the New Israel. With these stakes in mind, the *Colored American*'s staff repeatedly claimed an American national identity for the paper's black readers. As soon as he took over as editor, Samuel Cornish signaled this effort's centrality by changing the paper's name from the *Weekly Advocate* to the *Colored American*. Explaining the shift to readers, he wrote:

> Many would rob us of the endeared name, "AMERICANS" a distinction more emphatically belonging to us, than five-sixths of the nation, and one that we will never yield. In complexion, in blood and in nativity, we are decidedly more exclusively "American" than our white brethren; hence the propriety of the name of our paper, COLORED AMERICAN, and of identifying the name with all our institutions, in spite of our enemies, who would rob us of our nationality and reproach us as exoticks [sic].[18]

In *Freedom's Journal*, Cornish had implied that black Americans could gain entry into an American nation by acting right. In the *Colored American*, though, the editor argued that, rather than working for white acceptance into the national body, black Americans need only defend their inherent right to an American national identity. Indeed, invoking the nativist fear that white immigrants might have competing national allegiances, Cornish argued that black Americans held a greater claim to American "nationality" than many of their white countrymen. The phrase "Colored American," he contended, expressed an "exclusively 'American'" national identity. Though likely seen by many as a contradiction in terms, for Cornish the paper's new title captured the natural and undeniable Americanness of its black readers.

According to the *Colored American*, black Americans *already* possessed an American national identity. They need not prove their fitness for inclusion into the nation by acting in a certain way, since American nationality was not something for white Americans to bestow upon their black countrymen. The paper realized that white enemies could and would, though, try to "rob" black Americans of their national membership. White New Yorkers, for example, cast black men as un-American by preventing them from participating in the main ritual of American civic life: elections. Technically, black men in the state of New York could vote, but in 1821 the legislature added a property requirement for its black residents. Set at two hundred and fifty dollars, this stipulation effectively disenfranchised all but a handful of black New Yorkers. The *Colored American* relentlessly attacked this provision. In the first issue under its new title, the newspaper's front page carried a lengthy article, "On the Right of Colored People to Vote." A collection of speeches and writings from white legislators who had opposed the property clause, the piece provided readers with a primer on the arguments for increasing the franchise. Introducing the selections, Cornish framed disenfranchisement as a cruel violation of black New Yorkers' rights as Americans, especially since no such limitations confronted recent white immigrants. "Foreigners and aliens to the government and laws— strangers to our institutions—are permitted to flock to this land, and in a few years are endowed with all the privileges of citizens," he lamented, "but we, *native* born Americans, the children of the soil, are most of us shut out."[19] Cornish realized that, through disenfranchisement, the state legislature had attacked black New Yorkers' identity as Americans. And by extending the vote to recent white immigrants while keeping it from "native" black residents, the state reinforced whiteness as the key marker of national belonging.[20]

The *Colored American*'s fight against disenfranchisement only intensified after Charles Ray replaced Samuel Cornish as editor. In the summer of 1840, Ray threw the newspaper's support behind a "Convention of the Colored Inhabitants of the State of New York," to be held in August of that year. The Convention was specifically designed to address the issue of black voting rights, and Ray prominently placed its call for participants in the paper's pages, wrote numerous favorable editorials, and carried an account of the convention's proceedings after the fact.[21] Echoing Cornish's logic, the convention condemned New York's property provision for black voters "not because it restricts us socially with respect to the rest of the community, but because it unwarrantably withholds rights inherent to us as men."[22]

But elections, for Ray, not only provided black Americans with an opportunity to protect their "inherent" Americanness but also offered them a chance to directly affect the course of their country. The *Colored American* closely covered the 1840 election season, formally endorsed the Liberty Party, and urged its readers to vote accordingly. "We entreat all our brethren, who have a right to vote," wrote Ray on the eve of the election, "to be found at the polls in due time, and be careful not to drop your vote on the side of the oppressor." Rather, black voters should choose their candidates "from a sense of your own rights, and the rights of our oppressed brethren at the South," remembering always that their "vote will have a bearing upon those rights."[23] Despite their small numbers, Ray firmly believed that black voters could influence an election and help reform America's political institutions. And, as his predecessor Cornish had made so clear, institutional reform paved the way for the millennium.

In urging their readers to fight for an increased franchise and participate in elections, the *Colored American*'s editors implicitly accepted the United States as the legitimate earthly representative of God's chosen American nation. Consistent with its postmillennial message, the newspaper framed the United States as an inherently good political institution that could, through reform, achieve its potential perfection. While still titled the *Weekly Advocate*, for example, the paper carried a two-part series titled "A Brief Description of the United States." Compiled by printer Robert Sears, the piece offered readers detailed information on each state's population, terrain, and history. Sears composed a brief introduction lauding the United States' system of government. The country's "political system," he wrote, "has survived the tender period of infancy, and outlived the prophecies of its downfall. It has born the nation triumphantly through a period of domestic difficulties and external danger; it has been found serviceable in peace and in war; and may well claim from the nation it has saved and honored, the votive benediction of *esto perpetua*."[24] While casting the United States as the savior of the American people, Sears drew a clear distinction between the state and the nation. As Sears described it, the United States government represented and served an American nation that existed prior to and independent of any particular political body.[25] But while the United States' "political system" may not have been, in and of itself, the American nation, it offered the best hope for protecting the American people from foreign enemies and, indeed, from one another. In theory, a federalist system of government could balance and neutralize competing factions within the nation, allowing disparate peoples to live in harmony despite vast differences in geography, ideology, and culture. Black Americans could, Sears implied, find a home under such a system.

At least, that was the hope. But by the end of the *Colored American*'s first year, Sears's own frustration with the gap between the promise of the United States' political structure and the reality of life for black Americans boiled over. In an article on "Our Government," Sears lambasted the "political system" he had celebrated less than a year earlier. He focused in particular on the dismal character of public servants. "Swindlers and drunkards are appointed to office," the printer raged, while "[l]icentiousness exists to a most alarming extent among our men in power." Sears drew a straight line from the behavior of government officials to the poor moral condition of the people in general. Rattling off a litany of sins such as gambling, horse racing, dueling, and a general breaking of the Sabbath, the printer declared, "[o]ur Nation is corrupt to the very core." But, like Cornish in his attack on the American church, Sears intended his complaint as a wake-up call for reform. Like "a sentinel on the walls seeing the enemy approaching," he wrote, "we sound the alarm." Sears warned the *Colored American*'s readers that, if things continued on their current course, "the days of our Republic are numbered," but he remained hopeful that reformers could "regenerate our land—purify it from the curse and disgrace of slavery," and thus "enable us, as a nation, to stand forth before the world, redeemed and disenthralled."[26] For Sears, addressing the sins of the state would improve the character of the nation. Aiming his jeremiad at the government rather than the church, Sears echoed Cornish's vision of an American millennium ushered in through institutional reform.

At first glance, it may seem odd that the *Colored American* included pieces from its white printer. But Robert Sears did much more than just set type. During his time as the paper's official printer, Sears appears to have performed a number of roles including coeditor, business manager, and correspondent. And even after he officially left the newspaper in 1839, Sears continued to connect the *Colored American* to the world of book publishing, providing the paper with much of the raw material that made up its millennial message. Born in New Brunswick, Canada, in 1810, Sears moved to New York City in the early 1830s. He married a local woman, began a family, and set up his printing office.[27] Sears's writings for the *Colored American* reveal a man with deep religious convictions and a reformer's spirit, but the printer also had material ambitions. In 1840 Sears began editing and publishing books, and with a keen sense of readers' tastes as well as the size of their pocketbooks he built a thriving business. Sears produced ornate yet inexpensive educational volumes on a variety of subjects, though one feature in particular defined his list: illustrations.

The American appetite for pictures exploded in the 1840s and 1850s, and Sears made a fortune with titles like the *Pictorial Family Instructor* (1849), *Pictorial History of the United States* (1852), and *New Pictorial Library* (1856). He even went so far as to name his office and bookshop the "American Pictorial Book Establishment."

Sears carried his interest in images into the pages of the *Colored American*. With woodcuts provided by the printer, the newspaper's voice took a visual turn. The paper's first illustration appears on the front page of its second issue (see fig. 2.3). There, Sears continued his earlier "description" of the United States with a series of short pieces on some of the states that comprised the Union. These snapshots wrap around an image of the Capitol Building in Washington, D.C. Visually, this metonymic representation of the federal government binds the individual states together, as the paper's front page literally illustrates the theory of federalism that Sears had celebrated a week earlier. On the next page, Philip Bell informed his readers that they could expect more illustrations in the weeks and months ahead. "We hope the period is not very distant," he wrote, "when our weekly receipts will be such as to warrant us, in giving, at least, in every Paper, *One Engraving*, illustrative of some subject described."[28] New York newspapers like the *Sun* and *Herald* had begun including illustrations in their pages in the mid-1830s, and Sears and Bell expected their new journal to follow suit.

But producing a single image could involve a team of artists and engravers and cost as much as fifty dollars, and the fledgling black newspaper could barely stay afloat. Bell's hope proved premature, and the *Colored American* offered its readers very few images before 1840. That year, though, Sears released his first book, *Pictorial Illustrations of the Bible*. Hoping to drum up interest for his new volume, the ambitious publisher littered the *Colored American* with excerpts from the book accompanied by lavish illustrations. Upon his death in 1892, *Publisher's Weekly* described Sears not only as "one of the earliest pioneers in arousing and fostering the taste for pictorial representation" but also as "one of the first to recognize the value of judicious advertising."[29] Sears displayed both of these qualities when he provided the *Colored American* with images it could never have afforded otherwise. From 1840 to 1841, thirty-six major illustrations appeared on the *Colored American*'s back page. No other antebellum black newspaper, and indeed few white journals, carried such content.[30]

Rather than an exception, Sears's presence at the *Colored American* exemplifies the interracial production of early black newspapers. Despite the hope

Figure 2.3. Robert Sears. "A Brief Description of the United States—Continued," *Weekly Advocate*, January 14, 1837.

among some black elites that, as the 1847 Colored Convention's Committee on a National Press put it, "the compositors, pressman, [and] printers' help" who made black newspapers would "all, all be men of color," black editors routinely hired white staff members.[31] Like the *Colored American*, for example, the *North Star* and the *Provincial Freeman* each employed a white printer. Such arrangements provided a variety of reciprocal benefits. Philip Bell needed someone with a printing press, and Robert Sears needed steady work and a means to advertise his growing business. And Ray's inclusion of Sears's illustrations in the *Colored American* offers one example of how black editors used these relationships as entryways into otherwise unavailable cultures of print.

Plucked from *Pictorial Illustrations of the Bible*, many of the images in the *Colored American* predictably reproduced biblical scenes. The book's excerpts and illustrations served as advertisements, but they also became a crucial medium for the paper's millennial message. For example, in the summer of 1841 the paper printed a seven-part series describing the "Seven Churches of Asia." In Revelation, Christ appears to John and commands the apostle to convey his messages to seven Christian communities, or "churches," in cities scattered across Asia Minor. Each of the installments in the *Colored American* focused on one such city, reprinting the relevant passage from Revelation along with a brief account of the city's history from antiquity to the present. An illustration of the modern-day city, or its ruins, accompanied each description (see fig. 2.4).[32] The series in the *Colored American* explicitly advertised *Pictorial Illustrations of the Bible*, with that title introducing each installment.[33] But the Seven Churches carried a particular millennial relevance. Eager to discover when the millennium might arrive, many Americans read the Bible's apocalyptic prophecies (such as those in the book of Revelation) as a code that, once deciphered, would reveal the timing of Christ's return. In such a reading, the Seven Churches represented seven historical epochs that preceded the Second Coming.[34] The churches' order thus proved particularly important. In Revelation, John sends his final letter to the "lukewarm" church of Laodicea, implying that a lack of conviction among Christ's followers will directly precede his arrival. This sequence fits snugly within the premillennialist anticipation of a cataclysmic Second Coming that would awaken true Christians from their slumber. But the *Colored American* changed the order. Instead of Laodicea, the paper concluded its series on the Seven Churches with Philadelphia, a city John celebrates for its strong faith. This substitution reflects the paper's postmillen-

Figure 2.4. *Seven Churches of Asia—No. VII, Philadelphia. Colored American*, August 7, 1841.

nialist vision, where Christ returns after mankind achieves perfection through reform, and also clearly places the millennium on American soil.

Through editorials, illustrations, and advertisements, the *Colored American* imagined black Americans as one part of a larger, chosen American nation, politically represented by the United States. The paper urged its black readers to claim their American nationality and, as Americans with a millennial mission, to participate in and help perfect their country's institutions. As Charles Ray wrote in an 1840 editorial, "it is our duty and privilege to claim an equal place among the *American people*, to identify ourselves with American interests, and to exert all of [the] power and influence we have, to break down the disabilities under which we labor."[35] By removing the sins of slavery and racial oppression from the church and the state, black Americans would not only bring about their own liberation but indeed help create Heaven on Earth.

## The Destruction of Babylon

But conditions for black Americans in the North continued to deteriorate. Reforms faltered, slaveholders and their surrogates triumphed at the polls, and the United States became increasingly hostile to the free black men and women living within its borders. At the turn of the decade a postmillennial optimism seemed increasingly out of place, but the *Colored American* remained convinced that black Americans belonged to a chosen American nation. After 1840, however, the paper's prophetic tone darkened, and the specter of a premillennial catastrophe crept into its pages. Though certain that the millennium would begin on American soil, the paper increasingly wondered whether or not the United States would survive its arrival.

While still hoping that the United States might represent the American Israel, the *Colored American* explored the connections between the current American state and ancient countries that had enslaved and oppressed the Israelites. In the popular imagination, one city in particular symbolized these evil empires: Babylon. During the time of Jeremiah, Babylon's rulers had conquered Israel and carried its people back as slaves. Numerous prophets began predicting Babylon's destruction. Enraged at the enslavement of his chosen nation, God fulfilled these prophecies by eradicating Babylon and liberating the Israelites. The relationship of black Americans to the United States powerfully echoed that of the Israelites to Babylon. Perhaps, then, God would liberate his new chosen nation by destroying, rather than reforming, their oppressors. The *Colored American*'s vision of the United States as an American Babylon thus fit comfortably within a broader premillennial narrative centered around a sudden, divinely directed cataclysm.

Samuel Cornish had loudly linked the *Colored American*'s mission to Jeremiah's postmillennial message, but Charles Ray's prediction of an American apocalypse required a bit more circumspection. After all, while his predecessor had addressed white Americans as partners in a chosen nation, the new editor promised them that God would wipe their country from the face of the Earth. The paper's white allies might not embrace this fate, and Ray needed their support to keep his paper afloat. Less cynically, Ray never abandoned his hope that the state could be reformed through political means, and he continued such efforts even as the *Colored American* cast the United States as the American Babylon. The form of the newspaper allowed Ray to level a devastating critique against the United States without openly antagonizing his white readers. Rather than using his own voice to paint the United States as Babylon, the editor suggested the comparison by pasting together pieces from other publications. Through these reprints, a chorus of recycled voices carried the *Colored American*'s premillennial prophecies. Ray also took advantage of the newspaper's serial nature, building the association between the United States and Babylon across multiple issues. A regular reader of the paper would be able to connect articles appearing weeks apart to one another, but the *Colored American*'s premillennialist prophecies would slip past an enemy glancing at a single issue. With reprints and serial installments, Ray used the particular features of the newspaper form to shield the *Colored American*'s vision of an American Babylon from unsympathetic eyes.

The *Colored American*'s premillennialism also reflected the collaborative nature of newspaper production. Robert Sears had stopped printing the *Colored American* by May 1839. Taking over as sole editor and proprietor in March 1840, Charles Ray made clear in no uncertain terms that he and he alone determined the content of the *Colored American*'s pages.[36] But, in an effort to drum up interest for his new books, Sears provided Ray with reams of reprints that the editor then used to craft the paper's premillennial message. The look and feel of the *Colored American*'s envisioned apocalypse thus bore a striking resemblance to Sears's early catalogue. Before his own titles took off, for example, the fledgling bookseller republished and sold works of religious instruction to churches and schools. In one case, Sears packaged together sixty-four books into a "Christian Library," which he offered to "Clergymen, Teachers of Sabbath Schools, and Bible Classes" for a mere twelve dollars (noting that in "any other form they cannot be purchased for less than SIXTY").[37] This library predictably included biographies of prominent clergy, treatises from Christian philosophers, and primers on upright behavior. But Sears also tapped into the increasing American obsession with the modern-day Holy Land by offering accounts from contemporary visitors to biblical sites.[38]

Sears's interest in biblical geography deeply inflected the *Colored American*'s premillennial message. This influence clearly emerges in a five-part series titled "Sacred Geography and Antiquities," where Ray wove excerpts from various books and magazines (probably provided by Sears) into a patchwork filled with images of providential destruction.[39] Using the words of biblical prophets, ancient historians, and modern-day travelers, the series chronicles the rise and fall of Chaldea and Assyria, empires that conquered and enslaved the Israelites. These powers committed numerous sins, but Ray selected pieces that established a direct connection between their enslavement of the Israelites and their destruction. One reprint quotes the book of Jeremiah, where God promised his people, held by the Chaldeans, that "I will plead thy cause, and take vengeance for thee, and I will dry up her sea, and make her spring dry."[40] In another piece, the Assyrian emperor's command to have scores of enslaved Israelites "massacred every day" ultimately compels God to, in the words of another prophet, "stretch out his hand against the north, and destroy Assyria."[41]

"Sacred Geography and Antiquities" especially lingers over the destruction of the two empires' capital cities, Babylon and Nineveh. These selections reminded readers that God keeps his promises to his chosen people. Though some sections in the series read like a bland geographic primer, descriptions of these cities pop off the page.[42] For example, in trying to convey a sense of Nineveh's complete devastation to readers, the author of one reprinted passage exclaims, "The place is a desolation—an utter ruin—empty, void, and waste! The very ruins have perished; and it is reduced to even less than the wreck of its former grandeur. It shows not the least sign of the greatness of its kings, nobles, or merchants; but even the absence of those, amid the heaps of rubbish, proclaim most powerfully the vengeance of the Almighty against the wicked, and the infallible truth of the word of God!"[43] Such vivid accounts dot the landscape of "Sacred Geography and Antiquities," dramatically illustrating the value of God's word to his chosen people. Ray understood how difficult it could be for black readers in 1840 to soldier on in the face of increasing oppression. But the destruction of Babylon and Nineveh proved that God would not allow his people to suffer forever. Such assurances may have offered little practical support to black northerners beset by roving kidnappers and mob violence, but the conviction that God had not abandoned them provided a powerful defense against despair and resignation.

Taking full advantage of Sears's access to images, Ray punctuated the descriptions of Babylon and Nineveh with illustrations. The final two installments of "Sacred Geography and Antiquities" offered readers two woodcuts, *The Temple of the Sun at Nineveh* and *The Destruction of Babylon* (see Figs. 2.5 and 2.6).[44] Without saying a word, these pictures lifted the *Colored American*'s premillennialist prophecies from a whisper to a roar. The illustrations demonstrated that no earthly power, regardless of its seeming invincibility, could escape God's judgment. *The Temple of the Sun at Nineveh* imagines a thriving Nineveh, heart of one of the world's most powerful empires. But the *Colored American*'s readers knew that nothing of the grandeur displayed in the image

Figure 2.5. Detail, *The Temple of the Sun at Nineveh. Colored American*, June 13, 1840.

survived. A week later, *The Destruction of Babylon* accompanied a piece that focused exclusively on the fall of the Chaldean capital. As the text explains, the illustration exhibits Babylon "at the height of its glory."[45] Again, God freed his people from an empire whose strength appeared unassailable. The articles Ray selected for "Sacred Geography and Antiquities" assured the paper's readers that no earthly defenses could protect enslavers from God's judgment. And while the pieces Ray cut together for "Sacred Geography and Antiquities" addressed a highly educated reader, the *Colored American*'s illustrations carried the paper's prophecies to an audience unwilling or unable to sift through the series' dense prose.

Moreover, the images of Nineveh and Babylon illustrated an element of the *Colored American*'s premillennialism that the paper's text left unsaid. When uncoupled from their accompanying articles and considered together as a sequence, the pictures proclaim the suddenness of God's judgment. In this reading, *The Temple of the Sun at Nineveh* portrays a city before the terror portrayed in *The Destruction of Babylon*. The horror of the second image could arrive the next instant or, following the *Colored American*'s publication schedule, the next week. God's judgment was certain, but his timing was unpredictable. For his chosen people, this meant that liberation could arrive at any moment.[46]

Other pieces of American visual culture primed the paper's subscribers

*Prophecies for a Chosen Nation* 61

Figure 2.6. Detail, *The Destruction of Babylon*. *Colored American*, June 20, 1840.

to read *The Temple of the Sun at Nineveh* and *The Destruction of Babylon* in just this way. For example, the Nineveh-Babylon sequence overlapped with a broader tradition exemplified by Thomas Cole's *The Course of Empire*, a five-piece series of paintings that chronicled the rise and fall of an anonymous civilization. Cole exhibited his paintings in New York City in 1836, and the city's press commented widely upon the installation.[47] Cole's paintings narrate the life of an empire from its beginnings in a *Savage State* to its emergence in the *Pastoral or Arcadian State*, moving to its apex in the *Consummation of Empire* before illustrating its terrible fall in *Destruction* and concluding with its ruins in *Desolation*. Cole ostensibly painted an imagined empire, but along with references to biblical cities he filled *The Course of Empire* with allusions to the United States, leading a number of critics to read the series as an attack on Jacksonian America.[48] In a similar spirit, the *Colored American*'s "Sacred Geography and Antiquities" series in general suggested a parallel between biblical empires that enslaved the Israelites and the United States' oppression of black Americans, while its illustrations in particular echoed the sudden descent from "consummation" to "destruction."

62   Chapter Two

When planning *The Course of Empire*, Cole expected the paintings to hang together in the mansion of his patron Luman Reed, a wealthy New York merchant who had commissioned the series. The *Colored American*'s black readers did not live in mansions, but some undoubtedly decorated their homes with the images included in the newspaper. Clipping out and displaying illustrations from periodicals became a common practice in the 1840s, especially among those who could not afford to buy increasingly popular lithograph prints.[49] *The Destruction of Babylon* would have made an especially attractive addition to any black household. Adapted from a work by the famous English painter and engraver John Martin, the picture offered subscribers the opportunity to display a piece from a well-known artist. Moreover, its biblical subject matter made it perfectly suited for the homes of the pious men and women that Ray targeted. But most importantly, the image offered a quick and constant reminder of the paper's premillennial prophecies. The picture could greet a discouraged black New Yorker returning home after futilely protesting another kidnapping, or being again denied a place on an omnibus, or narrowly escaping white thugs unafraid of any legal consequences. In a glance, the image recalled God's promise to his chosen nation that their suffering would come to an end, that no power on earth could stand against his judgment, and that liberation could arrive at any moment.

## *Indigenous Chosenness*

In addition to reassuring its black readers of their liberation, the *Colored American*'s vision of the United States as the American Babylon redefined membership in a chosen American nation. When framing the United States as the American Israel, the *Colored American* imagined black and white Americans as equal members of a new chosen nation. But the paper's premillennial prophecies shattered this partnership. If the United States represented the American Babylon, then its people (i.e., white Americans) could not be a part of God's chosen nation. By contrast, black Americans could confidently claim to be the new Israelites precisely *because* the new Babylonians enslaved them. But while the *Colored American* defined the chosen nation as a community oppressed by, rather than a part of, the United States, the newspaper nevertheless remained convinced that being chosen meant being American. In 1841 Ray again turned to reprinted articles and illustrations, this time to present accounts and images not of the Holy Land but instead of indigenous American civilizations.

Through its coverage of contemporary Indian removal in general, and the plight of the Florida Seminoles in particular, the *Colored American* connected its black readers to a legacy of American nationhood far older than, and independent from, the United States. At a moment when that country seemed bent on destroying or enslaving all nonwhite Americans, the *Colored American* brought readers stories of an American past where the United States did not exist in order to help them imagine a similar future. Moreover, by underscoring how American Indians too were struggling for freedom from the new Babylon, the newspaper suggested that the chosen nation that rose out of the ruins of the United States would be made up of a variety of kinds of formerly oppressed American peoples.

By the early 1840s most eastern American Indian tribes had been forced west of the Mississippi River, but the Florida Seminoles continued to resist deportation. In the spring of 1841, Charles Ray made the Seminole cause the *Colored American*'s first priority. The United States had been waging war against the Florida tribes for decades, with the Second Seminole War erupting in the mid-1830s after the Seminoles refused to emigrate. By 1841 the war was largely over, but small bands of Seminoles continued to evade capture and strike at white settlements. The *Colored American* cheered on the Seminole fighters. The plight of an Indian tribe in Florida might seem an odd choice for the New York City–based black newspaper, but black Americans and Seminoles shared a long and special relationship. Though not averse to holding their own slaves, Seminole tribes offered sanctuary to many black Americans fleeing south to Florida from states such as Georgia. Beginning in the late eighteenth century, black communities sprang up alongside Seminole settlements. While never fully integrated into Seminole society, these "Black Seminoles" enjoyed more rights than the nominally free black Americans living in the northern United States, and could rely on their neighbors to protect them from slave hunters.[50]

The Second Seminole War cast a bright light upon this relationship, as Black Seminoles met white invaders in battle and acted as translators and advisers to Seminole chiefs. The conflict thus offered the *Colored American* an ideal opportunity to highlight the intimate relationship between black Americans and American Indians. In establishing this connection, the newspaper rooted black chosenness in an American national identity that transcended membership in the United States. Ray began his coverage in late March by reprinting a speech on the war from Ohio congressman Joshua Giddings. Giddings, a staunch abolitionist, placed the Black Seminoles at the heart of the conflict. Their presence, he argued, had led the United States into the war in the first place. Anxious to destroy a beacon of black freedom and increase their stock of slaves, officials from southern states such as Georgia called on the federal government to remove or destroy the Seminoles and capture the black Americans living under their protection. "[O]ur army was put in motion," cried Giddings, "*to capture negroes and slaves.*"[51] Like black Americans across the country, the Seminoles in Florida faced an enemy whose total commitment to slavery governed its policies. But the United States provided more than a common foe. Rather, a shared condition of oppression under the new American Babylon cast black Americans and American Indians as two parts of the new American Israel.

According to Giddings, moreover, far more than common suffering united black Americans and American Indians. The congressman explained that powerful familial ties kept the Seminoles from moving west and abandoning their black brethren. Rather than holding the Black Seminoles apart from their own society, Giddings asserted, the "Seminoles had intermarried with the negroes, and stood connected with them in all the relations of domestic life." By submitting to emigration, the Seminoles would condemn their "wives and children" to slavery.[52] Through Giddings's speech, the *Colored American* established kinship networks between black Americans and American Indians. In Florida, the paper imagined, Black and Native Seminoles joined together as husband and wife, mother and son, father and daughter. These intimate relationships bound black Americans and American Indians together as much if not more than a common oppressor. By reprinting Giddings's speech, the *Colored American* portrayed black Americans and American Indians as one people united through blood and circumstance.

As Charles Ray argued in a string of editorials, the Second Seminole War was the United States' attempt to deny American Indians their claim to an American national identity. This claim, Ray contended, rested not upon membership in the United States but rather on a native relationship to the land. In one piece, Ray cheered the decision by a Seminole chief to continue the fight after most of his brethren surrendered and moved west, urging him to "stick to your old, your native home, and be forced away at no man's will or bidding."[53] The wording of Ray's support echoes a line from the sixth canto of Sir Walter Scott's *The Lay of the Last Minstrel*, "This is my own, my native land!"[54] The editor had earlier reprinted a meditation on this line titled "Love of Country." "Whether it be the Greenlander in the realm of eternal winter," that article's author wrote, "or the Arab amid the scorching sands of Zahara, or the Indian in his solitary wild, it may be said of each, that in his own clime would he live, and there would he die."⁵⁵ The piece dwelled on the importance of a homeland, a place that linked a man to his neighbors as well as his ancestors. Samuel Cornish had invoked this sentiment when he had told his black readers that, "in blood and in nativity, we are decidedly more exclusively 'American' than our white brethren"; and Ray implicitly applied the same definition of "American" to the Seminoles. Black Americans and American Indians could thus each claim an American national identity that transcended citizenship in the United States.

Driving this point home to the *Colored American*'s readers, Ray reprinted articles exploring American civilizations that preceded European settlement. Through these pieces, the newspaper linked American Indians (and by extension black Americans) to a history of American nationhood that did not include the United States. The paper thus upended the idea of the United States as the natural, inevitable representative of the chosen American nation. Late in 1841, Ray reprinted two reviews of Alexander Bradford's new book, *American Antiquities and Researches into the Origin and History of the Red Race*.⁵⁶ Bradford described in detail the monuments and remnants of ancient peoples across the Americas, and explicitly linked the American Indians currently living in the United States to the remains he encountered. The "relics" Bradford examined carried readers "back several centuries, before the discovery of America by Columbus." Moreover, their builders were "of the same stock, with the present Indians."⁵⁷ Current tribes like the Seminoles were thus members of an American nation that had existed for hundreds of years before the arrival of the Europeans. They descended from a "rich, populous, civilized and agricultural people" who had constructed "extensive cities, roads, aqueducts, fortifications and temples."⁵⁸ These structures, Bradford concluded, were not the work of "migrating hordes" but rather "a population permanently established."⁵⁹

Of course, the civilizations created by the ancient American Indians had eventually collapsed, and the ruins Bradford described could be read as evidence of how far current tribes had fallen from their former grandeur. But the reviews of *American Antiquities* also dovetailed with the *Colored American*'s vision of a premillennial catastrophe. Bradford described thriving American civilizations whose reach extended far beyond that of the United States. Their destruction, like that of Babylon and Nineveh, proved once again the fragility of even the greatest earthly powers. "While our nation is vaunting of its greatness, and pushing westward its growth, and boasting of the States and Cities that are to be reared, in western forrests [*sic*]," wrote one reviewer, "we forget, that we are doing this on the very graves of more populous nations, that have been swept with the besom of destruction."⁶⁰ This reminder echoed the *Colored American*'s discussion of fallen biblical civilizations, promising the paper's readers that if the "more populous nations" that preceded the United States could be swept aside, so too could the current American civilization.

Through another set of reprints, Ray transported the *Colored American*'s visions of Babylon and Nineveh onto American soil. In the summer of 1841, the paper printed two reviews of *Incidents of Travel in Central America, Chiapas, and Yucatan*, a new book from the travel writer John Lloyd Stephens. Stephens's work provided Ray with an ideal opportunity to map the Holy Land onto an American landscape, as the author's books themselves charted a course from the Levant to the Yucatan Peninsula. Stephens's first book, the 1837 *Incidents of Travel in Egypt, Arabia Petraea, and the Holy Land*, chronicled the amateur archeologist's visits to biblical sites. Tapping into the American obsession with the Holy Land, the book became an instant sensation, and Stephens parlayed its success into financing for his subsequent trek across Central America.⁶¹ Even if readers knew nothing of Stephens's first book, Ray framed the recent work in a way that recalled the paper's section on biblical geography by placing the reviews under the title "American Antiquities," a phrase that not only referenced Bradford's work but also echoed the paper's "Sacred Geography and Antiquities" series.

Like "Sacred Geography and Antiquities," "American Antiquities" included an illustration. Ray chose an image that resonated with the earlier scenes of biblical prophecy. Stephens, like Robert Sears, hoped to capitalize on the American appetite for pictures. He enlisted the aid of the English artist Frederick Catherwood, who accompanied Stephens and sketched seventy-seven illustrations for the book. Having studied at the Royal Academy in London, Catherwood had learned his craft from leading artists including John Martin, whose depiction of Babylon had been adapted and appeared in the *Colored American* a year earlier.⁶² To accompany a review of *Incidents of Travel in Central America*, Ray inserted a copy of Catherwood's *Front View of an Idol at Copan* (see fig. 2.7). In its placement on the page, as well as through its status as the icon of a fallen civilization, this illustration especially resembles *The Temple of the Sun at Nineveh*. Indeed, the review drew an explicit connection between Copan and the sites of biblical prophecy. Describing how the remains of the Central American city consisted solely of temples—the homes constructed of "perishable materials" having "crumbled into dust"—the commentary reasoned that

Figure 2.7. *Front View of an Idol at Copan. Colored American*, August 14, 1841.

"no idea can be formed of the extent of the city when in its glory—it might have been as extensive as Babylon, Nineveh, or Thebes, and the ruins that are left to us may cover but a small portion of the perfect city."[63] Inviting readers to consider Copan through the lens of biblical history, Ray translated the prophecies of Nineveh and Babylon into an American tongue.

But Copan represented more than just an American version of Nineveh and Babylon. Rather, the city symbolized an American national identity uncoupled from the United States and available to the *Colored American*'s black readers. Though some critics contended that Copan's builders must have come from Europe (or Atlantis), Stephens believed that he had found the remains "of a people skilled in architecture, sculpture and drawing, and beyond doubt, other more perishable arts, and possessing the cultivation and refinement attendant upon these not from the Old world, but originating and growing up here, without models or masters, having a distinct separate, independent existence; like the plants and the fruits of the soil, indigenous."[64] This passage ostensibly addresses the native origins of American engineering. But within the context of the *Colored American*, Stephens's words elegantly define an American identity that transcended citizenship in the United States. The paper imagined an American nation "originating and growing up here" rather than in the "Old world" of Europe. Its members had no white "masters" (a particularly appropriate word choice), but rather enjoyed a "distinct," "separate," and "independent existence."

More than just describing the past, this image of an "indigenous" American nation free from white oppression brought the *Colored American*'s readers a hopeful vision of their future. Previewing his strategy with Bradford's work, Ray used the piece on Copan to link this past American nation to present-day American Indians and their black countrymen. Like Bradford, Stephens concluded that the members of current tribes descended from Copan's inhabitants. For the explorer and the author of one review, this genealogy gave Americans in the United States a material claim to Copan's treasures. Stephens hoped to transport his findings back to New York City, where he would establish a "museum of American antiquities," and his reviewer urged readers to support this scheme.[65] Copan's "ruins belong to us," the reviewer said, "they are the property of the people of this continent—the historical landmarks of the aborigines of our country."[66] On the one hand, this claim to Copan's relics represents an imperialist reading of all previous American civilizations as the rightful property of the United States, extending the borders of the country to encompass the lands and histories of Central America and beyond.[67] But references to the "people of this continent" and "aborigines of our country" take on a different meaning when situated within the *Colored American*'s discussion of indigenous American nationhood. Addressing its black readers, the newspaper could argue that the Central American city's "ruins belong to us" because black Americans belonged to the same chosen American nation as American Indians and their ancestors. As sites like Copan proved, the nation possessed a history of American civilization that predated white settlement by hundreds, if not thousands, of years. Its members had covered the continent long before the founding of the United States, continued to survive despite enslavement and attempted extermination, and would remain after that civilization fell.

Catherwood's illustration visualized the enduring power of this indigenous chosen nation. Unlike the imaginary scenes from Babylon and Nineveh, his *Front View of an Idol at Copan* showed an actual remnant of the city. Indeed, Stephens could dream of a museum filled with American antiquities because, unlike the biblical cities, scores of remaining relics testified to Copan's glory. As the *Colored American*'s "Sacred Geography and Antiquities" section made clear, *nothing* survived from the empires that enslaved God's chosen people. But Copan was not the capital of such an empire. Quite the contrary; as the city of an American civilization whose descendants suffered under the weight of the American Babylon, Copan recalled the ancient home of God's first chosen nation. The *Colored American* suggested that, in the jungles of Central America, Stephens had discovered the ruins of an American Jerusalem.

Like Martin's *Destruction of Babylon*, Catherwood's *Front View of an Idol at Copan* visually captured a key thread of the *Colored American*'s millennialist black chosenness. The first image promised readers that God would free them from their captors, and the second reminded them that they belonged to a chosen nation with deep roots in the American soil. Perhaps these two woodcuts hung side-by-side in the homes of black New Yorkers, offering hope and strength at a moment when the cause of black liberation seemed nearly defeated. From its earliest issues, the *Colored American* assured its readers that they were God's chosen people and would find freedom in America. Being a member of the chosen American nation brought with it certain responsibilities, and the paper urged its supporters to devote themselves to reforming oppressive institutions like the church and government. And when these efforts seemed hopeless, the *Colored American* reminded black Americans that no power could stand against God's wrath, and that he would not allow his people to suffer forever. But rather than move decisively from a commitment to reform to the promise of apocalypse, the paper presented its two millennial prophecies simultaneously. The *Colored American* thus offered its readers multiple paths to freedom, but the ultimate outcome of such efforts was never in doubt. Through reform or the divine destruction of their enemies, black Americans would be free. Whether or not the United States survived their liberation, though, remained an open question.

CHAPTER 3

# Revolutionary Chosenness

A revolution now cannot be confined to the place or the people where it may commence, but flashes with lightning speed from heart to heart, from land to land, till it has traversed the globe, compelling all the members of our common brotherhood at once, to pass judgment upon its merits.
—Frederick Douglass, "France," *North Star*, April 28, 1848


Frederick Douglass escaped from slavery in Baltimore on September 3, 1838. He arrived in New York City the next day (see fig. 3.1). Frightened and alone, Douglass spent his first night of freedom sleeping behind some barrels on one of the city's docks, and his second at the home of a kind stranger. On the third day, as Douglass would recall in his 1893 autobiography, *Life and Times*, this friend "went with me to Mr. David Ruggles, the secretary of the New York vigilance committee, a co-worker with Isaac T. Hopper, Lewis and Arthur Tappan, Theodore S. Wright, Samuel Cornish, Thomas Downing, Philip A. Bell, and other true men of their time." Through this list of names, Douglass highlights the collective nature of the fight for black liberation. Rather than focusing on Ruggles alone, Douglass frames his encounter with the "officer on the underground railroad" as an entry into a group of freedom fighters.[1] And the names Douglass selects reveal the specific contours of this community. By including Hopper and the Tappan brothers, three white men, Douglass points to the interracial nature of abolitionist activity. Wright and Cornish, both pastors of New York City's First Colored Presbyterian Church, represent not only a particular religious sensibility but also a link to the city's black middle class. Downing, part of the first generation of successful black businessmen in the city, reinforces this connection. Bell, by far the youngest member of the bunch, represents the continued vitality of the city's black elite.

Moreover, nearly every figure Douglass remembers helped create and spread

Figure 3.1. *Frederick Douglass*. Courtesy of the Library Company of Philadelphia.

printed materials. Hopper ran an abolitionist bookstore, the Tappans supported the *Colored American*, and Downing helped found *Freedom's Journal*. Cornish had edited that paper as well as the *Colored American*, which Bell cofounded. In addition to providing shelter for fugitive slaves like Douglass, Ruggles's home served as New York City's only black bookstore and reading room, and would have been littered with copies of the *Colored American* and his own magazine, the *Mirror of Liberty*.[2] One of Douglass's earliest experiences of freedom, then, was an immersion into a vibrant print culture. After a short stay in New York City, Douglass continued north to New Bedford. In Massachusetts, he began working closely with William Lloyd Garrison, whose faith in the power of the press manifested in his abolitionist newspaper, the *Liberator*. As another example of the newspaper as a tool for black liberation, the *Liberator* reinforced the lessons Douglass had learned during his stay at Ruggles's reading room.

But while Cornish, Bell, and Garrison may have laid the groundwork for Douglass's own entry into the editor's chair, international allies offered the moral and financial support necessary for starting a newspaper. Douglass cultivated these friends during an eighteen-month sojourn in the British Isles that began shortly after the publication of his 1845 *Narrative of the Life of Frederick Douglass, an American Slave, Written by Himself*. The *Narrative* quickly sold five thousand copies, and introduced Douglass to an international audience. But, since he was still legally a fugitive from slavery, the book also exposed Douglass to an increased threat of kidnapping and return to the South. In order to capitalize on the success of the *Narrative* and remove him from the reach of slave catchers who now knew his location, Douglass's supporters arranged for a speaking tour of the British Isles. In August 1845 he set sail, joining a string of black abolitionists who visited Europe in the 1840s and 1850s. Douglass toured Ireland, Scotland, and England, delivering speeches to packed houses and meeting with a range of allies sympathetic to the cause of black liberation. These new friends offered Douglass not only their applause but also their money, and raised enough funds to purchase his freedom so that he could safely return to the United States. But before he left Great Britain in April 1847, Douglass secured a promise for another two thousand dollars, earmarked for the purchase of a printing press and all materials necessary to start a newspaper.[3] Once he arrived in the United States, Douglass immediately set out assembling a staff for his journal and scouting locations for its base of operations. His British friends sent letters of encouragement along with the promised start-up funds. Such support proved invaluable since the white American abolitionists that Douglass turned to for help greeted his plans for a newspaper with open hostility. Such opposition, as Douglass wrote in his 1855 *My Bondage and My Freedom*, "caused me not only to hesitate, but inclined me to abandon the enterprise," but "[s]ome of my English friends greatly encouraged me to go forward, and I shall never cease to be grateful for their words of cheer and generous deeds."[4]

On December 3, 1847, Douglass released the first issue of his newspaper, which he titled the *North Star*. The paper would run until April 17, 1851, with Douglass as its only editor. Throughout its run, the *North Star* was four pages, with seven columns per page, and cost subscribers two dollars annually. Drawing support and readers from both sides of the ocean, the newspaper possessed a decidedly transatlantic character. As a result, in its first year of operation the *North Star* worked to link the revolutions rocking the Atlantic world in 1848 to the fight for black freedom in the United States. In doing so, the newspaper took up and revised some of the central tenets of black chosenness. Like the *Colored American*, the *North Star* promised its black American readers that they would achieve freedom from slavery and racial oppression. But whereas the earlier paper had filtered its vision of black liberation through American millennialism, the *North Star* saw black Americans as one part of a global army of liberation that was scoring repeated victories. As seemingly unassailable European empires fell in quick succession, Douglass and his staff sensed that the collapse of American slavery could not be far off. Indeed, in the spring of 1848 events in the United States reinforced their conviction that the spirit of revolution sweeping across Europe had crossed the ocean and arrived on American shores. By routing black chosenness through a transnational community of the oppressed rather than rooting it in a particularly American identity, the *North Star* upended the American exceptionalism that anchored the *Colored American*'s vision of a chosen nation.

But the *North Star*'s rejection of American exceptionalism did not mean that the paper abandoned wholesale the notion that black Americans had a particular gift to share with the world. Indeed, by bringing together on its pages accounts of and commentary on multiple insurrections, the paper offered a version of black exceptionalism that cast black Americans as uniquely able to blend and transform sometimes-competing tactics into an ideal strategy for transforming society. While the *North Star* struggled over the role that violence might play in such a struggle, the newspaper ultimately argued that personal transformation would produce a peaceful revolution. Like *Freedom's Journal* twenty years earlier, the *North Star* urged its black readers to conduct themselves with decorum and propriety. Rather than a retreat from the global fight for freedom, the newspaper saw upright behavior as a way to reproduce the transformations of Europe while avoiding the terrible violence that engulfed the continent. In 1848, the *North Star* argued, respectability could be revolutionary.

## *Making an Atlantic Newspaper*

In March 1848, the British steamship *Cambria* arrived in the United States. A year earlier, the ship had carried Douglass back from the British Isles. This time, in addition to its passengers, the ship carried copies of the *London Daily News*, whose pages were filled with reports of a new revolution in France. The paper relayed to readers how, on February 22, what had begun as a peaceful protest in Paris against the government of King Louis Philippe turned violent as marchers clashed with the city's police. The riots intensified over the next two days, as Parisians constructed barricades throughout the city. Louis Philippe called out the National Guard to put down the disturbance, but many of the troops joined the insurgents. On February 24, after unsuccessfully trying to placate the people by appointing new ministers, the king abdicated and fled the city. The revolutionaries quickly established a provisional government and proclaimed a new French republic. News of the "February days" in Paris sent shockwaves throughout Europe. By mid-March, bloody uprisings in Vienna and Berlin rocked the foundations of the continent's most powerful empires, and fighting broke out across the Italian peninsula. In a matter of weeks, Europe had been transformed by a revolutionary wave that had not yet come to rest.[5]

As news of the new French revolution spread across the United States, residents of large cities and small towns met to discuss the proper response to the events in Europe. Speakers at such gatherings often cast the French uprising as a descendant of the revolutionary tradition inaugurated by the United States. New York City mayor William Brady, for instance, embraced the role of the proud father who felt "paternal warmth" at the "birth of the [French] Republic."[6] But not everyone shared the mayor's sentiments. On April 27, a small group of community leaders in Rochester, New York, met in the city's courthouse. After laying the groundwork for a much larger gathering on May 8, those at the meeting listened to a series of speakers. Among them was Frederick Douglass, who had moved to Rochester the previous fall. Douglass initially expressed surprise at being called upon to speak, but reasoned that "it might well be supposed that on such a theme as this, I would have a word to say." Already an internationally renowned black abolitionist, Douglass made particular sense as a speaker because France's new provisional government had signaled its intention to abolish slavery in all its colonies. In his brief remarks, Douglass argued that France's moves toward emancipation shined a bright light on American hypocrisy. "[I]f anything can put our republic to the blush," he declared, "it is that glorious consistency with which the Provisional Government has made and set in operation measures which must bring about the entire overthrow of Slavery in all her dominions."[7] Rather than seeing the new French republic as an homage to the glories of the United States, Douglass surmised that France's consistent republicanism might shame Americans into abandoning their own inconsistent applications of the principles of liberty and freedom. While figures like Mayor Brady imagined a revolutionary spirit traveling from west to east across the Atlantic Ocean, Douglass reversed the direction of influence. In 1848, he hoped, Europe would teach the United States how to be truly free.

Though Douglass delivered his opinion on the events in Paris out loud to a small crowd, his speech reached a larger audience through the pages of newspapers. It first appeared in the Rochester *Democrat* on April 29, and then two weeks later in his own *North Star*. There, the short speech joined the paper's ongoing coverage of the European revolutions. Throughout the spring and summer of 1848, the *North Star* connected events in Europe to the struggle for black freedom in the United States, hoping that news of successful uprisings abroad would bring hope and inspiration to those fighting for liberation at home. Pointing to the steamships rapidly crisscrossing the ocean and the telegraph poles popping up across the United States, Douglass argued that the Atlantic world had become an interconnected field of revolutionary possibility.[8] "Thanks to steam navigation and electric wires," he wrote in an April 28 editorial on the Paris uprising, "we may almost hear the words uttered, and see the deeds done, as they transpire. A revolution now cannot be confined to the place or the people where it may commence, but flashes with lightning speed from heart to heart, from land to land, till it has traversed the globe, compelling all the members of our common brotherhood at once, to pass judgment upon its merits. The revolution of France, like a bolt of living thunder, has aroused the world from its stupor."[9] Here, Douglass sees no difference between a revolution and the news of its occurrence. For while the new information technologies of the 1840s carried reports of the Paris uprising to distant locations, Douglass imagines the revolution itself traveling at "lightning speed" across the wires. However, since only a select few had direct access to docking ships or telegraph offices, the newspaper provided a crucial conduit for the transmission of a revolution "from land to land." According to its editor, then, the *North Star* could in effect transport the European revolutions to American shores. Beyond just covering uprisings and insurrections in France and England, the newspaper made explicit and implicit connections between the antimonarchical battles in Europe and the fight for black liberation in the United States. Douglass saw black men and women in the United States as the American representatives of a chosen people that was international and revolutionary, and he used his newspaper to help them apply the lessons of Paris and London to their domestic battles against oppression. *Freedom's Journal* had equated the responsibilities of black chosenness with a certain kind of proper behavior, and the *Colored American* had connected them to the duties of the prophet. In the pages of the *North Star*, readers learned that being chosen carried with it a requirement to join the revolution.

Douglass had built a newspaper ideally suited to carry the 1848 revolutions from Europe to the United States since, from the outset, he had intended the *North Star* to be the organ of a transatlantic community. The *North Star*'s financing, production, and readership all underscored its international roots and routes. Though Douglass recruited Martin Delany and William C. Nell to serve as his paper's coeditor and publisher, many of the *North Star*'s day-to-day concerns seem to have fallen upon the paper's printer, a Scotsman named John Dick.[10] A year older than Douglass, Dick had moved from Edinburgh to London at the age of sixteen to learn the printing trade, and he immigrated to the United States in 1847 to work for Douglass.[11] Like Robert Sears at the *Colored American*, Dick performed a variety of duties beyond setting type. He wrote numerous articles for the paper, many of which focused on foreign affairs. And in the paper's early years, as Delany traveled the North in search of subscribers, Dick apparently served as an uncredited coeditor. On the multiple occasions when Douglass was away on speaking tours, most of the editorials were signed with Dick's initials (J. D.), and his writings concentrated in particular on events in Europe.[12] Dick's presence exemplified Douglass's interest in international collaboration, and his contributions advanced the *North Star*'s international agenda.

In addition to sending the *North Star* start-up capital and a central staff member, the British Isles provided numerous readers for the paper. With the contacts he had developed during his time abroad, Douglass built a healthy British subscription base. According to the *North Star*'s ledger, of the roughly four hundred and twenty readers subscribed to the paper during its first year, nearly half lived in the British Isles. In addition to individuals, the ledger also names institutional subscribers. Douglass sent copies of the *North Star* to a "Newsroom" in Leicester, to the office of the League of Universal Brotherhood in London, and to the Belfast Ladies Association. He also developed exchanges with newspapers such as the *British Friend* in Glasgow.[13] A single paper could be displayed in a reading room, passed around by members of an organization, or excerpted in an exchange paper. Such institutional allies provided Douglass with the means to spread the *North Star*'s message to a British readership beyond the paper's subscription rolls. And Douglass developed his editorial policies in response to the tastes of his British audience. In one case, for example, the editor apologized to his British readers in particular for reprinting an especially racist attack from the *Democratic Review*. "It is far from our purpose, in managing the editorial department of the NORTH STAR," he declared, "to as-sail the eyes of our readers, *especially our trans-Atlantic readers*, with all the low black-guardisms and vile abuse which the American press may see fit to lavish upon us."[14] Echoing a common strategy, Douglass imagined that the "low" and "vile" qualities of American racism offended the more sophisticated senses of his British audience. Such a portrayal not only flattered his readers abroad, but also cast white Americans as uncouth rubes.[15] Those fighting for black liberation, by contrast, belonged to a more advanced transatlantic culture, and the *North Star* served as the organ of that community.

The form of the newspaper page reinforced such transatlantic connections. Consider, for example, the third page of the April 28, 1848, issue of the *North Star*. There the newspaper pulls readers from both sides of the ocean into the space and time of a decidedly revolutionary Atlantic world. With seven evenly spaced columns, the page follows the paper's standard format and, aside from the image of the ship at the top of the third column, presents readers with a fairly uniform appearance. This uniformity creates a visual sameness over the distant geographies that come together on the page. The three center columns are devoted to the "Foreign News" section, which is filled with breathless accounts of revolutions erupting across Europe. Uprisings are reported from Ireland to Russia, and no space in between (either on the page or the continent) seems safe from the contagious and rapidly spreading revolutionary spirit. The page's second column carries a letter from the black abolitionist Henry Highland Garnet, who provides an account of the attempted escape of nearly eighty slaves in Washington, D.C., an event reportedly inspired by the recent revolution in France. The environment of the *North Star* places Washington next to Paris, making it all the more conceivable that the revolutions of Europe could make the jump to the United States.[16] By bringing together distant times and places on one page, the *North Star* creates a sense of simultaneity among the many fronts of the global war against tyranny.[17] The European revolutions covered in the paper's "Foreign News" section occurred weeks apart from one another, but in the newspaper they seem to happen all at once. And by appearing alongside the European uprisings, the escape attempt in Washington, D.C., joins the fray. The newspaper's spatial architecture thus creates temporal connections. There is an immediacy to the *North Star*'s form, a sense of present tense, which creates a unity of space and time between the multiple sites and moments of a struggle for universal emancipation waged by otherwise distant members of a revolutionary chosen nation.

But the timeliness of the *North Star* also exposes the vast distances that separated the two sides of the ocean. For while steamships and the telegraph increased the pace of transatlantic communication, the *North Star*'s April 28 accounts of the European revolutions reported news that was already weeks old. An insurrection in Madrid, for instance, had occurred on March 20. The newspaper clearly dated the events it described, forcing readers to confront the distance in time between the date on the newspaper's masthead and that of a European uprising that may have otherwise felt fresh and immediate. Indeed, the very sense of urgency that the newspaper conveyed underscored the fact that events abroad were moving at a fast pace, and that the shape of the revolutions may have dramatically changed by the time the news reached American shores.[18] By highlighting the distances that separated the Atlantic world's multiple liberation struggles, the form of the *North Star* revealed the difficulties of applying a single method of revolutionary change to different local circumstances. In other words, the newspaper recognized that the revolutionary character of acting chosen would not look the same in every time and place. Hence, while considering the insurrections erupting across the Atlantic world as fronts in a common war for liberation, the *North Star* urged readers on both sides of the ocean to carefully consider how their local conditions necessarily shaped the particular manifestations of this global struggle.

## Nearer Home Than Paris

Beginning in March 1848, the *North Star* devoted substantial space to covering the February revolution in France, exploring the implications of that uprising in the fight for black liberation in the United States. The newspaper repeatedly drew parallels between the administration of the deposed French king and the American slave power, suggesting that the fate of the first should serve as a warning to the second. "We call upon tyrants the world over, and especially American tyrants," wrote Douglass in his first editorial on the French uprising, "to look and reflect upon this late revolution in France," and remember that it "is impossible that the rebellious spirit of enslaved humanity can always be kept under." He concluded by warning "the slaveholder to learn anew, that human nature is still human nature, and that the time may not be distant when an illustration of the fact may be afforded nearer home than Paris."[19] Eight years earlier the *Colored American* had issued a similar warning by comparing the United States to biblical powers like Chaldea and Assyria. Since God had destroyed those empires for their sins against his chosen people, that paper suggested, the United States would face a similar fate if it continued to enslave and oppress black Americans. In 1840, this premillennial promise offered hope to black readers fighting against a seemingly indestructible slave power. The *North Star*'s reading of the new French revolution made a similar promise, though rather than rely upon biblical precedent the paper's black readers needed to only look to events abroad to gain faith in the success of their own liberation struggle.

In mid-April, events on the ground seemed to indicate that the revolutionary wave had reached American soil. On April 13, the schooner *Pearl* docked in Washington, D.C., and seventy-seven enslaved men, women, and children boarded the ship. Daniel Drayton, captain of the *Pearl*, sailed up the Potomac with the plan of transporting his passengers to the free states. But, disastrously, he chose to wait out bad weather in a cove at the mouth of the river, and was caught by a pursuing ship. The fugitive slaves and the crew of the *Pearl* were brought back to the nation's capital and paraded in chains through the city's streets on their way to the federal jail. Drayton and his crewmates were held for trial, and the vast majority of the recaptured slaves quickly were sold south. Despite its failure, the scale and audacity of the attempted escape set off a national firestorm. Pro-slavery advocates framed the escape attempt as an assault on the property rights of slaveholders, and blamed the entire affair on northern abolitionists and their allies in Washington. One correspondent to the New York *Herald*, for example, claimed to have "never heard of a more outrageous or audacious violation of constitutional and personal rights, than that perpetrated by a gang of abolitionists and kidnappers in Washington, D.C."[20]

The *North Star* folded the *Pearl* episode into its ongoing coverage of the 1848 revolutions. Douglass first commented on the events in Washington in his April 28 editorial, where he chided Americans for their cool reception of the French Revolution postemancipation. "While we write this," he explained, "a paper has been handed us containing a detailed account of the arrest and imprisonment in Washington of seventy-seven slaves, for an attempt to escape from the land of slavery to a land of liberty; and for helping these men to escape, three white American citizens are confined in an American dungeon." In the scene Douglass sets, news of the *Pearl* (carried in a newspaper) interrupts him in the midst of writing a piece on American reactions to French emancipation. But instead of distracting the editor from the task at hand, the plight of the fugitives provides him with a striking illustration of slavery in the nation's capital. And the presence of slavery in Washington, D.C., supports Douglass's larger claim that European revolutionaries should not expect support from the United States, since "it would be more consistent with our character for cruelty, (if not for cowardice,) to invade France with an army, with the avowed purpose of reinstating Louis Philippe, and restoring the emancipated slaves to their tyrant masters; than to sympathise with France in her struggles for a republic."[21] Throughout its coverage of the *Pearl* escape attempt and the aftermath, the *North Star* would follow Douglass's strategy in this editorial and relate happenings in Washington to a broader transatlantic revolutionary moment.

Indeed, the *North Star* seized upon reports that the February uprising in Paris had directly inspired the escape attempt of the seventy-seven slaves in Washington. In his April 28 letter to the paper Henry Highland Garnet included a lengthy excerpt from the Troy *Daily Post*, reporting that a "result of the grand sympathy meeting, got up in Washington, to glory in the success of Republicanism in France, with the fine speeches at them, in favor of the rights of man, appears to have been, to lead a number of slaves, who were probably listeners, to think that they too were to share in the glorious boon of freedom."[22] A week later, William C. Nell imagined the *Pearl*'s passengers "assembled at the Washington meeting of sympathy with the French," where the enslaved men and women heard "Senators glorifying a revolution which had made all the people in France free." As a result, Nell concluded, "the spark of freedom ignited their hearts, and behold their declaration of independence!"[23] In truth, speeches lauding the French revolutionaries had little to do with the meticulously planned escape attempt.[24] But in the pages of the *North Star*, it appeared that the news of the revolution in France had led American slaves to seize, however fleetingly, their own freedom.

By establishing the *Pearl* affair as an American echo of events in Europe, the *North Star* read the barricades of Paris as an inspiration for black freedom fighters rather than as a blueprint for resistance. But at times the paper envisioned, and even called for, a more direct application of French revolutionary tactics. Garnet, for example, argued that the men and women aboard the *Pearl* could have evaded recapture if they had borrowed the tools and techniques of the European insurgents. Rather than be caught unawares and unarmed by a pursuing vessel, he wrote in his letter to the *North Star*, the *Pearl*'s passengers "ought to have been better prepared." "One good cannon, well managed," Garnet reasoned, "would have crippled a dozen steamers. If white men were to undertake to runaway [sic] from human bloodhounds, they see to it, that the Telegraph wires were cut the distance of every ten miles in the direction of their flight. More than this they would do; they would pull up the rails of the rail-roads, and stop the speed of the iron horses." Cannons, of course, were not normally the tools of slaves running for freedom. Nor were cutting wires and ripping up railroads the typical tactics of black fugitives. Garnet critiqued the fugitives aboard the *Pearl*, then, for acting like runaways instead of revolutionaries. In order to be successful, he reasoned, the *Pearl*'s passengers needed to be prepared to use violence. Moreover, they should have recognized that technologies like the telegraph not only brought inspiring stories of foreign fighters to American shores but also carried news of the escaping slaves to their enemies. In other words, the black men and women aboard the *Pearl* should have taken up the tools and techniques of someone fighting in the streets of Paris, Berlin, or Vienna. White men and women fighting for liberation from tyranny engaged in these sorts of tactics. "Do you think friend Douglass," Garnet asked, "it would be an unpardonable sin for slaves to do the same?"[25]

Garnet's challenge to Douglass emerged from an ongoing debate among black activists over the use of violence in the struggle for black liberation. At the 1847 National Convention of Colored People, for example, Garnet had fiercely objected to a report, coauthored by Douglass, on the "Best Means to Abolish Slavery and Caste in the United States." The report denounced "any plan of emancipation involving a resort to bloodshed," and urged those in attendance to "set our faces against all such absurd, unavailing, dangerous and mischievous ravings, emanating from what source they may."[26] Six years earlier, Garnet had offered exactly this sort of plan in his "Address to the Slaves of the United States of America," and in 1847 he continued to resist Douglass's devotion to "moral suasion."[27] The 1847 convention registered the unsettled nature of the debate over violence by ultimately endorsing the report from Douglass's committee *and* passing a resolution recommending "to our people the propriety of instructing their sons in the art of war."[28] With the onset of the 1848 revolutions in Europe, Garnet renewed his call for violent tactics in the fight against slavery in the United States. In April of that year, in addition to composing his letter to the *North Star*, Garnet released a pamphlet that reprinted his 1843 address together with David Walker's *Appeal*. So, as black Americans considered the best way to fulfill the revolutionary responsibilities of being chosen, they were confronted, perhaps for the first time, by Walker's declaration that the "man who would not fight under our Lord and Master Jesus Christ, in the glorious and heavenly cause of freedom and of God—to be delivered from the most wretched, abject and servile slavery, that ever a people was afflicted with since the foundation of the world, to the present day—ought to be kept with all of his children or family, in slavery, or in chains, to be butchered by his *cruel enemies*"; and Garnet's conclusion that "[h]owever much you and all of us may desire it, there is not much hope of Redemption without the shedding of blood."[29] In and out of the newspaper, then, Garnet saw violence as an acceptable, and perhaps necessary, part of acting chosen.

In his writings on the 1848 revolutions Douglass, for his part, remained staunchly opposed to violence. But the *North Star* could transcend the views of its editor, and in the early summer of 1848 the newspaper imagined a course of action more in line with Garnet's reasoning, island-hopping its way to the United States. France's provisional government had declared emancipation in its colonies on April 27, but it took nearly two months for the declaration to reach the Caribbean. On May 23 slaves in Martinique successfully rebelled and forced the local governor to declare immediate emancipation. Then on May 27, the governor of the neighboring island of Guadeloupe followed suit in order to preempt a similar uprising. The provisional government's declaration arrived eleven days later.[30] On June 30 the *North Star* reprinted a piece from the Boston *Bee*, whose author trembled at the implications of the French Atlantic uprisings for the United States. "Do not the scenes now enacting in Martinique and Guadaloupe [sic]," the writer asked, "convey a warning to us as a people?" Reading the European uprisings and the Caribbean revolutions as fronts in a global "*war* of races," the author reasoned that white Americans "cannot expect that the negro race of this country will forever remain quiet."[31] Instead, the article concluded, the "spirit of rebellion, freedom, or whatever any one chooses to call it, will, sooner or later, arouse them to action, and the evil hour is unquestionably hastened on by the mad fanaticism of those who are crying out for immediate emancipation."[32] Though evidently written by an opponent of the abolitionists, the article's contention that antislavery agitation "unquestionably hastened" the "evil hour" of black liberation served in the pages of the *North Star* as a rallying cry for American and British readers. A week later, the newspaper reprinted a report of a suspected insurrection in Cuba. "There have," wrote the article's author, "been lately some serious symptoms of insurrection discovered among the slaves of this island." The writer surmised that news of the emancipation of the slaves in the French islands "and the terrible vengeance which they are inflicting upon their former masters" had likely "occasioned the present symptoms of outbreak, and may yet produce more decisive effects as they become more generally known among the slaves."[33] With the rumblings of a slave uprising in Cuba, it seemed that the "spirit of rebellion" detected by the writer for the Boston *Bee* had already spread from the Antilles, and now flourished just off the coast of Florida.

In the pages of the *North Star*, the Antilles exemplified the possibility that the Atlantic spirit of revolution could manifest as a slave rebellion as well as an escape attempt. For the newspaper, the *Pearl* proved that the revolutions rocking the Atlantic world could inspire slaves to flee from their oppressors, while the uprisings in Martinique and Guadeloupe presented another strategy for liberation—one that seemed to be working its way across the ocean. Like the *Colored American*'s millennial visions, the *North Star*'s picture of a wave of insurrections flowing toward the United States warned white Americans to abandon slavery before it arrived, and promised black Americans their liberation was at hand. But unlike its predecessor, the *North Star* routed its guarantee of freedom through current events rather than rooting it in scripture. Rather than erase the biblical typology so central to black chosenness, the *North Star*'s emphasis on worldly happenings simply clarified the timing of prophecy. According to scripture, God had worked through human armies to destroy Babylon and free the Israelites, and the specter of an Atlantic revolution crashing down on American shores suggested that the United States was on the verge of being destroyed by an uprising of God's chosen nation, whose members lived within and beyond its borders.

## *Barricades in the House of Commons*

But while the *North Star* held up the specter of a slave rebellion, its editor remained hopeful that an American version of the 1848 events in Europe would translate the urban warfare of Paris into a peaceful path to liberation. Indeed, despite the quick recapture of the fugitives aboard the *Pearl*, Douglass insisted that the escape attempt had provided a moral victory for abolitionists and paved the way for a successful legal challenge to slavery. The affair, he argued, had brought the practice of slavery in Washington to the attention of the nation, and this increased scrutiny could only help the abolitionist cause. "The broad eye of the nation will be opened upon slavery in the District as it has never before," Douglass wrote in a May 5 editorial; "the North and West will feel keenly the damning disgrace of their Capital being a slave mart, and a deeper hatred of slavery will be engendered in the popular mind throughout the Union." The editor saw the scene of seventy-seven men and women "running *from* the Temple of Liberty to be free," and then subsequently being paraded through the streets of the nation's capital and sold south, as a public relations disaster for American slavery.[34] Articles like those in the Troy *Daily Post* seemed to support this reading, and the *North Star* reprinted similar pieces from a variety of northern newspapers.[35]

In addition to its value as a rallying cry, the aftermath of the escape attempt provided antislavery activists with an ideal opportunity to challenge the legality of slavery in the nation's capital. The District of Columbia had long been a focus of abolitionists, since Congress had the power to do there what it could not in the various states: end slavery. Abolitionists in New England saw the impending trial of the crew of the *Pearl* as an occasion to force the issue, and on April 25 they held a meeting in Boston to discuss the affair. A report from the gathering, reprinted in the *North Star*, denied "that the Constitution confers on Congress any power to establish, or to maintain slavery, in territory over which it possesses exclusive jurisdiction," and those at the meeting set about hiring counsel that would bring "before the Supreme Court of the United States the question of the legality of slavery in the District of Columbia."[36] Douglass urged his readers to support a proposed defense fund. "Such a trial in the Supreme Court of the United States, with the present power of the anti-slavery press, the general anti-slavery sentiment at the North, and the great tide of moral influence setting in upon us from all parts of the civilized world," he wrote in the May 5 issue of the *North Star*, "might be made instrumental in the overthrow of slavery in the District of Columbia."[37] In addition to the progress in public opinion in the North (influenced by newspapers like the *North Star*), Douglass cited international pressure as a key reason why the spring of 1848 represented the right time to undertake such a challenge, implying that European revolutionaries would exert a "moral influence" over the Justices of the Supreme Court.

By casting the *Pearl* affair as a manifestation of the revolutionary sprit that had brought down Louis Philippe, the *North Star* imagined the American 1848 as a battle waged in the courtroom rather than in the street. The importance of the *North Star*'s British contributors and readers helps to explain this admittedly odd translation of a popular uprising from below into a fight for legal reform from above. For, as the newspaper's more explicitly British-directed pieces reveal, there was something decidedly English about Douglass's faith in the reasonableness of popular opinion and the government.[38] Through reprinted pieces from British newspapers and letters from its own London correspondents, the *North Star* covered in great detail the implications of the February revolution for readers in the British Isles. The *North Star*'s inclusion of such voices followed the practice of most American newspapers. Traveling by steamship en route to their distribution outlets, British newspapers represented the primary source of European news. Few American papers had correspondents in Paris, so American editors largely used British voices to tell the story of the French uprising.[39] While the *North Star* followed the general form of American newspapers by placing much of its British reporting under the heading of "Foreign News," its large and carefully cultivated British readership complicated this classification. Such readers would have considered accounts of British happenings decidedly domestic. Hence, a report reprinted from the London *Times* that declared, "[m]ore important, if possible, than even the momentous events of Paris, is the influence of those events upon us," reflected the priorities of nearly half of the *North Star*'s readers.[40]

Just as Douglass had worked through his editorials to establish a connection between the French revolutionaries and American abolitionists, the *North Star*'s British contributors asserted an affinity between republicans in Paris and reformers in London. One London correspondent to the paper, whose initials R. S. D. appear after every letter, wrote that the "great mass of the people of this country sympathise warmly, with the people of France and the noble spirit of the provisional government."[41] Jonathan Carr, who had spearheaded the British effort to raise the initial money for the *North Star*, composed an "Address, of the Inhabitants of Carlisle, England, in Public Meeting Assembled, to Their Brethren in France," which the newspaper reprinted. "Whilst the wonderful agencies of steam and electricity are almost bringing our two countries within speaking distance," proclaimed Carr, "let our hearts also draw near to each other in the communion and fellowship of true neighbors and friends, feeling the bond of a universal brotherhood."[42]

These very same voices, though, pointed out crucial differences between the French, who had turned to the barricades, and their British counterparts. Lest British readers fear that the spark of full-scale revolution would travel from Paris to London, the *North Star* focused on the tradition of reform that anchored British society. While cognizant that "the epidemic of popular excitement, prevalent throughout Europe, and bursting into revolution so near us, is not without its effects even upon our more staid and sober temperaments," the writer for the London *Times* saw no sign "that any class here is tainted with disaffection, or inclined to *emeute* [riot]."[43] The correspondent R. S. D. did report "some rioting in London and other large towns," but blamed the violence upon "the ignorant and degraded, who swarm in painful numbers in all the great centres of population in this country." "It is not by any such proceeding that Great Britain will work out its freedom," wrote the correspondent, "but by the energetic agitation of public opinion, acting in a constitutional way on the government and parliament, and thus obtaining gradually, yet surely, all necessary reforms."[44] The author of another reprinted piece explained how the French revolutionary spirit manifested in a British context: "Our emeutes are public meetings, and our barricades in the House of Commons."[45] The *North Star*'s subsequent interpretation of the *Pearl* escape attempt reflects precisely this faith in institutional reform to right society's wrongs.

But events in the British Isles seemed to contradict this faith in British reserve. Antitax riots broke out in Glasgow and London on March 6, and the London *Times* reported that the violence, "coupled with the late events in Paris, gave rise to a general dread of some political disturbance."[46] Tensions escalated when, on March 18, the Chartist newspaper the *Northern Star* announced that members of the movement would present a petition with their demands to Parliament on April 10. The Chartists, who had been fighting for political reform for over a decade, planned a mass meeting and procession to accompany the presentation of the petition. The government, remembering that the revolution in Paris had begun as a peaceful protest, responded by banning the gathering, deploying troops and cannons throughout London, swearing in and arming thousands of special constables to the police force, and sending the Queen to the Isle of Wight for her safety. "After such extraordinary preparations," wrote R. S. D. to the *North Star*, "people began to talk of a revolution here."[47] But April 10 proved anticlimactic. Chartist organizers had hoped for a gathering of two to three hundred thousand, but fewer than ten thousand marchers materialized. After a meeting with the police, the Chartist leader (and editor of the *Northern Star*) Feargus O'Connor agreed to disperse the gathering and presented the petition with only a small entourage. Upon inspection, it was revealed that the petition itself contained less than half of the reported 5,700,000 signatures, and that a number of these were forgeries. The correspondent R. S. D. concluded that April 10 was "a day in which people had apparently conspired to make fools of each other."[48]

In the pages of the *North Star*, Douglass unequivocally condemned the Chartists for bringing Great Britain to the brink of violent revolution. In a May 5 editorial titled "Chartists of England," he described their attempt to "overawe the government" through a show of force as a "wild and wicked measure," and rejoiced that the Chartists had "wisely abandoned the mischievous and useless project." Unlike the revolutionaries on the continent, Douglass argued, the British had avenues for reform besides a violent uprising. "While the liberty of speech is allowed—while the freedom of the press is permitted, and the right of petition is respected, and while men are left free to originate reforms without, and Members are left free to propose and advocate them within the walls of Parliament," he wrote, "no excuse can be valid for resorting to the fearful use of brute force and bloodshed."[49] While sympathetic to the overall aims of the Chartist movement, Douglass could not countenance violence when alternative avenues to reform remained. The revolutionaries in cities like Paris and Berlin had no voice in an elected parliament, nor could they print their views in newspapers without fear of government reprisal. By contrast, the Chartists could elect sympathetic representatives and publish a number of journals. For Douglass, the very fact that the Chartists could present their petition to Parliament, and have their concerns taken up by that body's members, demonstrated the openness of the political process. Violent revolution had no place in such a society.[50]

The details of "Chartists of England" explicitly addressed the concerns of the *North Star*'s British readers. But Douglass's take on the role of violence in liberation struggles not only made up a part of the paper's coverage of the 1848 revolutions in Europe but also represented an indirect commentary on how black men and women should translate those uprisings onto American soil. The May 5 editorial dovetailed in particular with the paper's approach to the *Pearl* escape attempt and its aftermath. The *North Star*'s reading of the *Pearl* episode as an opportunity to challenge slavery in court offered an American version of Douglass's insistence upon a nonviolent, parliamentary solution to oppression in Great Britain. Moreover, the paper emphasized how the escape attempt itself had been a peaceful affair. A week before composing his editorial on the Chartists, Douglass contrasted the peacefulness of the fugitive slaves, who had attempted "in the most harmless way possible, without violence or injury to any one, to gain their freedom," with the violence of their captors, "a band of armed menhunters [sic], who compel them, at the musket's mouth, to surrender."[51] For Douglass, the *Pearl* episode revealed violence as a tool of oppressors, not of the oppressed.

But while Douglass chided the Chartists for trying to transport continental revolutionary tactics to London, other articles pointed out the ways in which a British model of parliamentary reform might not apply to the antislavery struggle in the United States. In "Chartists of England," Douglass cited freedom of speech and freedom of the press as preconditions for peaceful reform. The aftermath of the *Pearl* episode had, however, revealed the fragility of these freedoms in the United States. After the fugitives had been returned to Washington, D.C., a rumor spread that Gamaliel Bailey, editor of the local antislavery newspaper *National Era*, had played a part in the attempted escape. A mob attacked the newspaper office, demanding that Bailey shut down his presses and leave the city. Though Bailey and his newspaper ultimately survived, the *North Star* used the attack to highlight the precarious position of a free press in the nation's capital. Three columns over from "Chartists of England," the paper reprinted, under the title "The Riot in Washington," a detailed account of the attack. "What a commentary on our free institutions," Douglass snidely remarked in his introduction to the excerpt.[52] A week earlier, the *North Star* had included a letter from Bailey decrying the attack as "aimed at the freedom of the press." "It is a damning disgrace," the *Era*'s editor continued, "that at the very moment we are rejoicing with the people of France at their triumph over a despot who undertook to enslave the press, an attempt should be made to strike down the freedom of the press in this capital city of this Republic, in sight of the National Legislature."[53] For Bailey, the actions of the mob suggested a parallel between Washington, D.C., and Paris before the February revolution. Like France under Louis Philippe, Bailey portrayed the United States as a land where a newspaper could be destroyed for voicing an unpopular opinion.

Lest readers mistake the attempted suppression of the *Era* as an isolated incident unrepresentative of the position of the government, the *North Star* covered in detail congressional debates surrounding the affair. These debates revealed that United States senators not only supported suppression of the press but also sought to silence even the most tangential discussion of slavery. A report from the Senate floor covered the front page of the paper's May 12 issue. In response to the attack on the *Era*, Senator John Parker Hale from New Hampshire, who had been elected in part because of his antislavery leanings, asked leave to introduce a bill "for the Protection of Property in the District of Columbia—making any city, town, or corporate place liable for injuries done by mobs." Senators Jefferson Davis and John C. Calhoun erupted in a fury, charging Hale with attacking the institution of slavery. For Calhoun, the attack on the *Era* had been an appropriate response to the charge that Bailey may have been involved in the *Pearl* escape, and any measure designed to forestall similar reactions in the future would "prevent the just indignation of our people from wreaking their vengeance upon the atrocious perpetrators of these crimes, or those who contribute to them." Here, the anger of the slaveholder clearly trumped the freedom of the press. Southern senators objected not only to the substance of Hale's bill but also to his temerity in introducing legislation that even slightly touched upon the subject of slavery. Hale indignantly responded that though he realized that the "right of speech was sacrificed long ago . . . it is to be proclaimed that we cannot even introduce a bill looking to the execution of the plainest provisions of the Constitution, and the clearest principles of justice, for the protection of human rights, because gentlemen choose to construe it into an attack upon that particular institution."[54] At the same time that Douglass urged the British to pursue peaceful means because they lived in a society with a free press, free speech, and political representatives free to introduce legislative reform, the *North Star* showed its readers that none of these conditions existed in the United States.

Without such freedoms, the United States resembled Europe's most oppressive powers rather than the more liberal British state. In light of the failure of the *Pearl* escape, the attack on the *National Era* in the United States, and the progress of revolutionary movements in Europe, Garnet's excerpt from the *Daily Post* announced "that soon, Moscow in Russia, and Washington in the United States, will be the only national capitols [sic] that can furnish a mob to destroy a free press; and that the only victory against human liberty this year is in our national capital, over sixty negroes."[55] In linking the United States to Europe's authoritarian regimes, the *North Star* echoed the *Colored American*'s image of the United States as an American Babylon. In Douglass's paper, though, the true character of the American government (like the certainty in black liberation) emerged not from reading the Bible but rather from studying foreign affairs. The *North Star* invited its readers to compare conditions in the United States to those in France and England, examine the means and ends of the liberation movements in those countries, and apply the lessons learned to their own struggles for freedom at home. In doing so, Douglass's newspaper leveled a quiet but thorough critique of the American exceptionalism that had shaped the *Colored American*'s vision of black chosenness. The earlier newspaper defined God's chosen people not only by their oppression but also by their claim to an American nationality. By contrast, the *North Star* cast black Americans as one part of a global army of liberation whose members fought against tyranny in all its forms.

## Revolutionary Character

The *North Star* imagined an Atlantic world made up of a series of interconnected revolutionary struggles, as its pages created connections between the establishment of a republic in France, the Chartist movement in England, and the *Pearl* episode in the United States. But the newspaper also urged its readers to carefully consider local circumstances when developing a course of struggle. For black Americans, this meant not only recognizing the similarities that linked the antislavery struggle in the United States and battles being waged at the barricades or in the House of Commons but also understanding the differences that separated Washington, D.C., from Paris and London. The paper's coverage of the escape attempt aboard the *Pearl* and its aftermath revealed that the freedoms that made legislative reform possible in England did not exist in the United States. And while the policies of the U.S. government may have resembled those of Louis Philippe's, black Americans lacked the strength in arms and numbers that had allowed the French republicans to overthrow the king. In its search for a liberation strategy that could succeed given the conditions in the United States, the *North Star* turned to public propriety. In taking up the theme that had dominated *Freedom's Journal* two decades earlier, but now within the larger context of the 1848 uprisings, Douglass's newspaper clarified the revolutionary potential of acting chosen.

On July 14, Douglass presented his readers with a lengthy editorial that asked the question, "What Are the Colored People Doing for Themselves?" While "the oppressed of the old world" had risen up against their tyrants, he lamented the fact that "we, who are enduring wrongs far more grievous than any other portion of the great family of man, are comparatively idle and indifferent about our welfare."[56] Black Americans may not have been able to echo their European brethren and overthrow their government or bring their concerns before Congress, but Douglass saw these limitations as no reason for paralysis. Instead, he urged his black readers to cultivate and display proper morals. Douglass insisted that "[w]hat we, the colored people, want, is *character*, and this nobody can give us."[57] He defined "the great elements of character" as "[i]ndustry, sobriety, honesty, combined with intelligence and a due self-respect," and assured the *North Star*'s readers that in the presence of such qualities "prejudice is abashed, confused and mortified." As a means of translating the revolutionary energies of Europe onto American soil, Douglass asked his readers to focus on self-improvement and have faith that "by an honest, upright life, we may at last wring from a reluctant public the all-important confession, that we are men, worthy men, good citizens, good Christians, and ought to be treated as such."[58] *Freedom's Journal's* editors had assured readers that their theory of acting chosen, based on certain class norms, would when put into practice convince state legislatures to end slavery in the United States. Having connected black Americans to a community that stretched far beyond local, state, and national boundaries, Douglass adopted a strikingly similar version of acting chosen as the practices of an international revolution.

Just as the Fourth of July celebrations in 1827 had provided *Freedom's Journal* with an opportunity to test this theory, the *North Star* saw the 1848 commemorations of emancipation in the British West Indies as proof that public propriety could help the cause of black liberation.[59] On August 1, between four and five hundred black men, women, and children gathered in front of Rochester's Ford Street Baptist Church. Led by marshals on horseback and Adams' Brass Band, the procession wove its way through the city streets before arriving at Washington Square, where an audience of nearly two thousand revelers listened to a series of speakers that included Douglass. In a review for the *North Star*, Douglass underscored how "the day passed harmoniously, soberly, and pleasantly, without any of those riotous manifestations which are too apt to disgrace the rejoicing days of both the blacks and the whites." Because of this proper behavior, he implied, the "cause of human equality has been advanced by the proceedings of this day."[60] In order to highlight the positive impression that the day's decorum had left with white onlookers, the *North Star* reprinted numerous accounts from local newspapers. A writer for the Rochester *American* declared that the "proceedings were conducted with entire decorum and propriety throughout," while the *National Reformer* went so far as to "express an humble wish that our fourth of July might in all future time be as orderly and appropriately celebrated by our white friends, as was the first of August by our colored citizens."[61] Like *Freedom's Journal* had done two decades earlier, the *North Star* used such reports to show its black readers that white onlookers responded to public propriety. Though neither violent insurrection nor legislative reform seemed like viable paths to black liberation, the newspaper urged its readers not to fall into despair but rather to focus on building support for their cause through upright conduct.

Rather than a retreat from the fight for black freedom, then, the *North Star* considered public propriety to be the most effective way that black Americans could practice the spirit of revolution in their daily lives. Moreover, the newspaper implied that, as a strategy for siphoning northern white support away from the slave power, black decorum could set the stage for a successful slave insurrection. In his August 1 address, which the *North Star* printed in its entirety three days later, Douglass argued that southern slavery could not survive without support from northern whites. "Slavery exists in this land," he charged, "because of the moral, constitutional, political and religious support which it receives from the people of this country, especially the people of the North." Such support doomed any attempted slave uprising, since "the Constitution guarantees to the slaveholder the naval and military support of the nation." Rather than simply a fight between slaves and their masters, then, an insurrection would pit "[s]eventeen millions of armed, disciplined, and intelligent people, against three millions of unarmed and uninformed." But if black freedom fighters could rely upon northern whites to stand aside when an uprising occurred, then, Douglass surmised, "the slave might instantly assert and maintain his rights."[62] So for black Americans to successfully reenact the scenes of Paris, Martinique, or Guadeloupe on U.S. soil, they had to first convince northern whites that they deserved freedom. Public propriety could do just that. Displays of black morality and decorum, Douglass argued, shattered antiblack prejudice by forcing white Americans to grapple with the fact of black humanity. *Freedom's Journal* had followed a similar line of logic, expecting this kind of conversion to prompt whites to give slaves their freedom through legislative acts of emancipation. By contrast, the *North Star* only needed white northerners to remain neutral while black Americans fought for their own liberation. Convincing northerners not to fight would be no small task but, as Douglass had pointed out, an insurrection that confronted a united American nation would be suicidal. As the white response to Rochester's August 1 celebration suggested, the first stage of the strategy, at least, was working. The newspaper reports reprinted in the *North Star* showed that public propriety could convince white onlookers to accept black humanity. Through their personal and collective conduct, then, black Americans could participate in the global fight against tyranny. While not as dramatic as the barricades in the streets of Paris or even the arguments in London's House of Commons, the *North Star* showed its readers that a display of character could be revolutionary.

In the pages of the *North Star*, public propriety emerged not as a retreat from the promise of 1848 but rather as a valid manifestation of its revolutionary energies. By working through the connections between the struggles for black freedom in the United States and the 1848 revolutions in Europe, Douglass and his staff imagined black Americans as one part of a global community of the oppressed engaged in a common struggle against tyranny of all sorts. By placing the struggles of black Americans within this broader context, the *North Star* hoped to transform seeming defeats, like the recapture of the *Pearl*'s passengers, into potential victories. Like *Freedom's Journal* and the *Colored American*, Douglass's paper offered its black readers hope in the face of seemingly insurmountable odds. But rather than root its confidence for black liberation in faith in white legislators or millennial prophecy, the *North Star* routed its hopes through events in the larger Atlantic world. In doing so, the paper uncoupled the promise of black chosenness from American identity. Indeed, black Americans could be sure of their eventual victory because they belonged to a revolutionary force that transcended national boundaries.

CHAPTER 4

# The Limits of Black Chosenness

We repeat, that, no "negro" be he King of Dahomey, Emperor of Timbuctoo or Frederick Douglass, can advance one lot the interests of colored British subjects, but the reverse is the fact as the superior influence of British subjects, without complexional distinction, is made to bear upon other nations and people, and to the benefit of the downtrodden everywhere.
—Mary Ann Shadd Cary, "Plastering, &c.," *Provincial Freeman*, July 19, 1856

On February 16, 1849, Frederick Douglass's *North Star* printed a letter from its itinerant coeditor Martin Delany. Delany, who had been regularly reporting back on the progress of his lengthy subscription tour, provided in his February missive the usual commentary on the black communities he had visited and individuals who had caught his eye. On this occasion, he related how, during a stop in Wilmington, Delaware, he was particularly taken with a young woman who had spoken up during an antislavery meeting. "Among the people," he wrote to Douglass, "a choice character is found in the person of Mrs. Mary Ann Shadd." Delany described his new acquaintance—somewhat condescendingly—as "an excellent girl," and he explained that she had recently completed a pamphlet "on the elevation of our people." He considered this work "an excellent introduction to that great subject, the Moral Elevation of the colored people," and he seemed pleased that Shadd would "henceforth give her whole attention to writing."[1]

Douglass, for his part, seemed less interested in the work of the young woman from Wilmington. He made no more mention of her pamphlet in his newspaper until June, when a Philadelphia correspondent quoted at length from the twelve-page document, which Shadd had evidently titled *Hints to the Colored People of the North*. The correspondent explained that he had been try-

Figure 4.1. *Mrs. Mary Ann Shadd Cary*. Courtesy of the Library and Archives Canada.

ing to distribute the piece in Philadelphia, and though he believed the work to be "widely circulated in this city," he had "not been able, as yet, to sell more than three or four in about two months." The Philadelphia writer likely hoped that a mention of the pamphlet in the *North Star* would increase its sales, though he admitted that "some have said that had they known that the work contained some things which it does, they would not have had it as a gift." While the letter's author claimed, "what the objectionable part is, I have yet to learn, unless it be its telling too much truth," the section he quoted from took up the very same argument that had alienated so many of *Freedom's Journal*'s readers. In her pamphlet, Shadd criticized the tradition in black communities of holding "processions, expensive entertainments, excursions," and "public dinners and suppers." She lambasted those who participated in such extravagances as merely seeking the "praise" of onlookers, which served as "incense to our susceptible imaginations, instead of gall and wormwood to our souls, as it should have been, and as it really is to our hopes, if we continue to follow this policy."[2] Evidently, given the pamphlet's poor sales (a fact that could partially explain why no extant copies remain), black Philadelphians in 1849 rejected such unsolicited advice as strongly as black New Yorkers had twenty years earlier.

This response did not, however, dissuade Mary Ann Shadd from moving boldly into the public arena of print. In March 1848, perhaps frustrated that Douglass had yet to endorse her pamphlet, Shadd wrote directly to the *North Star*. Cannily, she offered a letter attacking black clergymen, a topic near to Douglass's heart and likely to find a place in the pages of his newspaper. Yet, before she moved into the meat of her missive, Shadd alluded to the theme that would occupy her for the next decade. Commenting on the results of black conventions, she lamented that "[w]e have put forth few practical efforts to an end." "We should do more," she concluded, "and talk less." Impatient with discussions of black liberation that seemed increasingly to operate only on the rhetorical level, Shadd yearned for a practical, immediate plan that she could follow. Though she would search for three more years, in 1851 she found such a solution: emigration to Canada. After her relocation north, Shadd quickly became a leading voice among black American communities in Canada. Toward this end, she deepened her already-demonstrated investment in print, composing another pamphlet and founding and editing the *Provincial Freeman*, thus becoming the first black woman to edit a newspaper in North America. Apparently, Shadd had written in multiple registers when, in her letter to the *North Star*, she declared, "in anything relating to our people, I am insensible of boundaries."³

Like Douglass, Shadd possessed a personal connection to her predecessors in the black press. Shortly before emigrating to Canada, Shadd worked as a teacher at Primary School No. 1 in New York City. The school was located on Centre Street, steps away from the site of *Freedom's Journal*'s founding, and run by an organization that counted Samuel Cornish (that newspaper's coeditor) as a main member. During her time in New York, Shadd also developed a friendship with Charles Ray, former editor of the *Colored American*. By the time she left New York in the fall of 1851, Shadd felt that her friendships with Cornish and Ray were strong enough to list the two men as references.⁴

But despite such connections, the male-dominated institutions of black activism did not always offer Shadd a warm welcome. For example, Shadd encountered fierce resistance when she attempted to attend the 1855 Colored National Convention in Philadelphia. According to the convention's minutes, a motion to approve her as a corresponding member "gave rise to a spirited discussion."⁵ Shadd was ultimately accepted into the convention by a vote of thirty-eight to twenty-three in favor, but out of the numerous motions to approve corresponding members hers was the only case that created a controversy. In every other case, all involving men, the applicant was approved without discussion or the need for a ballot. Shadd was allowed to join the convention, then, but only after a fight. Shadd's entry into the world of black newspapers was greeted with similar hostility. Douglass, to his credit, consistently supported her efforts, and Delany would become one of her most loyal allies. But Henry Bibb, editor of the Canada-based *Voice of the Fugitive*, leveled a series of brutal attacks against his potential competitor. Such opposition helped shape the *Provincial Freeman*, as the newspaper consistently challenged the authority of the black men who would silence its founding editor.

As a newspaper designed by and for women and men who existed at the margins of U.S. black activism, the *Provincial Freeman* took aim at the two exceptionalisms that anchored the black chosenness developed by earlier black newspapers: American and black. Similar to the *North Star*, the *Provincial Freeman* uncoupled the promise of black liberation from the claim to an American identity. But whereas Douglass's paper had nevertheless argued that black Americans could point the way toward peaceful revolution, Shadd and her staff saw no value in anything emanating from the American hemisphere. In the mid-1850s British soil seemed to offer the only sanctuary for black freedom, and so the *Provincial Freeman* urged its black readers to move to Canada, abandon all claims to American identity, and embrace their status as subjects of the British Crown. In privileging Britishness over all other markers of identity, the *Provincial Freeman* upended black exceptionalism. Having experienced firsthand how self-appointed black leaders used the idea of racial unity to silence dissenting voices, Shadd remained deeply suspicious of any talk of race-based communal identity. Emerging as a challenge to the patriarchy of black activism, at a moment when British soil seemed to offer the only sanctuary for black freedom, the *Provincial Freeman* tried to convince its readers that being British was more important than being black. In doing so, the newspaper revealed the limits of black chosenness.

### Making a Competing Newspaper

Mary Ann Shadd was born on October 9, 1823, in Wilmington, Delaware. Her parents, Abraham and Harriet Shadd, were nominally free, her father being a successful cobbler and respected voice in the black abolitionist movement. When she was ten years old, the family moved to West Chester, Pennsylvania, a community roughly fifteen miles south of Philadelphia. Shadd was well educated, most likely in a Quaker setting, and in her late teens returned to Wilmington as a schoolteacher. Over the next decade she would work as a teacher in Pennsylvania, New Jersey, and New York City before deciding in 1851, at the age of twenty-eight, to emigrate to Canada. Shadd initially settled in Windsor, a border town located at the terminus of the Great Western Railway. There, she continued her work as a teacher and opened a school for black and white children. At the same time that Shadd fought to keep her struggling school afloat financially, she continued to write and publish. She wrote letters to abolitionist newspapers and, by June 1852, had composed *A Plea for Emigration; or Notes of Canada West, in Its Moral, Social and Political Aspect, with Suggestions Respecting Mexico, W. Indies and Vancouver's Island, for the Information of Colored Emigrants*, a forty-four-page pamphlet published in Detroit. *Notes of Canada West*, as the pamphlet became known, defies any easy generic classification, acting simultaneously as a travel narrative, almanac, and work of political theory.[6] By the end of 1852 Shadd concluded that, while a pamphlet and letters to the editor had provided her an entry into the public arena of print, the impact of these efforts paled in comparison to the power wielded by those who edited their own newspapers. She thus began to lay the groundwork for the *Provincial Freeman*, a paper designed for Canada's black citizens.

In stepping across the northern boundary of the United States, Shadd joined a train of black emigrants to Canada. Indeed, by the time she arrived in 1851, black men and women had been living in Canada for over two hundred years. The first black person arrived in Canada in 1628, when a young boy from Madagascar who had been enslaved by a British privateer was carried to what was then New France and sold to a resident of Quebec. The numbers of black Canadians increased substantially after the American Revolution and again after the War of 1812 when, in both cases, black loyalists fled north from the United States. Canada became particularly attractive as a destination for fugitive slaves after 1834, when Great Britain abolished slavery in its colonies; and the 1850 Fugitive Slave Act also prompted a number of nominally free black Americans from the northern United States to move across the border.[7] In 1852, the Anti-Slavery Society of Canada estimated the black population of Canada West (the modern-day province of Ontario) at thirty thousand. While this number represented just over 3 percent of the colony's total population, black immigrants settled in concentrated areas and thus made up a far greater percentage of the population in their local communities. For example, in the mid-1850s black residents of Chatham made up roughly 20 percent of the town's inhabitants.[8]

Though they had escaped from the threat of slavery, black Americans immigrating to Canada confronted hostility and discrimination from their white neighbors. White Canadians largely opposed the institution of slavery, but that position did not necessarily mean that they welcomed their new black countrymen and -women. As the editor of the Toronto *Colonist* wrote in 1851, "[p]eople may talk about the horrors of slavery as much as they choose; but fugitive slaves are by no means a desirable class of immigrants for Canada, especially when they come in large numbers."[9] Throughout the 1850s white newspapers like the *Colonist* and the *Canadian Oak* published antiblack articles and editorials, pieces that provided justification for the racial discrimination that black Canadians faced in their daily lives. In his 1855 *Autobiography of a Fugitive Negro*, the black immigrant Samuel Ringgold Ward chronicled his experiences in Canada. While his text largely painted Canada as a safe haven for black Americans fleeing the United States, Ward did remark upon a variety of kinds of discrimination faced by the black immigrant. "In many cases," wrote Ward, "a black person travelling, whatever may be his style and however respectable his appearance, will be denied a seat at a *table d'hôte* at a country inn, or on a steamer."[10] Ward himself had experienced such treatment, which exemplified how in Canada freedom from slavery did not necessarily equal freedom of movement.

In an echo of the conditions that helped spark the beginnings of the black press in the United States, the discrimination that black Canadians suffered combined with the racism of white newspapers spurred on the birth of Canada's black press. On January 1, 1851, nearly a year before Mary Ann Shadd arrived in Canada, Henry Bibb published the first issue of his bimonthly newspaper, the *Voice of the Fugitive*. Henry, a fugitive slave, had moved with his wife, Mary, to Canada West in 1849 and settled in the hamlet of Sandwich. There, the Bibbs established themselves as leaders of the province's black community, with Mary opening and administering a school for fugitive children and Henry becoming heavily involved in the Refugee Home Society, an effort to purchase lands for fugitive emigrants.[11] In 1852, *Frederick Douglass' Paper* described the *Voice of the Fugitive* as a "spirited little sheet, devoted to the cause of the fugitives in Canada."[12] Bibb coedited the *Voice of the Fugitive* with James T. Holly, and the paper called for black emigration to Canada and defended those who had already arrived against attacks from papers such as the Toronto *Colonist*. Bibb also used the *Voice of the Fugitive* to promote the Refugee Home Society, a cause that brought him into direct conflict with Shadd, who despised any endeavor that cast black immigrants as charity cases or created separate institutions for black and white Canadians. In 1852 Shadd wrote a series of unsigned letters to the *Western Evangelist*—a paper whose articles were at times reprinted in the *Liberator*—criticizing Bibb's venture.[13] Bibb quickly and correctly identified Shadd as the author, and he castigated her as an "insignificant anonymous scribbler" who "merits the contempt, indignation, and execration of the whole community, and should not be allowed to eat bread amongst a people, whose interest is thus abused."[14] Such a brutal response reveals not only Bibb's contempt for Shadd but also, perhaps, his fear of a potential rival in the world of black Canadian print production.

Bibb had reason to worry, as it would not be long before Shadd began work on the *Provincial Freeman*. Like her predecessors in the black press, including Bibb, Shadd justified her new paper on the grounds that the community it represented had been suffering attacks from hostile newspapers and lacked a venue to answer such charges. But in this case the offending paper was edited by a black man. From its inception, Shadd and her supporters explicitly framed their new paper as an answer to Bibb's *Voice of the Fugitive*, a journal that they claimed distorted the views of black Canadians. In March 1853, for example, Mary Ann's father, Abraham Shadd, held a fundraising meeting for the *Provincial Freeman* in West Chester, Pennsylvania, after which a writer for the *Pennsylvania Freeman* reported that the paper's founders were trying "to establish a newspaper that will correctly represent their conditions and express their views; as the Voice of the Fugitive, a paper thought by many to express the views and represent the condition of the Refugees in Canada, does not do so, but on the contrary misrepresents them, and has refused to publish their sentiments."[15] Bibb and his coeditor Holly struck back only a few days later at a meeting in Sandwich, where they passed a series of resolutions against the creation of a new black newspaper in Canada. They saw no "necessity for another paper devoted to the interests of the colored people of Canada," especially since the *Voice of the Fugitive*, "the first standard unfurled on the free soil of Canada, specially devoted to the anti-slavery cause," had not been "as extensively patronised as its merits demand."[16] Struggling with the same economic difficulties as earlier black newspapers in the United States, Bibb's paper now faced a new threat: competition. During their respective runs, *Freedom's Journal* and the *Colored American* had each been the only black newspaper in New York City, and Douglass had launched the *North Star* from Rochester in order to avoid competing with established papers in places like Boston. By contrast, Shadd entered into an already crowded print marketplace, and her battles with Bibb and the *Voice of the Fugitive* imparted lessons that she would carry into her own newspaper. A fierce battle for authority within and among Canada's black communities created the *Provincial Freeman*, and Shadd consistently used her newspaper to challenge existing black norms and power structures.

Perhaps due in part to Bibb's opposition, the *Provincial Freeman*'s March 1853 issue was not as successful at attracting subscribers as Shadd had hoped, and it would be another year before the paper would begin full production. During that time, Shadd moved her base of operations from the village of Windsor to the metropolis of Toronto, hopeful that the city's larger black population would be better able to support a weekly paper.[17] Shortly after her arrival, Shadd began fundraising for the *Provincial Freeman*, setting up the Provincial Freeman Association and selling stock in the venture. By March 1854, she was able to rent a printing office at Five City Building, King Street East—in the heart of Toronto's business district—from a Mr. James Stephens, for eighteen pounds annually. For an additional two hundred and fifty pounds, she also purchased Stephens's printing press and materials. Funds raised through stock sales, subscriptions, and a loan from Reverend J. B. Smith allowed Shadd to make a one-hundred-pound down payment, with an agreement that she pay the remaining amount in installments over three months.[18] To assist her in the physical production of the paper Shadd enlisted the aid of John Dick, the white printer who had originally moved from his native Scotland to Rochester, New York, where he had joined the staff of Frederick Douglass's *North Star* as printer and sometime editor. After marrying Eliza Griffiths—the sister of Douglass's business partner and confidante, Julia Griffiths—Dick had moved to Toronto in 1850 and established his own printing business.[19] Just as Shadd was preparing to fully enter into the realm of the press, her greatest competition began to fade from view. In late 1853 a fire destroyed Henry Bibb's printing press, effectively marking the end of the *Voice of the Fugitive*. Though Bibb would attempt to revive the paper and sporadically published a single-sheet version, any hope for the *Voice of the Fugitive* ended at three o'clock in the morning on August 1, 1854, when Bibb, its thirty-nine-year-old founder and editor, died.[20]

## Choosing Canada

One year and a day after its trial issue, the *Provincial Freeman* reappeared. The paper was published from March 25, 1854, until September 13, 1857, contained four pages with six or seven columns per page, and cost one-and-a-half pounds annually. The masthead of the March 25, 1854, number named Samuel Ward as editor and Alexander McArthur as corresponding editor, but instructed readers to send their correspondence and subscriptions to "M. A. Shadd." This editorial hierarchy was, however, a ruse. In March 1854 Ward was on a speaking tour in England, and McArthur was en route to Scotland. Neither would ever play a major role in the day-to-day operations of the paper, and Shadd exercised near-total control over the *Provincial Freeman*.[21] Though she would at times enlist coeditors such as H. Ford Douglass and her brother Isaac, Mary Ann Shadd would remain the driving force behind the paper throughout its run.

From the outset, Shadd framed the paper as a distinctly Canadian publication. An editorial in the *Provincial Freeman*'s March 25, 1854, issue (most likely written by Shadd) explained that the new paper existed "[b]ecause the interests of the large and growing colored population of Canada demand such an organ," and also because "none of the papers published by our people, in the States, answer our purpose." Black newspapers in the United States, Shadd continued, "either pass us by, in cold contempt" or "by opposition or neglect disparage us, as much as convenient."[22] Shadd thus echoed the early editorials of papers such as *Freedom's Journal*, the *Colored American*, and the *North Star*. But rather than pitch her paper as the organ of all black Americans, or even a publication for an international black community, Shadd explicitly marked the *Provincial Freeman* as the voice of black Canada. The paper's readership reflected this emphasis. Black newspapers like *Freedom's Journal* and the *Colored American* had listed subscription agents across the United States and the Caribbean, thus highlighting the potential reach of the journals; but the *Provincial Freeman*'s March 25, 1854, number named only four agents, all of whom resided in Toronto. And whereas the *North Star* had openly addressed its subscribers abroad, Shadd fiercely rejected the idea that her paper relied upon international support. "We have English exchanges," she wrote in an October 1854 editorial, "but we *have not one English or other foreign subscriber, nor has one copper ever been collected abroad or been sent to America for this paper, to the best of our knowledge*, so that to the people of Canada and the few subscribers we have in the States, is the paper indebted alone for its support."[23] The *Provincial Freeman* reinforced this point when, in late 1855, the paper printed the names of twenty-seven delinquent subscribers. Twenty-five of these "dodgers" lived in Canada.[24] The paper's financing and subscribers (paying or not) firmly rooted the *Provincial Freeman* in Canadian soil.

Shadd emphasized the Canadian character of her paper because she believed that Canada offered black Americans the best chance for freedom from slavery and oppression. *Freedom's Journal*, the *Colored American*, and the *North Star* all promised black readers that their membership in a chosen nation guaranteed their eventual freedom in the United States. But rather than offer her black American readers any hope of or strategies for achieving liberation in the United States, Shadd relentlessly urged them to abandon their homeland and settle in a land that already recognized their freedom. Accordingly, she filled the *Provincial Freeman*'s pages with pieces celebrating Canadian superiority and urging black Americans in the United States to make the journey north. The paper thus continued the strategies that Shadd had begun to use in her 1852 pamphlet, *Notes of Canada West*. In that work, for example, it seemed that every observable feature of Canada compared favorably to the United States. Sickness, for example, was virtually unheard of, as "epidemics are not of such frequency as in the United States" and "local diseases are unknown."[25] The temperature was neither too hot nor too cold, but instead, "exempt from the enfeebling warmth of southern latitudes, and the equally injurious characteristics of polar countries, it is highly conducive to mental and physical energy."[26] Samuel Ringgold Ward made a similar point in his 1855 *Autobiography*, writing that "the climate is the most pleasant and the most salubrious on the American continent" and that he had never "heard, or read, of a more healthy country."[27] This strain of argument continued in the *Provincial Freeman*. The author of a reprinted January 1855 letter, for example, found Canada to be "a healthy place" with "little sickness except the ague and fever."[28] At first glance, such descriptions can seem a bit outlandish. But these commentaries displace a comparison between the moral worth of the United States and Canada onto each land's geographic features. For example, the absence of slavery as much as any climatological feature left Canada free from the "enfeebling warmth of southern latitudes" for its black residents. Nor need black Canadians worry about becoming afflicted with "drapetomania," the fictional disease that, according to the American physician Samuel Cartwright, caused black men and women to run away from slavery.[29] Canada's physical features, in other words, reflected its moral superiority to its southern neighbor.

While painting Canada as an ideal site for black settlement, the *Provincial Freeman* also imagined the province in the midst of improvement, reprinting multiple pieces that framed Canada as a place on the rise. One traveler's letter, reprinted in the paper's October 28, 1854, issue, declared "that in almost all quarters there prevails a very decided spirit of improvement—a steady progress towards a great and prosperous condition."[30] Some pieces located that spirit in tangible markers such as infrastructure projects and the growth of cities. The author of an April 21, 1855, reprinted piece, for example, celebrated "the railroads now in course of formation," the investment in "interminable water communication," and the creation of "extensive fisheries."[31] And the author of an article reprinted from the *Canadian News* marveled at the "astounding progress" of places like Toronto, which had been transformed from a "small village" into "one of the most splendid cities in British America."[32] But the spirit of improvement also manifested in less physical ways. The author of a May 19, 1855, reprinted selection announced that "Canadians live in an age of improvements." This age produced not only railroads and waterways but, more crucially, "*great people*, for Canada will compare favorably with any other nation, so far as advancement in all that tends to the elevation—morally and pecuniarily—of her people is concerned."[33] Like the *Colored American*, the *Provincial Freeman* invited its readers into a world on the way to moral and material perfection. But whereas the earlier newspaper had linked its postmillennialism to an American identity, the *Provincial Freeman* described a distinctly Canadian "age of improvements." In order to participate in such progress, then, black Americans would need to settle in Canada.

Indeed, the *Provincial Freeman* saw black settlers as a primary engine of Canadian progress. Again connecting moral and material conditions, the *Provincial Freeman* repeatedly located the Canadian spirit of improvement in the economic successes of the province's black inhabitants. In January 1855 Shadd reprinted a letter from E. R. Johnson, a white American abolitionist who had visited Canada and written about his experiences for the *Liberator*. Johnson found "much wealth among the colored people," and encountered black Canadians as owners of "large farms" and tradesmen "engaged in mechanical pursuits."[34] Another reprinted letter, appearing in the *Provincial Freeman*'s November 24, 1855, issue, made a similar claim about black economic progress. Its author found "the majority of the colored people in Canada" to be "industrious, moderately enterprising and decidedly thriving in their circumstances."[35] Such descriptions from outsiders dovetailed with the accounts provided by black Canadians. In 1855 the white abolitionist Benjamin Drew visited Canada's black communities and collected dozens of testimonials, which he published a year later in a volume titled *A North-Side View of Slavery; The Refugee: Or The Narratives of Fugitive Slaves in Canada*. Drew himself frequently commented upon the wealth and industry of black Canadians, and his interviews supported these claims. William Howard, of Toronto, remarked that he knew a number of black residents of that city "who own houses and lands," while Edward Hicks, from Chatham, revealed to Drew that he had "got a little property together, worth some $2000."³⁶ J. C. Brown, who had settled in Chatham in 1849, also told Drew that "[t]here is a great deal of property owned here by the coloured people," but he saw black economic industry and achievement as not only the fruit of Canadian progress but also a driving force behind such improvement.³⁷ He described how, when he arrived in Chatham, "[t]here were no masons, bricklayers, or plasterers among the coloured men. I went for some, and got them here, and we are now able to build a house from the stump. We can cut the timber and make the brick. The greater part of the bricklaying and plastering is in the hands of the coloured mechanics."³⁸ Far from being poor refugees dependent upon the charity of their white neighbors, such accounts cast black Canadians as the builders of an improving Canada.

But while the *Provincial Freeman* and writings by and about black emigrants highlighted the ways in which black Canadians contributed to the perfection of their adopted country, the newspaper's writings and other narratives never forgot that black emigrants could help uplift Canada in terms of infrastructure and moral character because they did not have to fight against legal slavery and discrimination. "Canada is the freest country in the world," proclaimed the *Provincial Freeman* in an April 1854 editorial, since "[i]n the eyes of justice both white and black, slave and free-born, rich, and poor, learned and unlearned are the same."³⁹ As the narratives provided to Benjamin Drew made clear, black emigrants understood freedom as a legal category. Explaining his warm feelings toward Canada, Thomas Hedgebeth, from Chatham, declared, "I like the laws, which leave a man as much freedom as a man can have."⁴⁰ "In Canada," wrote Samuel Ringgold Ward in his *Autobiography*, "we are not on trial as to whether we shall have our rights: we have them."⁴¹ In Canada, guaranteed legal protections existed independently of any demonstration of a fitness for freedom. Relieved of the burden of obtaining their "rights," black Canadians could focus their energies on improving the conditions of their communities and their country.

Writings that celebrated Canada as a space of black freedom and advancement represented one piece of an ongoing debate within and among black communities over the question of emigration from the United States. While *Freedom's Journal*'s conflicted position on the question of black emigration to Liberia in the late 1820s illustrates the long history of this debate, the 1850s witnessed an uptick in pro-emigration sentiment in some quarters. Publications like Martin Delany's 1852 *Condition, Elevation, Emigration, and Destiny of the Colored People of the United States* (published just two months after Shadd's *Notes of Canada West*), and national emigration conventions held in 1853 and 1854, point to the increasing visibility and institutional organization of emigration's advocates. But powerful voices, foremost among them Frederick Douglass, relentlessly attacked the pro-emigration position.[42] For while the *North Star* had asked its black readers to see themselves as members of a global revolutionary community, such international solidarity was always framed as a way to improve conditions in the United States rather than as a precursor to emigration. And in the mid-1850s, Douglass used the pages of *Frederick Douglass' Paper* to answer pro-emigration arguments. The call for the 1854 convention, for example, occasioned an exchange of letters to the paper from James M. Whitfield, a staunch ally of Delany, and William J. Watkins, Douglass's associate editor.[43] Watkins rejected the emigrationist argument that black Americans could "never be the equals of the whites in this country, and we must, therefore, prepare for our exodus," and instead urged his brethren to embrace their role as "part and parcel of the *American Nation*."[44] Whitfield dismissed such a claim, writing to Watkins, "I have no country, neither have you, and your assumption that you are an *integrant* part of *this* nation, is not true."[45] White Americans, he continued, would only accept a black presence in their country if the relations of master and slave were maintained and strengthened. Black Americans committed to liberation, Whitfield concluded, thus had a "duty to get out of a situation where all the profits of their labor go to strengthen their oppressors, and rivet the chain upon themselves; and take a position where their labors will help to improve and elevate their race."[46] As the Watkins-Whitfield exchange reveals, the debate over black emigration centered on the question of whether or not black liberation could ever be achieved in the United States.

Accordingly, many of the *Provincial Freeman*'s emigration articles focused not only on the glories of Canada but also on the unredeemable character of the United States. This effort clearly emerges in a series of letters written to the paper in early 1855, debating the merits of emigration. The letters came from John Gaines and Samuel Lowery, two black men living in Cincinnati. The Queen City had become a flashpoint in the emigration debate, as the renewed enforcement of Ohio's oppressive black laws compelled a number of its black residents to move to Canada. The thirty-four-year-old Gaines, a successful businessman who concentrated most of his activist energies on improving educational opportunities for Cincinnati's black youth, steadfastly opposed emigration.[47] In a January letter to the *Provincial Freeman*, he argued that progress had been made in the United States, thus making emigration a retreat from a winnable war for black liberation. Focusing on his hometown, Gaines declared that "Cincinnati has improved much during the last ten years." Its white citizens had become "more tolerant to anti-slavery men," and its black residents had found success as "lawyers, doctors, editors, orators, divines, professors, musicians, merchants, mechanics, and capitalists." For Gaines, the fact that black men could enter into such a variety of professions refuted the argument that black freedom was impossible in the United States, instead proving that "competent colored men can do as well in the professions as competent whites."[48]

Samuel Lowery disagreed.[49] In a February letter provocatively titled, "Gaines on Submission, or an Anti-Emigrationist Reviewed," Lowery contested Gaines's implication that black economic success could be used to measure the state of black freedom in the United States. He wrote that "in the south, there are men of color possessing wealth equal to nine-tenths of the community in which they reside, and their condition is as honorable, as far as wealth is concerned, as man can wish or heart desire," but that these same men "are deprived of every principle of manhood," and indeed feared to protest their unfair treatment lest they be summarily deprived of the money they had earned. Without the law to protect them, Lowery argued, "those in the most affluent circumstances have to bear more social and personal oppression from the foul demon of prejudice against color than many of their fellows not so well provided with the necessaries of life, because they fear being divested of their wealth, in case they should repudiate their many wrongs."[50] Tragically, according to Lowery, economic success prevented black men and women from becoming leaders in the fight against racial oppression. Without equality under the law, then, economic gains were fleeting at best, and potentially an obstacle to racial progress.

In the Gaines-Lowery debate, the question of whether or not the United States could be redeemed as a space for black freedom dovetailed closely with the language and logic of millennialism. In his final letter to the *Provincial Freeman*, Gaines acknowledged that conditions for black Americans in the United States appeared to be worsening, but read setbacks to black liberation like the Fugitive Slave Law as part of a jeremiad, and thus signs that freedom was close at hand. "I see clouds before me and around me," he wrote, "but everything portends the rise of a glorious morn, when the master shall lie down with the slave."[51] Since liberation was imminent, Gaines argued, to leave the United

States "now, when the vessel is well nigh ready to bear us safely into port," was to walk away from the fight for freedom at the moment of victory. This retreat, he warned, would send a powerfully negative signal to the world about the commitment of black Americans to fight against oppression. "I trust, however, in this the noon of our regeneration," Gaines concluded, "that we may prove to the world that we are not poltroons and cowards, and unfit for the condition of freemen."[52] In 1827 *Freedom's Journal* had advanced a version of acting chosen rooted in ideas of propriety as a way for black Americans to demonstrate their fitness for freedom. Gaines too believed that black Americans needed to behave in a manner that proved that they deserved to be free. But rather than looking to norms of industry and frugality, Gaines anchored his understanding of such behavior in a rejection of emigration. For Gaines, acting free meant remaining in the United States.

Lowery, too, saw the fight for black liberation coming to a close. But rather than a resolution that involved a reconciliation between former masters and slaves, Lowery invoked a premillennial version of sudden and catastrophic divine intervention. "The groans of the black man have ascended to God for vengeance against this iniquitous Government," he wrote in a March 17 letter, and as a result "there is to be a reckoning with this Babylon of the world, the *American Government!*"[53] Making explicit the analogy that the *Colored American* had implicitly offered fifteen years earlier, Lowery assured the *Provincial Freeman*'s readers that the United States' oppression of black Americans would result in that country's divinely inspired destruction. But whereas the *Colored American* had not put any specific timetable on God's judgment, Lowery saw the fall of the United States as imminent. "God," he concluded, "is *now* preparing her desolation."[54] Like Gaines, Lowery urged the *Provincial Freeman*'s readers to take action in advance of the oncoming millennium. But, rebutting Gaines's interpretation, Lowery's expectation of an American apocalypse led him to advance emigration as a strike for liberty. For Lowery, Canada represented a sanctuary, provided by God, where black Americans could gain immediate freedom while awaiting the destruction of the United States. "In this time of revolution," he wrote, "we must come out, as other people; the Canadas are now awaiting us, by the protection of an Almighty Being, as one point, where we can secure that which will never be gained here, until the American Government is burst into a thousand atoms."[55] Rather than wait for divine intervention, however imminent, black Americans could secure their freedom immediately by crossing the border into Canada. While leaving the door open to a possible return after the fall of the "American Government," Lowery cast emigration from the United States as the ultimate proof that black Americans would go to any lengths to be free.

In its broader coverage of the emigration question, the *Provincial Freeman* reinforced Lowery's position. Rather than a retreat from the battle for black liberty, the newspaper saw emigration from the United States as not only a practical and realizable path for personal freedom but also a strike for immediate racial uplift. *Freedom's Journal*, the *Colored American*, and the *North Star* had taught readers to fulfill the responsibilities of black chosenness by acting properly, prophetically, or revolutionarily. Each of these earlier black newspapers saw acting chosen as a weapon in the fight for black liberation in the United States. The *Provincial Freeman* also called upon its readers to take action. But given Mary Ann Shadd's certainty that black freedom could never be achieved within the boundaries of the United States, her newspaper held up emigration as the primary responsibility of black Americans. In an 1856 editorial commenting upon another planned pro-emigration convention in Cleveland, Shadd urged her paper's readers to "[g]o to the Cleveland Convention, and determine to remove to a country or to countries, where you may have equal political rights, and thus be *elevated* at *once*."[56] Whereas writers like Benjamin Drew had highlighted the potential for black economic improvement in Canada, Shadd focused on "equal political rights" as the most important marker of elevation.

The *Provincial Freeman* would devote a great deal of time to counseling its black Canadian readers on proper behavior, but the paper separated this instruction from the question of how to achieve legal rights. Regardless of their efforts, Shadd argued, black Americans would never convince the United States, "a government that begins its depredations upon the rights of colored men, and ends by destroying the liberties of white men," to recognize their freedom.[57] For pro-emigration activists like Shadd, *Freedom's Journal*'s theory of acting chosen in order to demonstrate a fitness for freedom represented a strategy for black liberation articulated before the British had abolished slavery in their colonies. By the mid-1850s, with a free Canada sitting just next door, all black Americans had to do to prove their fitness for freedom was move to a land that required no such demonstration.

## *The Importance of Being British*

In addition to its revision of acting chosen, the *Provincial Freeman* called into question the link between black chosenness and American identity. Beginning with *Freedom's Journal*, black newspapers in the United States had consistently envisioned God's chosen people as members of an American community of some sort. By acting chosen, argued the editors of *Freedom's Journal*, black Americans could convince their white neighbors to support their cause and thus find freedom in the United States. The *Colored American*, while imagining the divine destruction of the United States, always located the beginning of the new millennium on American soil. Indeed, the possibility that the United States was the new Babylon only reinforced the argument that oppressed Americans were the new Israelites, hence God's chosen people. And even while connecting black Americans to an international revolutionary movement, the *North Star* never went so far as to argue that membership in this global community erased an American identity. On the contrary, the paper urged its readers to translate the lessons from abroad to their particular local struggles and to achieve freedom in their American homeland. The *Provincial Freeman*, by contrast, cast American ideals, institutions, and people as dire threats to black freedom. Only by renouncing their American connections and stamping out American influences wherever they could be found, Shadd and her staff argued, could black people secure the freedom they had achieved by crossing into Canada. For in doing so they had set foot on British soil, and the promise of black liberation emanated from that Empire rather than any American nation.

Despite periodic outbursts against the constraints of imperial rule, by the 1850s Canada's English-speaking majority overwhelmingly saw themselves as "British" rather than Canadian (though the exact contours of Britishness remained unsettled), and accepted some degree of imperial oversight.[58] From her earliest writings on the subject, Shadd argued that this imperial connection guaranteed black freedom. Given that black Americans fighting for freedom confronted the full power of a pro-slavery United States government, she wrote in *Notes of Canada West*, "there seems to be no safe alternative left but to be satisfied with that government now existing that is most reliable and most powerful," and "[t]hat government is Great Britain; her dependencies for a *secure* home for the American slave, and the disgraced *free* man."[59] No other government on earth, Shadd claimed, was "so powerful and so thoroughly impartial as Her Majesty's; so practically anti-slavery, and so protective."[60] As her use of italics implies, Shadd understood security as a precondition for black freedom. And given the strength of the United States, black Americans could only gain such security through the protection of a government "powerful" enough to defy the United States. As one of Great Britain's "dependencies," Canada could carry the protection of the Queen's government to North America.

In order to strengthen their connection to the British Empire, and as a result secure their freedom, the *Provincial Freeman* urged its black readers to fully embrace their new status as British subjects. In a January 31, 1857, editorial, Shadd urged the paper's black readers, who had "come under British rule from necessity, to become British at heart in reality." To become "British at heart," she contended, black Canadians needed to forget their "yankee training," which had schooled them in "ignorance" and "servility," and instead carry themselves with "confidence, intelligence," and "independence."[61] Four months later Shadd reiterated her argument, writing that among the things most needed "[b]y the colored people of Canada, are a good British Education, thorough instruction to the young by means of British school books, by teachers British at heart."[62] But black Canadians could only benefit from these teachers if they would "consent to let American books, teaching, pro-slavery republican preaching, negro-hating separate institutions, Yankee old clothes and new clothes, and Yankee habits alone."[63] Again, Shadd contrasted her preferred Britishness to the harmful American ideas and institutions. Part of being "British," then, was renouncing any claim to an American identity.

While the *Provincial Freeman* urged its readers to become "British at heart" by adopting certain values, the paper also translated these attitudes into concrete actions. Being British, like being chosen, required adherence to a particular set of practices. For example, in order to be truly British black Canadians could not participate in any racially exclusive institutions. Shadd had long railed against separate schools, churches, and settlements, and the *Provincial Freeman* linked this protest to its idea of British identity. In a March 28, 1857, piece on "The Duties of Colored Men in Canada," coeditor H. Ford Douglass pronounced, "Colored men should become as thoroughly British as they can. We are opposed to all separate organizations, whether civil, political or ecclesiastical, that can have no other effect than that of creating a line of demarcation." In the same breath, then, Ford Douglass linked becoming "thoroughly British" to a firm opposition to "all separate organizations." He went on to explain that separate institutions "are dark and hateful relics of Yankee *negrophobia*, contrary to that healthy, social and political equality, recognized by the fundamental principles of British common law, and should never be permitted to take root upon British soil."[64] Like Shadd, Ford Douglass drew a firm line between British and American identities, here represented through particular kinds of institutions. Separate organizations, for him, carried with them the legacy of American racism, a tradition incompatible with true British values. Part of being British, then, was defending British soil from American encroachment, in this case by opposing certain kinds of institutions.

The fear that the values and institutions of the United States could creep across the border and threaten black freedom was not entirely unreasonable. Canada West's close proximity to the border, coupled with the expansionist policies of the United States, made the very land that black Canadians lived on vulnerable to invasion or annexation. Two years before he himself moved to Chatham, Martin Delany rejected Canada as a permanent destination for black emigrants because, he announced, "according to political tendency, the Canadas—as all British America—at no very distant day, are destined to come into the United States."[65] The United States' invasion of Mexico and bellicose rhetoric in regards to the disputed Oregon territory in the 1840s exemplified that country's "political tendency" to conquer the continent. Moreover, an incipient annexation movement within Canada presented black Canadians with the specter of their white countrymen willingly joining forces with a government that would never tolerate black freedom.[66]

According to the *Provincial Freeman*, only the British imperial government could defend black Canadians against the threats to their freedom, foreign and domestic. Hence, the paper urged its black readers to use their political rights to maintain the Empire's control over its province. By the 1850s Canadian politics had largely fallen into a two-party system, with the Conservatives representing the interests of the Crown while the Reformers advocated for, among other issues, increased local autonomy.[67] Just as it had read separate institutions as an encroachment of American values on British soil, the *Provincial Freeman* saw the Reform party in Canada as an echo of similar formations in the United States, and this connection transformed the Reformers into a dire threat to black freedom. "This reform party," wrote Ford Douglass in another April 11 piece, "is nothing more nor less, than the old Locofoco party of the United States galvanized," and "[w]e have seen enough of democracy and slavery in the United States, without wishing to see it introduced here." Linking support for the Conservative Party to the fight against American encroachment into Canada, Ford Douglass warned his "colored fellow citizens to be careful in the exercise of the right of suffrage; be argus eyed in guarding your interest, in sustaining the honor and dignity of the British Empire."[68] Connecting the interests of black Canadians and those of the British Empire, Ford Douglass urged his readers to protect themselves by sustaining the imperial influence.

Ford Douglass's argument followed a logic that had, historically, convinced black Canadians to support Conservative candidates. In the mid-1830s the radical reformer William Lyon Mackenzie complained that black immigrants were "opposed to every species of reform in the civil institutions of the colony."[69] In the same period the American abolitionist James Birney visited Toronto and, in a letter back to Lewis Tappan, observed that "the colored people generally . . . belong to the Government party."[70] But in the late 1840s this support began to fade. William King, who had established the Elgin settlement for black immigrants, encouraged its residents to vote as a bloc for whichever candidate best represented their interests, regardless of party. King's strategy proved effective and spread to other black communities. By the time the *Provincial Freeman* arrived, Conservative politicians could no longer rely on the blanket support of their black constituents. In an April 11, 1857, article Ford Douglass, as part of a biting critique of drunkenness in Chatham, related how, while walking home from the newspaper's office, he encountered a very drunk black man "delivering a Reform Speech" on a street corner.[71] While framing support for the Reformers as a product of intoxication, this notice also reveals a certain anxiety that Reform had gained a foothold on the doorstep of the *Provincial Freeman*.

For the *Provincial Freeman*, the danger of black voters abandoning the Conservatives, and thus threatening their own security, seemed particularly real in the summer of 1857. Colonel John Prince, a Conservative politician, enraged Toronto's black residents when he came to the defense of two local magistrates who had been dismissed for handing over a black emigrant to U.S. authorities. In response many of the city's black voters organized an "Indignation Meeting" to censure Prince. Prince did not respond well to such criticism. In a letter to the Toronto *Colonist*, which the *Provincial Freeman* reprinted in its entirety, Prince railed against the meeting of Toronto's black citizens, which gave "evidence of their natural conceit, their vanity, and their ignorance." He repeatedly referred to black Canadians as "Darkies," who he found to be "a graceless, worthless, thriftless, lying set of vagabonds." And lest readers mistake his meaning, Prince pronounced black Canadians "the GREATEST CURSE ever inflicted upon the two magnificent western counties which I have had the honour to represent in the Legislative Council of this Province."[72] Black voters had previously supported Prince, but his defense of the dismissed magistrates and racist tirade almost guaranteed that his black constituents would vote for his Reform opponent in any subsequent election.[73]

Prince presented a problem for the *Provincial Freeman*. The paper could not let his racist attacks go unchecked but, given its reading of the Conservative Party as a bulwark for black freedom, it could not advocate his removal. In order to simultaneously support black Canadians and the Conservative Party, the paper responded to Prince's direct attacks while downplaying the seriousness of his outburst. Defending Toronto's black residents against Prince's slanders, Shadd placed a rebuttal piece from the Toronto *Times* just after Prince's letter. According to the writer for the *Times*, the "colored people of Toronto are an example, in point of industry, sobriety, and morality, to their white neighbours."[74] In an editorial on the next page, Shadd explained that when it came to the Prince affair, beyond reprinting the article from the *Times*, the *Provincial Freeman* "will *neither do nor say anything* at present."[75] The paper would continue to "look after and interest ourselves in those measures designed to promote the *general* good," rather than spend more time on "the indignation meetings that may be called to fight such verbose but harmless opinions."[76] Shrugging off Prince's "verbose but harmless opinions," Shadd tried to frame the Conservative's comments as mildly offensive but ultimately unimportant. Her paper's readers apparently disagreed, as in the next issue Shadd returned to the topic to defend her stance and, this time, Prince himself. She lamented the fact that the paper had been attacked for "not choosing to be irritated by such evident nothings as the term 'darkies,' 'blackies,' &c," and reminded her readers that "Mr. Prince was and is an active and working member" of the government.[77]

Shadd's unwavering defense of Prince, despite his obvious disdain for black Canadians and over the strong objections of her readers, underscores the stakes involved in keeping Conservatives in power. In the pages of the *Provincial Freeman*, American people, places, and ideals represented an existential threat to black freedom, and only Canada's connection to the British Empire allowed the province to offer black men and women sanctuary on a continent increasingly dominated by an aggressively expansionist, pro-slavery United States. Shadd and her staff passionately believed that if the Reformers prevailed this imperial link would fade or disappear, and the guarantee of black freedom would vanish. As local stewards of the Empire, Conservative politicians garnered the *Provincial Freeman*'s unqualified support, regardless of their racist rhetoric.

## Black Chosenness without Guarantees

For the *Provincial Freeman*, the British Empire secured black freedom in Canada. Accordingly, the paper tolerated no competing allegiances to British identity. These included not only American affections but also racial ties. This is not to say that the *Provincial Freeman* discounted the bonds of race, or counseled its black readers to abandon their racial brethren. But the *Provincial Freeman* rejected racial solidarity as a pathway to liberation. Freedom came from being British, not black. Such views marked a radical departure from those held by the paper's predecessors in the black press. *Freedom's Journal*, for example, had been founded upon the principle that a newspaper could unite a scattered black population, with the assumption that such unity was necessary for black liberation. But by the 1850s it must have seemed like the increasing interconnectedness of black Americans, both to one another and to other diasporic communities, had done very little for the cause of black freedom. Perhaps, then, the most devastating piece of the *Provincial Freeman*'s critique of black chosenness was the paper's refusal to assign any inherent values or possibilities to racial identity. Blackness, for the newspaper, came with no guarantees.[78]

Unsurprisingly, perhaps, the *Provincial Freeman* offered its clearest critique of blackness during a dispute with another black newspaper. On July 4, 1856, *Frederick Douglass' Paper* carried an editorial titled "Canada—Liberia—H. Ford Douglass—*Provincial Freeman*—Mary A. Shadd," in which Douglass argued that race, more than anything else, defined and united black people worldwide. "We are one people," he wrote, "[w]hether of mixed or unmixed blood, we are the heirs of a common inheritance." Echoing the arguments of Cornish and Russwurm in *Freedom's Journal*, and anticipating at least in part the idea of race as a social construct, Douglass understood that white observers created and enforced the notion of a homogenous blackness and ignored intraracial distinctions of class, character, and national affiliation. He reminded readers that "[o]ne drop of African blood degrades a gallon of Saxon, and flings the possessor among the outcast and despised." Hence, he continued, a black man "may live in Canada and call himself a British subject, or in the States and call himself an American citizen; but neither his subjection to Britain, nor his citizenship of the States will save him from being mainly recognized as a *colored man*, identified with *colored people*, and a sharer in the common destiny of the colored people."[79] In this formulation, white recognition creates the racial subject, and this subjectivity (or, to borrow from Douglass, subjection) makes membership in any community defined in terms other than race irrelevant. Hence, Douglass argued that the "common identity" of race "overmasters all conventional and [geo]graphical changes and conditions," refuting the rationale that drove Shadd's investment in being British.[80]

As *Freedom's Journal*'s editors had understood, the idea of a homogenous black community allowed hostile whites to use isolated incidents of bad behavior to indict the entire race. In his 1856 editorial Douglass used the same logic of synecdoche, but to opposite ends, arguing that instances of black success in spaces like Canada and Liberia could be used to paint the entire race in a positive light. "Looking thus upon our people as a whole," he explained, "we feel proud to mention any facts, indicating an upward tendency of the race, any fact which contradict and resist the tide of disparagement now setting heavily against us." Focusing on Canada, Douglass pointed to Mary Ann Shadd's work at the *Provincial Freeman* as an example of black industry. He celebrated Shadd's "unconquerable zeal" in the face of "lukewarmness, false friends, open enemies, ignorance and small pecuniary means," and professed, "[w]e do not know her equal among the colored ladies of the United States." Douglass also singled out Shadd's coeditor H. Ford Douglass, whom he described as a "young man of excellent natural abilities." Addressing the editors of the *Provincial Freeman*, Douglass exclaimed, "[e]very noble example you set us in Canada, is a contribution to the common stock of excellence which we are rolling up for the redemption of our race."[81] As representatives of a global black community, the successes of Shadd, Ford Douglass, and the *Provincial Freeman* reflected back upon the entire race.

Ironically, Douglass's celebration of racial solidarity dovetailed with the writings of his earlier adversaries in the debates over emigration. In 1853, for example, James M. Whitfield championed plans for black emigration from the United States to areas in Central and South America already possessing a black majority. The purpose of emigration, he argued, was to create and display to the world a "powerful nation in which the black is the *ruling* element, capable of maintaining a respectable position among the *great* nations of the earth."[82] And in 1854, before he had changed his mind and himself emigrated to Canada, Delany declared that a "people, to be free, must necessarily be *their own rulers*."[83] Like Whitfield, Delany had linked black freedom to black rule, an equation that disqualified Canada as a destination for emigration. Canada, he reminded his listeners, "is, and ever must be, white." In such a space, he argued, "colored people might never hope for anything more than to exist politically by mere sufferance."[84] While stopping short of the black nationalist position of Whitfield and Delany, Douglass's 1856 editorial similarly held up racial solidarity as the path to black liberation. And again echoing his earlier adversaries, Douglass explicitly dismissed the importance of the British Empire.

Douglass's case for racial solidarity, then, stood in open opposition to the

*Provincial Freeman*'s vision of black freedom secured through British identity, and these larger stakes help explain Shadd's blistering response to his editorial. Two weeks after Douglass's piece appeared in *Frederick Douglass' Paper*, Shadd offered a rebuttal in the pages of the *Provincial Freeman*, where she took particular offense at Douglass's assumption that a shared racial identity united black people everywhere into a single community. Shadd argued that "bigotry and fatuity" fueled the "absurd notion" that "color must be a bond of union among colored elements," and opposed "any attempt then, to connect the men of Canada and Africa, or, of the United States and Canada." Roundly rejecting Douglass's contention that the positive effect of black achievement transcended geographic boundaries, Shadd proclaimed that "no 'negro' be he King of Dahomey, Emperor of Timbuctoo [sic] or Frederick Douglass, can advance one lot the interests of colored British subjects, but the reverse is the fact as the superior influence of British subjects, without complexional distinction, is made to bear upon other nations and people, and to the benefit of the downtrodden everywhere."[85] In the course of defending British identity against the competing claims of a transnational black community, Shadd shattered the notion that the struggles and triumphs of black people would light the way for oppressed peoples across the globe. If any group had been chosen to lead the world to freedom it was the British, a fact that made black efforts to achieve British identity all the more urgent.

*Freedom's Journal*, the *Colored American*, and the *North Star* each offered black Americans a potential avenue to emancipation and equality. But by the mid-1850s proper behavior had not changed the pro-slavery stance of the United States government, the millennium had not arrived, and the transnational revolutionary wave of 1848 had broken against counterrevolutionary forces in Europe and an increasingly powerful slave power in the United States. The promises of black chosenness, as they appeared in black newspapers, seemed increasingly hollow. So rather than continue the apparently quixotic quest for freedom in the United States, the *Provincial Freeman* turned its attention to practical pathways to liberation. The newspaper urged readers to move to Canada, abandon their claims to American nationhood, and consider themselves British before black. Disavowing race and nation would be no easy task, but in the eyes of Mary Ann Shadd and her supporters it was a small price to pay for immediate and enduring freedom and equality.

CHAPTER 5

# Joining the Chosen Army

God is carrying on a war with this guilty nation, that they may know that
he has not forgotten us, and his justice would not sleep forever.
—"Letter from Rev. J. W. Loguen," *Weekly Anglo-African*, August 31, 1861

On April 12, 1861, southern artillery surrounding Fort Sumter in South Carolina fired the first shots in the American Civil War. In an eerily prescient passage in his 1829 *Appeal*, reprinted in 1848 by the black activist and writer Henry Highland Garnet, David Walker had imagined just this sort of conflict. Promising black readers that God, "being a just and holy Being will at one day appear fully in behalf of the oppressed, and arrest the progress of the avaricious oppressors," Walker wrote that "although the destruction of the oppressors God may not effect by the oppressed, yet the Lord our God will bring other destructions upon them—for not unfrequently will he cause them to rise up one against another, to be split and divided, and to oppress each other, and sometimes to open hostilities with sword in hand."[1] When the newly formed Confederate forces struck at the Union Army's fort in South Carolina, a definitive sign that the United States had become "split and divided," it seemed to many black Americans that Walker's prophecy had come to pass. The war, they argued, was part of a providential design to finally free God's chosen people. "God is carrying on a war with this guilty nation," wrote the Syracuse-based Reverend Jermain Loguen, "that they may know that he has not forgotten us, and his justice would not sleep forever."[2] Watching events unfold from London, Garnet believed that the "set time has come when the numerous promises of God to Africa is about to be fulfilled," and he concluded that the "system of negro slavery is rapidly passing away, and ere long it will thunder to the ground."[3] And Frederick Douglass, writing for his *Douglass' Monthly*, urged white Americans to "*Repent, Break Every Yoke, let the Oppressed Go Free for Herein alone is deliverance and safety!*"[4] Despite the Union's enduring reluctance to endorse abolition, writers like Loguen, Garnet, and Douglass immediately recognized the war as a divinely directed means of black liberation.

Loguen gave his interpretation of the war in an August 1861 letter to the *Weekly Anglo-African*. The New York–based black newspaper had folded in the spring of 1861, but in July of that year editor Robert Hamilton relaunched the journal, and Loguen welcomed the paper's reappearance. "I think there never was a time when we as people needed a weekly paper as we do at this time," he wrote. Loguen heaped praise on *Douglass' Monthly* but argued that such "fearfully interesting times" required a more regular publication. Douglass had been publishing his monthly periodical since 1858, but the pace of war could move quickly, and only a weekly newspaper could bring news of the conflict to black readers in a timely manner. At the same time, black Americans needed a sustained voice in the press to display their wartime efforts to a white audience. "Our people are deeply interested in this war and are doing much," wrote Loguen, "[b]ut without a faithful organ like the Anglo-African sustained by us, the world would not know the fact."[5] Echoing the arguments of *Freedom's Journal*'s founders, Loguen saw the black newspaper as a means to provide white onlookers with a positive image of black Americans. The context of the war made this mission all the more crucial, since the paper could potentially help convince white northerners to embrace the cause of black liberation. According to the paper's war correspondent George E. Stephens, who was embedded with the Union Army in Maryland, the *Weekly Anglo-African* did just that. Stephens passed copies of the paper around the camp, and related how "[o]ne individual could hardly believe when he saw the ANGLO 'dat niggers could do dat.'" "I am importuned continually by men in the army for chances to read your paper," he concluded, because soldiers "find in it matter of interest and importance which they can gather from no other source."[6] By bringing accounts of black accomplishments to the front, where black soldiers were not yet welcome, the *Weekly Anglo-African* could potentially convince those most directly involved in the war to embrace the cause of black liberation.

But, like its predecessors in the black press, the *Weekly Anglo-African* did far more than simply announce the achievements of black Americans. As a wartime newspaper, the *Weekly Anglo-African* not only covered but also helped shape the black response to the Civil War. While endorsing the view that God had sent the war to finally free his chosen nation, the paper explored the appropriate worldly ways in which northern black men, in particular, should respond to the conflict. Prior to Abraham Lincoln's 1863 Emancipation Proclamation, it was not at all clear that the Union represented the interests of its black inhabitants. Moreover, the government expressly forbid black men from joining the army, and black northerners disagreed as to whether or not they should prepare to fight despite this prohibition. Through letters to the editor, war correspondence, and a serialized novel, the *Weekly Anglo-African* explored this dilemma. Ultimately, the newspaper counseled black men to prepare for battle. But, in order to remind the would-be soldiers that they fought for their enslaved brethren rather than for any government, the paper cast black military preparations as akin to a slave conspiracy. Companies of trained and armed black men, secretly lodged in northern towns and cities, would form God's chosen army. And this force, the newspaper argued, would guarantee black liberation by either joining the Union cause or, if neither the United States nor the Confederacy abolished slavery, striking down both governments.

After the January 1, 1863, Emancipation Proclamation, the *Weekly Anglo-African* reasoned that the United States had become the best hope for black liberation. With the Union Army now admitting black soldiers, the newspaper urged northern black men to formally join the fight. But despite the fact that these volunteers would now be Union soldiers, the newspaper reminded them that they ultimately fought not for any government but instead for those still enslaved. Throughout its Civil War coverage and commentary, the *Weekly Anglo-African* focused on the duty that black northerners had toward their southern brethren. Indeed, as the paper began imagining life after emancipation, and after the war, it called its black readers in the North to go south and help educate the newly free. In doing so, the paper articulated the new mission of black chosenness. Before sharing their God-given gifts with the world, or even with their own country, the newspaper reasoned, black Americans would need to minister to one another.

## Making a Wartime Newspaper

Robert and Thomas Hamilton grew up surrounded by black newspapers. Their father, William Hamilton, traveled in the same circles as the men who had founded *Freedom's Journal*. William was the first president of the New York African Society for Mutual Relief and an original trustee of the city's African Methodist Episcopal Zion Church. During the furor over public celebrations, *Freedom's Journal* lauded the elder Hamilton's Fourth of July oration (delivered at the Zion Church) as "distinguished throughout for originality and beauty," and Samuel Cornish and John Brown Russwurm printed a lengthy excerpt from the speech in the pages of their paper.[7] A decade later, both Hamilton brothers worked for the *Colored American*. That paper's editors appointed eighteen-year-old Robert to the important post of "City Agent and Collector," and fourteen-year-old Thomas wrapped papers for delivery and carried them to city subscribers.[8] In adulthood Robert became a powerful activist renowned, like his father, for his oratorical skills. After the passage of the Fugitive Slave Act in 1850, Robert joined the Committee of Thirteen, a collective that protected black New Yorkers from roving slave catchers. During the 1850s, he also served as a delegate to state and national black conventions. Thomas, meanwhile, thoroughly learned the newspaper trade in the offices of papers like the *Evangelist*, and in the early to mid-1840s launched his own short-lived publication, the *People's Press*.[9]

In 1859, Thomas Hamilton again tried his hand at publishing and editing, this time founding two publications in quick succession: the *Anglo-African Magazine* and the *Weekly Anglo-African* newspaper.[10] The newspaper was a four-sheet production with six to seven columns per page, which ran, with some interruptions, from July 23, 1859, to December 1865. Subscriptions were initially two dollars per year, but by 1865 had been raised to three and a half dollars annually. The magazine, a monthly, offered readers just over thirty pages per issue. The *Anglo-African Magazine*'s early issues cast Hamilton as not only a seasoned newspaperman but also an editor highly conscious of his black predecessors. In his opening editorial, Hamilton informed readers that the "publisher of this Magazine was 'brought up' among Newspapers, Magazines, &c.," and that the "training of his boyhood and the employment of his manhood have been in the arts and mysteries which pertain to the neighborhood of Spruce and Nassau streets," an area commonly referred to as "Publisher's House Square" and home to papers such as the New York *Tribune*, New York *Herald*, and *World*.[11] With such a claim, Hamilton situated his publications within a culture of print that included the city's greatest newspapers.

In the magazine's second number, a vignette by William J. Wilson linked the *Anglo-African* to a tradition of black newspapers now over thirty years old. Wilson, writing under his pseudonym "Ethiop," composed a series of short pieces for the magazine titled "Afric-American Picture Gallery." In the series, the narrator peruses and critiques an imagined set of paintings, statues, and sketches. After pausing over an image of a slave ship docked in Jamestown, Virginia, at the beginning of the seventeenth century, Ethiop turns to a small painting titled "The First and the Last Colored Editor." In the scene, "The Last Colored Editor" sits in his editorial chair reading "the first number of the Freedom's Journal," and surrounded by "piles of all the journals edited by colored men from the commencement up till the present, among which the Freedom's Journal, Colored American, People's Press, North Star, and Frederick Douglas's [sic] paper are the more prominent."[12] Looking over the shoulder of the Last Editor, "unperceived," is the First Editor, who discovers his descendant reading "his own first editorial, and the first ever penned and published by a colored man in America." Wilson's sketch not only illustrates the existence of a black periodical tradition but also suggests that the success of "The Last Colored Editor" (and by implication Thomas Hamilton) depends upon his knowledge of and engagement with his predecessors. Moreover, Ethiop concludes that "[t]he scene is the linking together of our once scarcely hopeful past with the now bright present."[13] In this final remark, Ethiop reads black periodicals as representatives of epochs in black American history. *Freedom's Journal* stands in for a "scarcely hopeful past," while the newest publication (perhaps the *Anglo-African Magazine* itself) represents the "now bright present." The history of the black press is, in this reading, the history of black America.

As if he had indeed been reading *Freedom's Journal*'s first editorial, Thomas Hamilton justified the *Weekly Anglo-African* newspaper in language deeply reminiscent of that earlier publication. In his own opening editorial, Hamilton began, "[w]e need a press—a press of our own," because "[o]ur *cause* (for in this country we have a cause) demands our own advocacy."[14] Again echoing Cornish and Russwurm, Hamilton not only addressed a black audience but also hoped that his newspaper would act as a kind of connective tissue, binding together black readers scattered across the country. "We shall endeavor, by a continuous correspondence from nearly every city and town in the country," he wrote, "to connect and keep astir our whole people, thus bringing them together weekly, to compare notes and learn of each others' prosperity."[15] By the end of the Civil War the paper could indeed claim a wide reach, as it listed subscribers located not only in the northeastern states but also as far away as Florida, Louisiana, and California. In another illustration that subscriber rolls only begin to tell the story of a paper's actual readership, the *Weekly Anglo-African* noted instances where one individual held multiple subscriptions. William E. Matthews of Baltimore, for example, paid for five subscriptions to the paper, and Mrs. Martha A. Starr of New Orleans paid for two.[16] George Stephens noted that the *Weekly Anglo-African* began appearing in Union camps early in the war, and after 1863 the paper became especially important to black soldiers who read it aloud to one another and wrote back letters that appeared in its columns.[17] While the paper's subscription lists and presence at the front demonstrate its distribution across the United States, Hamilton also hoped that the *Weekly Anglo-African* would, through its coverage of international affairs, relate black readers in the United States to happenings beyond their country's borders. "Of all that transpires in our common country or throughout the world that will have any bearing upon our *cause*," he explained in his 1859 editorial, "we shall take a view so broad and so comprehensive that none will fail to see either the danger or the advantage, and be thus enabled to act accordingly."[18] Drawing upon the *North Star*'s approach to the 1848 revolutions in Europe, Hamilton emphasized the local relevance of international affairs. The *Weekly Anglo-African*, he promised, would draw connections between liberation struggles no matter where they occurred, and help readers apply lessons from abroad to their own immediate circumstances.

In another, less desirable echo of his predecessors in the black press, Thomas Hamilton struggled to keep his publications financially solvent. Like the *Colored American*'s printer Robert Sears, Hamilton doubled as a book publisher and seller, and tried to use this trade to entice subscribers for his own publications and as a means of supplementing his income. As he explained in an 1859 letter to John Jay, agents for the *Anglo-African Magazine* offered potential subscribers copies of George B. Cheever's temperance tale *The Dream, or The True History of Deacon Giles' Distillery*, and Hamilton hoped that in the future he could "offer the productions of colored authors," as well as J. R. Beard's *The Life of Toussaint L'Ouverture*.[19] But the editor required capital to publish or purchase these works; he asked Jay for a loan of five hundred dollars, offering his two thousand dollar life insurance policy as collateral. It is unclear if Jay granted Hamilton's request, but regardless the *Anglo-African Magazine* folded after less than two years. The *Weekly Anglo-African* struggled on until March 1861, when financial difficulties forced Hamilton to sell the paper to George Lawrence and James Redpath. In exchange for eleven hundred dollars Thomas reportedly agreed not to start a rival paper.[20] But after Redpath quickly changed the name of the paper to the *Pine and Palm* and used it to advertise Haitian emigration, Robert Hamilton relaunched the *Weekly Anglo-African* in July 1861.

The new version of the paper listed Robert as editor, but Thomas undoubtedly stayed active in its operations. The *Weekly Anglo-African*'s offices remained at 48 Beekman Street, a location that placed the paper in the vicinity of Publisher's

House Square. The paper's office also served as a meeting place for black New Yorkers and visitors to the city. For example, William Gould, a black sailor serving in the Union Navy, stopped by the newspaper's offices at least five times in April and May 1864, while his ship was docked in New York City.[21] Gould would have found more than fellowship at 48 Beekman, as Thomas Hamilton used the same location as a book- and drugstore. As advertisements in the *Weekly Anglo-African* attested, visitors to the office could purchase not only copies of the newspaper but also bound publications including the first volume of the *Anglo-African Magazine*, Douglass's *My Bondage and My Freedom*, Solomon Northup's *Twelve Years a Slave*, and Harriet Beecher Stowe's *Uncle Tom's Cabin*. Or, if a customer's ailments could not be cured by a good book, Thomas offered medicines such as "Mrs. Winslow's Soothing Syrup," "Dr. Clarke's Sugar-Coated Herb Pills," and "B. T. Babbitt's Superior French Chemical Erasive Soap."[22] From 1861 to 1863 Thomas also published a series of books including Martin Delany's *Official Report of the Niger Valley Exploring Party*, Robert Campbell's *A Pilgrimage to My Motherland*, and William Wells Brown's *The Black Man*.

In 1863 Thomas and Robert together published *Turning the Tables on the Overseer*, a stunning illustration depicting southern slaves gathered together to enjoy the whipping of a white overseer (see fig. 5.1). The Hamiltons transformed the image, which had originally appeared in the New York *Illustrated News*, into a stand-alone print available for purchase. Black New Yorkers could hang on their walls a scene of black men, women, and children taunting and whipping a white man, making crystal-clear their views on the proper treatment of southern slaveholders. The decision to move into print publishing also indicates that, like Charles Ray and Robert Sears, the Hamiltons keenly understood the power of visual culture. With the two brothers working together in their publishing pursuits, it seems likely that the *Weekly Anglo-African* was in truth a coedited publication.[23] The Hamiltons thus adopted the model of Samuel Cornish and John Brown Russwurm. And by the summer of 1864, in an almost too-neat historical coincidence, the brothers had moved their newspaper to 184 Church Street, only steps away from the last offices of *Freedom's Journal*.[24]

## Standing Still in the Promised Land

The new *Weekly Anglo-African*, launched in July 1861, emerged into a country and city in the throes of Civil War fever. Eight days after the attack on Fort Sumter, over one hundred thousand New Yorkers had gathered to show their sup-

Figure 5.1. *Turning the Tables on the Overseer.* Courtesy of the Library Company of Philadelphia.

port for the Union. Covering the rally (held, appropriately, in Union Square), a reporter for the New York *Times* described how "everywhere, on house-tops and mastheads, and on men's hats and next to their hearts, and even in ladies' bonnets were the Stars and Stripes—the emblem of a Union which the people have declared 'must and shall be preserved.'"[25] The *Times* also announced that a "Commissioner of the Federal Government is now in the City making arrangements for the transportation by water of all the New-York troops needed at Washington and intermediate stations," and within three days of the Union Square rally six regiments had been formed and sent off with great fanfare.[26] Though officially discouraged from following suit, black New Yorkers organized throughout the summer and, in July, offered New York's governor three fully funded regiments. The governor declined.[27]

But the official prohibition against black enlistment in the Union Army did not foreclose the possibility that black men would be called on to take up arms at some point in the conflict. Indeed, from the earliest days of the war, black northerners spent considerable ink debating the merits of preparing themselves for battle. In May 1861, for example, Frederick Douglass wrote a series of pieces for his *Douglass' Monthly* magazine, in which he counseled black northerners to begin military preparations and urged white northerners to accept black regiments. Despite the current stance of the federal government, wrote Douglass, "we do most earnestly urge our people everywhere to drink as deeply into the martial spirit of the times as possible; organize themselves into societies and companies, purchase arms for themselves, and learn how to use them." For, he predicted, "[t]he present war may and in all probability will reach a complexion when a few black regiments will be absolutely necessary."[28] And, in a companion piece titled "How to End the War," Douglass urged the government to "*[l]et the slaves and free colored people be called into service, and formed into a liberating army*, to march into the South and raise the banner of Emancipation among the slaves."[29] In such public pronouncements, Douglass extolled black enlistment as the key to northern victory, a fact that made black preparations for military service all the more necessary. But in private he revealed more ambivalence about loyalty to a government that had not yet come down on the side of black liberation. In a letter to Samuel J. May, Douglass declared that he would support the Union "[w]henever the government is ready to make the war, a war for freedom and progress," but asserted that "[n]othing short of an open recognition of the Negro's manhood, his rights as such to have a country, to bear arms, and to defend that country equally with others would induce me to join the army in any capacity."[30] Regardless of his feelings toward the U.S. government, though, Douglass never wavered in his public advocacy of black military preparations.

During the summer and fall of 1861, debates over the wisdom of black military activity raged across the pages of the *Weekly Anglo-African*. Building upon discussions in earlier black newspapers, the Hamiltons' paper offered competing visions of acting chosen in wartime. For example, a quick exchange in early October approached the issue of military preparation through the lens of black propriety and decorum, recalling the fight over Emancipation Day celebrations that had played out in *Freedom's Journal* in the late 1820s. The author of an unsigned piece titled simply "Let Us Drill!" concluded that even "[i]f the Government sees fit to refuse the enrollment of black soldiers, that is no reason why black men shall refrain from organizing themselves into military companies for purposes of drill." Such practice, he argued, in addition to preparing for the inevitable time when "there will be a great and pressing need for colored men well drilled in military tactics" would "add to our carriage and demeanor, take away the slouchy slip-shod step too frequent among our young men, and replace it by the firm self-confident, self-reliant tread of the soldier-citizen."[31] Drilling, the writer argued, would transform unruly black youth into proper, orderly men, thus performing the very function that Samuel Cornish and John Brown Russwurm hoped that their newspaper could accomplish decades earlier.

But the author of "Let Us Drill!" also proposed a public procession, that event so denounced by *Freedom's Journal*'s editors. Once organized and well schooled in military formation, the author imagined a striking display of black military readiness. "Ten such companies," he wrote, "amounting to about one thousand men, with black field and company officers, marching down Broadway, at the date of these presents would send a thrill through the country such as would elevate us in our own, and also in the public opinion to a height we have never won before."[32] While couched in the rhetoric of public propriety, with the decorum of the marchers elevating themselves and their race in the eyes of "public opinion," the specter of one thousand armed and organized black men marching down Broadway invoked more than just a display of black propriety. Like the Fifth of July procession in 1827, such a march could be read not simply as a demonstration of black fitness for freedom but also a warning to white onlookers of the threat of insurrection if they failed to acknowledge the inherent rights of their black countrymen. And whereas the marchers in the 1820s carried banners and represented the city's black mutual improvement societies, the men marching down Broadway in 1861 would carry guns and be organized into well-trained military companies. The "thrill" that such a display might send "through the country," then, was the possibility of black military intervention in the war, with or without the sanction of the government. Welcomed into the fold of the Union Army, such a force could provide the key to victory, but if the United States continued to oppose black liberation the marchers represented a fifth column lodged in the heart of Union territory. Drilling would not only give black men lessons in proper behavior, but it might also provide the federal government with an added incentive to embrace the cause of black freedom.

"Let Us Drill!" appeared in the *Weekly Anglo-African*'s October 5, 1861, issue. The next week the paper printed a rebuttal piece titled, appropriately, "We Should Not Drill." The article's anonymous author, like the writer a week earlier, framed the issue of military action within the larger context of black propriety. But rather than read drilling as a tool for cultivating respectability, this writer saw military preparations as distractions from that effort, arguing that "it is infinitely of greater importance that we strain every energy to drill our young men into habits of sobriety, frugality, chastity and economy." In addition to training in these values, the author of "We Should Not Drill" argued that a thorough education in "scientific and mechanical knowledge" needed to precede any efforts at military organization, "for what would appear more droll, or excite greater well-deserved ridicule than a Broadway parade of a regiment of our young men armed with all the implements of warfare, and not two in the whole regiment understanding the process of manufacturing a fire-arm, an accoutrement, or even the simple ammunition." A week earlier, such a procession had been imagined as a means of racial elevation and, potentially, motivation for the Union government to make the cause of black liberation its own. But, echoing the position taken by the editors of *Freedom's Journal*, public processions in this account could lead only to black embarrassment and degradation in the eyes of a white audience. Rather than wasting time and energy on such ridiculous displays, then, the opponent of military drilling concluded that "we should all immediately lay hold with might and strength, not first to drill as military companies, but in the more important essentials, to the formation of character, so when in the Providence of God, the time comes when we must act, that we may be all fully prepared to do our part in totally annihilating the demon slaver, and all other unrighteous systems."[33] For this author, black men in the North needed character, not companies, to fight slavery.

While most obviously revolving around the question of public propriety, the letters sent to the *Weekly Anglo-African* in early October also expressed a fundamental disagreement over the timing of the black response to the Civil War. Those who agitated for black military organization argued that the war demanded an immediate response. But some black northerners believed that the divinely appointed time for action had not yet arrived. As another exchange of letters to the newspaper reveals, the debate over timing stemmed from a fundamental disagreement over the biblical typology of black chosenness. In a series of letters printed sporadically in the *Weekly Anglo-African* from September to December 1861, New Yorker Robert H. Vandyne and Philadelphia's Alfred M. Green engaged in a spirited debate over black enlistment that hinged, ultimately, upon which epoch in biblical history was being repeated on American soil.[34] Vandyne argued that black Americans were like the Israelites in the second book of Chronicles. They had reached the Promised Land, but hostile armies threatened their kingdom. The Civil War, in this reading, was

God's way of destroying the forces arrayed against his chosen people by having them fall upon one another. Green, though, contended that black Americans were living in an age reminiscent of Exodus. Suffering under the lash of Egyptian enslavement, the Israelites would have to take action to gain freedom. But unlike their biblical counterparts, black Americans were separated from their Promised Land by time rather than space. They could be free on American soil, but would have to fight through the waves of the Civil War (as the Israelites crossed the Red Sea) to reach safety. For Vandyne and Green, then, how black northerners should respond to the Civil War, and when, depended upon which period in the history of God's chosen people black Americans were currently reliving.

Robert Vandyne began the conversation in a September letter. The New Yorker asked those who advocated black participation in the Union war effort why black Americans should support a Union government that had never been an ally and had, up until the outbreak of the Civil War, been perceived by many black Americans as the ultimate obstacle to liberation and equality. "Is this country ready and anxious to initiate a new era for down-trodden humanity," he wrote, "that you now so eagerly propose to make the sacrifice of thousands of our ablest men to encourage and facilitate the great work of regeneration? No! no!! Your answer must be: No!!!" Rather, he argued, black Americans would be wise to watch and wait, throwing their support behind a government only after a commitment to emancipation was assured. Since, he reasoned, the prospect of international aid could potentially lead the Confederacy to abolish slavery first "rather than submit to Northern dictation or subjugation," black Americans should refrain from too quickly supporting either side, and should instead remain "neutral, ever praying for the success of that party determined to initiate first the policy of justice and equal rights." The uncertainty of war demanded, according to Vandyne, extreme caution, and he finished his letter by imploring his black readers to "do our duty to each other—use care in all our public measures—be not too precipitous, but in prayer wait and watch the salvation of God."[35]

Alfred Green could not have disagreed more. His October letter passionately argued for an increase in black military training and warned that the consequences of inaction could be disastrous. "No nation has ever or ever will be emancipated from slavery," Green argued, "but by the sword wielded too by their own strong arms." He was particularly irked by the argument that God had commanded his followers to sit idly by and refuse to fight for their own liberation, lamenting as "most unfortunate" those black leaders who would "counsel sitting still to see the salvation of God." Such reasoning was, Green argued, a fundamental misreading of how God worked in the world. He contended that the Civil War was "nothing less than God's means of opening the way for us to free ourselves by the assistance of our own enslavers if we will do it." A failure to act and determine the course of the war—and ultimately force the Union to declare the conflict a war for black liberation—could, Green continued, lead to the South emancipating its slaves and enlisting them into the Confederate Army. Black northerners could then be drafted into the Union ranks, and find themselves in the surreal position of fighting against their southern brethren. "Sitting still," Green concluded, "shirking the responsibility God has thrown upon our shoulders, alone can engender such a dilemma."[36] Only through action could black northerners ensure that the Union enacted emancipation first, and hence avoid such a scenario.

Vandyne's next letter reiterated his earlier argument, and directly addressed Green's reading of God's intentions for black Americans. Far from reading the war as an opportunity for liberation provided by God, he saw no "evidences of God's will or demands upon us in that direction," and expressed his pleasure at having "the honor of being termed one of those unfortunate who are willing to wait and see the salvation of God." "I abide time," Vandyne wrote, "clinging to my avowed policy, humbly trusting in Him who I have every reason to think has taken the cause of the oppressed of our people in this land out of our weak hands, and has or is about to answer our many appeals in his own glorious way, while we continue to lift our hearts, our hands, in praise and thanksgiving to His holy name."[37] Rather than an opportunity for action, Vandyne saw the Civil War as irrefutable evidence that God had directly intervened in the antislavery struggle. Nominally free black Americans had struggled for decades to achieve freedom and equality for themselves and their enslaved brethren, but now God had taken that fight out of their "weak hands," and would complete the task himself. The appropriate black response to the war, then, was simply to give thanks and praise to God for answering the cries of the oppressed.

Increasingly frustrated, Green argued in his final rebuttal that the logic of "this stand still policy," as he termed it, was based upon a misreading of scripture. Invoking the biblical context of "stand still, and see the salvation of the Lord," Green thundered:

> When the slaves have raised the standard of rebellion against their masters, and have broken every yoke, and then by some great impending danger are about to yield and go back again to slavery, I like Moses, rather than retrograde, would readily counsel standing still at least for a while. When we of the north by indefatigable exertion (and sacrifice if required) have armed and equipped ourselves, and become proficient in all that pertains to self defence [sic], as men in our condition should be; and then find ourselves environed with some of the difficulties that my friend predicts would follow such a significant result; and we like Israel are about turning back to our present unhappy and significant condition; I for one should steadfastly counsel standing still with fixed bayonets and iron cartridges, to see the salvation of God.[38]

Through his invocation of Moses, Green routed his reading of black chosenness, as well as his interpretation of current events, through a specific biblical typology rooted in the book of Exodus. As he implied, a command to "stand still" appears in that scripture as the Israelites, fleeing from the Egyptians, meet the apparently impassable barrier of the Red Sea. Seemingly trapped, and with the Egyptians closing fast on their heels, the Israelites ask Moses why he had taken them out of Egypt, if they were only to die in the wilderness. Better, they reason, to have remained in slavery. Moses responds, in the King James translation, "Fear ye not, stand still, and see the salvation of the Lord: for the Egyptians whom ye have seen today, ye shall see them again no more for ever."[39] Moses then leads the Israelites to safety across a parted Red Sea, and when the Egyptians attempt to follow the waters return, drowning the would-be enslavers. In Green's reading, this context shows how Moses' words came only after a great struggle, when all seemed lost and the Israelites contemplated retreat. Concerning black involvement in the Civil War, then, "stand still, and see the salvation of the Lord" could be used as a rallying cry for black troops suffering on the battlefield, but held no purchase as a call for inaction.

Green's letter provides an important challenge to the reading of the command to "stand still, and see the salvation of the Lord" as the basis for a passive policy. However, the phrase possesses another scriptural context, appearing again in the second book of Chronicles when the Israelites, this time rulers of an established kingdom surrounding Jerusalem, turn to God for help against an oncoming invasion. Through a prophet, God instructs King Jehosophat to take his army down to meet the enemy, but then to sing their praises to the Lord rather than fight: "Ye shall not need to fight in this battle: set yourselves, stand ye still, and see the salvation of the Lord with you."[40] Following God's command, Jehosophat goes out to meet Israel's enemies, appointing "singers unto the Lord" to go "out before the army, and to say, Praise the Lord."[41] After they begin "to sing and to praise," the opposing armies fall upon each other, destroying themselves while the Israelites stand by and watch.[42] Rather than a command to stand fast in the face of adversity, here the command to "stand still and see the salvation of the Lord" instructs God's followers to stand aside and let their enemies destroy themselves. Vandyne's argument seems to be firmly rooted in this moment of scripture, rather than in the book of Exodus. Indeed, this passage offers a powerful lens through which to read the question of black involvement in the Civil War, a conflict between two governments that, in 1861, each endorsed the oppression and slavery of black Americans.

Both Green and Vandyne, when faced with the question of black involvement in the Civil War, based their reading of current events on the biblical typology that lay at the heart of the theory of black chosenness. Critically, however, the two men related their present to very different moments in the history of the Israelite nation. Green drew the now familiar parallel between black Americans and the Israelites in the book of Exodus, fleeing from enslavement by the Egyptians. Hence, "stand still, and see the salvation of the Lord" clearly references Moses' command to continue toward freedom rather than retreat back into slavery. Within this typological association, the Civil War—the splitting of the Union, as it were—could be read as akin to God parting the Red Sea. The coming of the war was God's intervention, but it was now the responsibility of black Americans to move forward, into the breach, and take full advantage of the opportunity. Vandyne, however, invoked a different typological association, one that saw black Americans as akin to a later Israelite nation, one already in the promised land, but under siege from hostile forces bent on its subjugation. In this reading, as exemplified by the *Colored American*'s illustrations, the United States usually occupied the position of Babylon. This civilization, like the Egyptians, enslaved the Israelites, but as a consequence of this oppression Babylon would not merely allow the Israelites their freedom, but would be wiped from the face of the earth. Within this typology, the Civil War could be read as the God-given conflict that would destroy the United States and leave black Americans free to establish a new American civilization. Given this context, Vandyne quite understandably read "stand still, and see the salvation of the Lord" as an invitation to sit back and marvel at the power of God, as the United States, the entity that had since its founding enslaved and oppressed black Americans, destroyed itself.

## "A Deep Laid Secret Organization"

On November 16, 1861, in the midst of the debate between Robert Vandyne and Alfred Green, Robert Hamilton informed the *Weekly Anglo-African*'s readers that "in our next number we will commence the publication of a story of thrilling interest, from the able pen of Dr. Martin R. Delany, entitled 'BLAKE: OR THE HUTS OF AMERICA,—A Tale of the Mississippi Valley, the Southern United States and Cuba.'"[43] The appearance of a novel in the paper was not especially remarkable, since black newspapers had been serializing fiction since the early 1828 issues of *Freedom's Journal*.[44] Indeed, as Robert admitted, his brother Thomas had serialized a "portion" of *Blake* two years earlier in the *Anglo-African Magazine*, though less than half of the supposed eighty chapters had appeared in the magazine. Robert promised his readers that, "[a]s we have the entire manuscript in our possession, a similar interruption is improbable."[45] The novel's first installment appeared in the *Weekly Anglo-African*'s November 23, 1861, issue and, true to the editor's word, ran on the paper's front page without interruption until at least April 26, 1862.[46]

*Blake* sprawls across seventy-six chapters, with action taking place in the United States, Canada, Cuba, and Africa. Henry Holland, the protagonist, flees from his home on a Mississippi plantation after his wife, Maggie, is sold to a planter in Cuba. Yet, instead of immediately seeking her out or running north to freedom, Henry travels throughout the southern states in order to transmit his plan for a general insurrection to slaves across the South. His task complete, he flees with his son and some other slaves to Canada, resting there only briefly before he continues on to Cuba. There, he finds Maggie and secures her freedom. Readers also learn that Henry descends from an elite Cuban family, and his real name is Henrico Blacus, which he anglicizes to Henry Blake. In Cuba, Henry continues to foment a slave insurrection, pausing only when he signs on for a brief voyage (as the sail-master) aboard a slave ship traveling to and from Africa. At the novel's close an uprising seems imminent, with the butcher-knife-wielding Cuban chef Gofer Gondolier ominously declaring, in the closing line, "Woe be unto those devils of whites, I say!" The novel never reveals the details of the plan that Henry imparts to his fellow conspirators, of what precise action he has asked them to take or what the fruits of his revolutionary plan might look like. Such ambiguity potentially lent an element of suspense to *Blake*, keeping readers interested in the story and, by extension, the newspaper in which it appeared.

But the context of the *Weekly Anglo-African* suggests one way to fill in the gaps that Delany left in his novel. In particular, the newspaper's Civil War coverage transforms *Blake* into a commentary on the debates over black military preparations in the North.[47] In a brief synopsis designed to entice his paper's readers, Robert Hamilton explained that, "at the instance of his wife being sold from him," *Blake*'s hero Henry sought his "revenge through the medium of a deep laid secret organization."[48] Tracing the creation of a vast, transnational conspiracy to overthrow the slave power that dominated the American hemisphere, Delany's novel focuses on the work that precedes an uprising—on the preparations necessary for a successful revolution.[49] As he travels across the U.S. South, and then into Cuba, Henry asks his coconspirators not to fight but rather to prepare themselves for the moment when they would be moved to rise up and free themselves and their brethren. As one piece of the *Weekly Anglo-African*'s attempts to define the responsibilities of the chosen nation in wartime, *Blake* picked up where Vandyne and Green left off, displacing the black response to the conflict onto an imaginary conspiracy. In doing so, the novel called upon black northerners to act chosen by preparing themselves for battle in an imminent war for black liberation.

The language of Delany's novel invited the *Weekly Anglo-African*'s regular readers to connect *Blake* to the paper's ongoing Civil War coverage and commentary. Echoing the debate between Robert Vandyne and Alfred Green, for example, *Blake*'s early episodes repeatedly invoke the contested scriptural command to "stand still, and see the salvation of the Lord." In the novel's first installment Henry—enraged that his wife Maggie has been sold away—returns to his home plantation and informs an older slave, Joe, of his intention to go after her. Joe counsels patience, reminding Henry that "[d]e wud say 'stan' still an' see de salbation.'" Henry harshly answers, "That's no talk for me, Daddy Joe; I've been 'standing still' long enough—I'll stand still no longer."[50] Henry here resists the passive implications of a "stand still" policy but later, like Alfred Green, recognizes that the biblical phrase can inspire God's chosen people to resist their oppressors. As Henry indoctrinates coconspirators into his "secret organization," he transforms the command to stand still into a watchword for black revolution. After imparting his plan to two slaves on his home plantation, Henry commands the men to "Stand still, then, and see!" Similar scenes dot *Blake*'s early installments in the *Weekly Anglo-African*. For example, the paper's December 14, 1861, number follows Henry across the southern United States as he periodically pauses to impart his revolutionary message to trusted

*Joining the Chosen Army* 135

slaves at plantations along his route. In one such instance, the slave Nathan exclaims (after hearing Henry's plan), "[m]y eyes has seen, and meh yeahs heahn, an' now Laud! I's willin' to stan' still an' see dy salvation!" Later, at a neighboring plantation, Henry brings the aptly named Uncle Moses into the fold. Upon being questioned by his family after Henry's departure, "all that could be elicited was, 'Stan' still child'en, and see da salvation uv da Laud!'"[51] By using this line from scripture as a revolutionary shibboleth, Henry and his compatriots echo Green's understanding of the biblical phrase as a call to remain steadfast in the face of adversity.

Henry's initial suspicion of religion, but ultimate embrace of its revolutionary potential, echoed the approach to religion that Delany had articulated in his 1852 treatise, *The Condition, Elevation, Emigration, and Destiny of the Colored People of the United States*. There, Delany had worried that the deep religious faith held by the "colored races," which he deemed "an excellent trait in their character," could lead them to "stand still—hope in God, and really expect Him to do that for them, which it is necessary they should do for themselves."[52] Not discounting the importance of faith, Delany concluded that "[t]o depend for assistance upon God, is a *duty* and right; but to know when, how, and in what manner to obtain it, is the key to this great Bulwark of Strength, and Depository of Aid."[53] Like the hero in his novel (and Alfred Green), Delany here refuses to see faith and action as mutually exclusive. Freedom, he suggests, cannot be achieved without God's help, but in order to "obtain" divine assistance black men and women will need to take action. Recognizing the revolutionary potential of religious faith, Delany urges his black readers to be ever watchful for God's aid and prepare themselves for the moment of divine intervention. In *Blake*, Henry's command to his fellow conspirators to "stand still" dramatizes the relationship between faith and action that Delany had theorized in *The Condition*. Rather than ask his fellow slaves to abandon their reliance upon God, Henry urges them to use that certainty in divine aid as a springboard for their own uprising.

Like the conspirators in Delany's novel, the *Weekly Anglo-African*'s northern black readers could follow scripture's command to adopt a position of revolutionary readiness by preparing themselves for battle. Indeed, an April 1861 editorial cast black military preparations in the North as akin to the "deep laid secret organization" in Delany's novel. The editorial centered around the question of the paper's "war policy," which it saw as "simply confined to this one point—how can we so use our strength to best aid the slave?"[54] While "against the policy indicated by the movements in this city, Boston, and elsewhere, to organize volunteer companies, to be offered to the Government," the newspaper urged black men in the North to "organize for military purposes, drill efficiently, procure arms, and hold ourselves as Minute Men, to *respond when the slave calls*."[55] Such preparations, the editorial concluded, should be "quietly conducted and efficiently carried forward." In April, then, the *Weekly Anglo-African* endorsed black military activity in the North. But rather than forming companies so that they could join the Union war effort, the paper counseled black northerners to prepare themselves to support a slave uprising. This organizing would need to proceed in secret, since the force being arrayed would not be used in the service of the United States. "This is then briefly our war policy," the editorial concluded, "[t]o let the Government take care of itself, and give our labors for the slave, and the slave alone."[56] Early in the war, then, the *Weekly Anglo-African* separated black military preparations from loyalty to the United States. Members of God's chosen nation had a responsibility to fight for one another, rather than for any government.

During *Blake*'s serialization in the *Weekly Anglo-African*, the paper routinely printed letters from a war correspondent that reiterated the fact that the Union could not be trusted to fight for the slave, and so it was the responsibility of black northerners to ensure the liberation of their enslaved brethren. On November 2, 1861—three weeks before the first installment of *Blake* appeared—the *Weekly Anglo-African* introduced its readers to a new correspondent, George E. Stephens, a black Philadelphian who had signed on as cook for a Union officer and provided the newspaper with regular reports from the front.[57] Stephens's letters, written from a Union encampment in Maryland, consistently chastised the Union for its unwillingness to fight for black freedom. In one December 1861 letter, for example, Stephens surmised that the white northern public would be only too happy to accept slavery in the South as a condition of reunification. White northerners might find slavery onerous, he wrote, but "could they restore what was supposed to be by the credulous a 'Glorious Union,' and the Constitution and laws, with all of the crimes and iniquities which hover around it, they would passively submit and forget under the sophistries and blandishments of polished rhetoric, the claims of millions of enslaved men, to all of the blessing and benefits of liberty and civilization."[58] And even if the Union had possessed the will to free the enslaved, Stephens relentlessly attacked the impotence of an army that could not even conquer the muddy roads of Maryland. In a February 1862 letter, the correspondent imagined that even if

"Richmond, the metropolis of rebeldom presented an easy conquest, this army, this 'slumbering giant,' could not budge an inch; here it would have to lie at its huge length, barricaded in the mud."[59] With the Union unwilling and unable to fight for black freedom, it would seem the height of folly for black Northerners to align their efforts with that of the government.

But far from seeing Union ineptitude as a death knell for black liberation, Stephens shared numerous stories of black men and women liberating not only themselves but also their brethren and sisters in bondage. Through such episodes, Stephens painted a picture of black freedom secured through the efforts of black Americans. In one January letter, for example, Stephens told the story of Henry Young, an enslaved black man in Maryland. After an altercation with his owner, Young had fled across the Potomac, where he had been arrested as a runaway and imprisoned in a Virginia jail. Young "remained there four days with four others beside himself," Stephens wrote, before he "broke goal [sic], released his comrads [sic], and found his way to the banks of the Potomac, signaled a passing steamer, was taken on board and carried to Washington." Reading Young's actions as exemplary rather than exceptional, Stephens concluded by assuring readers that "[t]here are many of the same sort about here."[60]

And readers of the *Weekly Anglo-African* could find an account of "the same sort" on the front page of the very same issue as Stephens's letter. For in that week's installment of *Blake*, another Henry had performed a similar feat of communal liberation. In a chapter aptly named "The Escape," Henry Holland and five other fugitive slaves had been captured and imprisoned in an Indiana stable. Their captors, celebrating their expected bounty in the tavern, leave their quarry alone for the night. "So soon as the parties left the stable," the narrator relates, "the captives lying with their heads resting on their bundles, Henry arising, took the knife, cutting loose himself and companions, but leaving the pinions still about their limbs as though fastened, resumed his position on the bundle of straw," after which Henry and his allies proceed to subdue a guard and make their escape.[61] As in Stephens's letter on Henry Young, Delany's Henry "broke goal" and "released his comrads." The *Weekly Anglo-African*'s two Henrys demonstrated the importance of communal liberation since, in each episode, the hero frees himself in order to liberate his companions. In the newspaper, such scenes reinforced the sense that black men in the North had a responsibility to use their nominal freedom in the service of their enslaved brethren. Indeed, by embedding *Blake* within the broader conversation surrounding black participation in the Civil War, the *Weekly Anglo-African* cast black military preparations in the North as akin to Delany's imagined conspiracy. Such a comparison rendered the question over Union policy moot, since the black companies organized in the North would offer their allegiance to the slave rather than any government.

## The New Mission of Black Chosenness

But on January 1, 1863, the cause of the slave and that of the Union seemed to come together, as Abraham Lincoln's Emancipation Proclamation officially linked Union victory to the abolition of slavery. The *Weekly Anglo-African* read Lincoln's proclamation as evidence that the Union had, finally, joined the fight for black freedom. And so, after the Union Army began accepting black recruits in early 1863, the newspaper wholeheartedly endorsed black enlistment. The paper never wavered in its insistence that free black men should devote their efforts to the liberation of their enslaved brethren, but it now seemed like they could best accomplish this goal by swearing allegiance to the Union government. In a January 17, 1863, editorial, Robert Hamilton urged his black readers to "organize one regiment in every large northern city, and send our offer of services directly to the President or the Secretary of War." In line with the logic offered by Alfred Green, Hamilton now saw the Civil War as the God-given opening for black Americans to gain their freedom, and urged his readers to seize the opportunity. "If we rise in tens of thousands, and say to the President, 'here we are, take us!,'" Hamilton declared, "we will secure to our children and our children's children all that our fathers have labored and suffered and bled for!"[62] In an April 1863 letter to the paper, George Stephens urged his northern brethren to enlist, reminding them that "[w]e have more to gain, if victorious, or more to lose, if defeated, than any other class of men."[63] Hamilton expanded upon this point in a June editorial, promising black readers that "if successful, the blessings attendant upon an enlightened christian civilization will be ours; but if we fail—if the Union is overthrown—then a night of darkness and horror comes upon us, the like of which no people ever saw."[64] Black men in the North apparently agreed with the apocalyptic stakes that Hamilton laid out. By war's end, nearly 200,000 black men had served in the Union military.[65] Unsurprisingly, the *Weekly Anglo-African* accompanied black regiments to the front. The newspaper noted that a sergeant major for the 29th U.S.C.T. ordered sixteen subscriptions for his regiment.[66] And, in a regularly appearing notice, Hamilton informed readers that he was "receiving daily from the various regiments, applications for our paper," and asked for contributions toward this cause.[67]

Supporting the Union war effort may have been the most immediate way that black northerners could advance the cause of black liberation, but the *Weekly Anglo-African* saw military activity as only the first step toward black Americans gaining and maintaining true equality. Echoing the arguments of Cornish and Russwurm in 1827, and Frederick Douglass two decades later, Robert Hamilton emphasized the necessity of proper black conduct in a post-emancipation United States. But rather than casting black northerners as students who required lessons in propriety, Hamilton saw black men and women in the North as teachers who could carry the message to those who needed it most: the newly free in the South. "The process of transforming three millions of slaves into citizens," wrote Hamilton in his January 17 editorial, "requires the aid of intelligent colored men and women." According to Hamilton, black northerners were uniquely suited to the task of uplifting their southern brethren. "We are, and can be, nearer to them than any other class of persons," he wrote, "we can enter into their feelings and attract their sympathies better than any others can." Indeed, concluded Hamilton, the limited freedom that black northerners had possessed during the previous decades had been provided by God specifically to fit them for this service. "It is for this trial," he wrote, that "God has given us the partial freedom, and such education, and the irrepressible desire for equality which consumes our souls." "This labor of love and humanity His Providence has assigned to us," Hamilton concluded, "and we will be false to our destiny if we fail to do it."[68] Seeing the work of racial uplift in the South as divinely ordained, the editor here echoed the sentiments of Douglass, who had, in a November 1862 article written in response to Lincoln's preliminary proclamation, imagined that after the war, "[t]he whole South, as it never was before the abolition of slavery will become missionary ground."[69] This idea of the newly free as the not-yet-converted, requiring the attention of missionaries, applied the understanding that certain kinds of behavior needed to be learned and performed in order to demonstrate fitness for entry into the chosen nation to the aftermath of the Civil War.

Moreover, Hamilton's vision of northern missionaries using the tenets of acting chosen to transform "slaves into citizens" conflated being a member of God's chosen nation with being a citizen of the United States. A Union victory might not result in the hemispheric revolution envisioned in *Blake*, but the possibility of freedom from slavery for all black Americans in the United States was enough to convince even that country's most vociferous critics to embrace the Union cause. Martin Delany abandoned his plans for emigration to Africa and signed on as an Army recruiter, while Mary Ann Shadd returned from Canada and took up a similar position. Rather than contradicting her earlier position, Shadd's return remained consistent with her search for the path that seemed most likely to lead to immediate, enduring freedom. Nevertheless, the shift of figures such as Shadd and Delany from fierce opponents of the United States to boosters of the Union Army exemplified the ways in which the Civil War, and especially the Emancipation Proclamation, transformed the idea of black chosenness. Black newspapers from *Freedom's Journal* to the *Weekly Anglo-African* had struggled over the relationship between God's chosen nation and the United States and debated whether or not God's plan for his people's liberation would help reform or ultimately eradicate that American government. The Emancipation Proclamation, however late and incomplete, suggested that the United States would survive God's judgment. And, according to the American jeremiad, the crucible of the Civil War confirmed the chosenness of the United States and its people. If such logic held true, then citizenship in the United States would not only provide black Americans with earthly rights and privileges but also confirm their membership in God's new chosen nation.

## Conclusion

### THE ENDS OF BLACK CHOSENNESS

It would seem that it was regarded as a greater crime to be black than to be a rebel. If this is the ethics which is to prevail, then we have more judgments in store for the nation.
—Samuel Childress, Untitled Letter, *Weekly Anglo-African*, December 16, 1865

On June 16, 1864, a soldier in the 54th Massachusetts, a black regiment, sat down to write a letter. Now stationed on Morris Island, South Carolina, the 54th had been in the field for a year and seen tremendous action. Indeed, the black soldier who signed his letter with the initials "E. W. D." composed his missive from the very site where, eleven months earlier, the 54th had lost nearly half its number in the bloody assault on Fort Wagner. Despite such sacrifice, and the incredible bravery that black troops had shown in battle, the letter writer complained that the "Fifty-fourth Regiment Massachusetts Volunteers is still in the field without pay, and the Government shows no disposition to pay us."[1] Though the United States initially promised black men enlisting in its army the same pay as their white counterparts, the War Department decided in June 1863 that black men fighting and dying at the front deserved just over half of what white soldiers earned. Black soldiers protested this betrayal in a variety of ways. Like E. W. D., many wrote letters decrying their unequal treatment. Some black regiments, like the 54th Massachusetts, refused to accept any pay that was not the same as that for whites. The members of the 21st U.S. Colored Infantry went one step further and stacked their arms as a sign of protest. In response, the Union executed the 21st's sergeant, William Walker, for inciting mutiny.[2] In his letter, E. W. D. reasoned that by refusing to pay its black soldiers an equal wage yet demanding their service, the Union had in effect established a new form of slavery. "They cannot tell us that we do not fight as well nor die as freely as the white man," he proclaimed, "but they can tell us they are a majority, and, therefore, assume presumption of their power, and intend to compel us to involuntary servitude, or, in other words, compel us to work for half pay, which is involuntary servitude."[3] Despite the Emancipation Proclamation, despite finally welcoming black enlistment, the Union's refusal to honor its promise of equal pay to black soldiers signaled, yet again, the country's enduring commitment to black oppression.

Building upon decades of black activism, E. W. D. turned to black chosenness as he envisioned a pathway to black liberation within, or without, the Union Army. "If the Fifty-fourth must be as the leaders of Israel," he wrote, "let us suffer in the wilderness until a second Moses shall rise up and smite the rock, that we may drink of the spring of freedom, and the spring of learning." Drawing upon the now-familiar biblical typology between black Americans and the Israelites, the letter writer from the 54th imagined serving in the Union Army as an echo of God's first chosen nation wandering in the desert after escape from Egypt. They had left slavery, but had not yet reached the Promised Land. For black Americans, then, the Civil War was the space in between bondage and freedom, and more trials remained before liberty would be secured. "No nation has ever risen to dignity without self-sacrifice, none has ever triumphed in victory without undergoing great hardships and long forbearance," E. W. D. reasoned, "but we still abide in faith, and look forward to the time when Ethiopia shall stretch forth her hand and rise from obscurity with healing in her wings." The reference here to the Ethiopian prophecy, from Psalms 68:31, makes clear that the "nation" that E. W. D. refers to is not the United States but rather the black Americans currently "undergoing great hardships" in the camps of the Union Army. The Civil War represented another step toward the liberation that black Americans, as God's chosen nation, would surely achieve. But again, the United States' commitment to black oppression made that country's fate less certain. "If a strong power crush the weak and deprive them of the blessings which God has ordained for them," concluded E. W. D., "it must fall." And if the United States failed to live up to its promises to God's chosen people and was destroyed as a result, black Americans would emerge from its ruins ready to follow God as he directed them "in the establishment of the most pure Government."[4]

The black soldier E. W. D. wrote his letter to the editor of the *Christian Recorder*, and his missive appeared on the front page of that paper's June 25, 1854, issue. Founded in 1852 as the official organ of the African Methodist Episcopal (A.M.E.) Church, the *Recorder* had been sporadically printed in the 1850s before being reinvigorated under the editorship of Elisha Weaver in 1861. While the paper certainly spent time on topics specific to the A.M.E. Church, like other black newspapers it provided coverage of and commentary on a range of current events, and it also printed a considerable amount of poetry and fiction.[5] The *Recorder* also became a major forum for letters from black soldiers. Often distributed by black army chaplains affiliated with the A.M.E. Church, the *Recorder* found its way into the hands of the black men serving at the front. As its correspondent Henry McNeal Turner, a chaplain who would later become bishop of the A.M.E. Church, wrote in 1864, the "Recorder is looked for weekly, as a precious visitor, in this part of our noble army."[6] As readers and writers, black soldiers used the newspaper's pages to practice their spelling, learn of goings-on back home, and share their experiences with northern readers.

The *Recorder* devoted considerable ink to the issue of unequal pay for black soldiers. Unlike correspondents like E. W. D., though, the newspaper's editorials consistently framed the army's policy as a departure from the policies of an otherwise gracious and reliable United States government. In a December 1863 piece on "The Pay of Colored Soldiers," editor Weaver acknowledged reports of unequal pay but saw it as the practice of a few corrupt individuals rather than the policy of the U.S. government. "We cannot believe," he wrote, "that the Government sanctions this." Instead, Weaver imagined that the discrimination against black soldiers was "some fraudulent scheme being practised on them by some rascally paymaster," and concluded his piece confident that "Congress is already moving for equal pay to ALL soldiers, and will no doubt pass a bill to that effect."[7] It is tempting to read Weaver's faith in the U.S. government as tongue-in-cheek, as a feigned incredulity that underscores the shocking hypocrisy of the army's treatment of black soldiers. But the editor's framing of a reprinted letter from Colonel Thomas Wentworth Higginson less than a year later suggests that Weaver meant what he said about the government's innocence. On August 1, 1864, the War Department declared that black soldiers who had been free on April 18, 1861, would be paid the same as white soldiers, and that they would receive back pay to that effect. But the Union refused to pay the more recently free an equal wage. Higginson, the white colonel of a black regiment, wrote a letter to the New York *Tribune* decrying this inconsistency. By refusing to honor its initial promise to pay all black soldiers the same as whites, Higginson reasoned, the government taught white Americans that they did not have to honor contracts with former slaves. Invoking the infamous words of Chief Justice Roger Taney's *Dred Scott* decision, Higginson complained that the government's policy said in effect "that a freedman (since April 19, 1861) has no rights which a white man is bound to respect." "Any employer, following the example of the U.S. Government," he continued, "may make with him a written agreement, receive his services, and then withhold the wages." Such conditions made a man declared free after April 18, 1861, "virtually a slave, and nothing else, to the end of time." Weaver reprinted Higginson's letter on the front page of the *Recorder*'s August 20, 1864, issue, and framed it with editorial comment. Introducing Higginson's letter as "a voice from one who ought to know," the editor cryptically remarked that "[t]hose who complain will do well to note it." Focusing it seems on Higginson's opening report that some black soldiers would now be paid the same as their white counterparts, rather than the injustice that occupied most of his missive, Weaver concluded that the colonel, "a model officer," was "endeavoring to show that if one party fulfils [sic] one side of the contract, the other part will endeavor to do its share—that is, when the colored volunteer does what the Government requires of him, the United States, in turn, will satisfy him."[8] The fact that Higginson had made the opposite point seemed irrelevant. According the editor of the *Christian Recorder*, in order to secure their freedom black Americans needed to first demonstrate loyalty to the United States and then trust that the government would honor its side of the bargain, despite all evidence to the contrary.

Regardless of Weaver's stance, the *Christian Recorder* continued to print letters from black soldiers complaining of unequal treatment. Weaver thus continued the tradition of black editors like Frederick Douglass, Mary Ann Shadd, and Robert Hamilton, all of whom gave space in their papers to opposing voices. And like Shadd and Hamilton, in particular, Weaver answered such disagreement with letters from correspondents who supported the editor's position. On August 27, 1864, for example, the paper printed a letter from J. H. Hall of the 54th Massachusetts. Hall had likely not learned of the War Department's August 1 change in policy when he sent in his missive again accusing the United States of betraying its promise to black soldiers. Echoing his regimentmate E. W. D., Hall too turned to earlier visions of black chosenness and proclaimed that "God will avenge the wrongs of him who is oppressed—and no Government can prosper that is deceptive and false at its very foundation and rules of doing things."[9] Three weeks later, the *Christian Recorder* printed a letter from Garland H. White, a reverend in the A.M.E. Church who served with a black regiment from Indiana. White, a regular contributor to the *Recorder*, had been reading the newspaper and lost patience with the soldiers from the 54th.

*The Ends of Black Chosenness* 145

"Those few colored regiments from Massachusetts make more fuss," he wrote, "and complain more than all the rest of the colored troops in the nation." Echoing Weaver's rosy view of the U.S. government, White stunningly contended that "[u]p to the present time, under the present Administration, no colored man has any right to complain," and charged his New England brethren with an incurable "spirit of dissatisfaction and insolence." He assured readers that most black soldiers, like those in his Indiana regiment, were loyal subjects of the United States. "For the flag of our beloved country," he proclaimed, "we are willing to die to defend, or live to honor." This was a far different reason for fighting than that articulated in the *Weekly Anglo-African* earlier in the war. There and then, God's chosen army fought for the slave rather than for any particular government. But by 1864 the growing consensus that conflated being chosen, and being free, with being a citizen of the United States apparently made dissent against that nation-state dangerous and unwelcome. The letters from the 54th complaining of unequal treatment were, according to White, "doing themselves and their race a serious injury." So until the troops from Massachusetts had learned how "to be quiet and behave themselves like men and soldiers," the chaplain concluded, "it would be far better for them to cease to write or speak."[10] Better to be silent, White reasoned, than to question the integrity of the United States.

From 1827 to the onset of the Civil War, black newspapers had imagined and enacted a chosen nation that existed in relation to but was not synonymous with the United States of America. Navigating the contested terrains of middle-class propriety, millennial prophecy, transnational revolution, emigration, and military enlistment, black newspapers offered their readers pathways to liberation, which could end either in a reformed United States that championed black freedom and equality or, if the United States refused to abandon its commitment to black oppression, in the ruins of that civilization. The Emancipation Proclamation suggested that black men and women had finally reached the former destination, as the Civil War turned the United States at last toward a future where all Americans would be greeted as full and equal citizens. Accordingly, black newspapers like the *Weekly Anglo-African* and the *Christian Recorder* began urging their black readers to join and support the United States. Black chosenness had always been, at least in part, a means to the end of freedom from bondage, and with the Emancipation Proclamation it appeared that black Americans had achieved that goal. White's response to his brethren in the 54th vividly demonstrates how, in the wake of emancipation, practices of black chosenness that challenged the legitimacy of the United States faced fierce hostility from those who equated U.S. citizenship with freedom. It remained to be seen, then, whether black chosenness could survive emancipation, or whether its appeal to black Americans had come to an end.

Even before the Civil War's conclusion, though, some black Americans began to wonder whether the United States would ever keep its promises. The Union Army would eventually equalize the pay of all its soldiers, including those held as slaves at the onset of war, but whether or not it would defend its new black citizens in the years to come remained in doubt. In an April 15, 1865, editorial in the *Weekly Anglo-African*, Robert Hamilton gave voice to such concerns. "If we feel less disposed to join in the shouts of victory which fill the skies," Hamilton began, "it is because with the cessation of the war our anxieties begin." The editor worried that, though "there will be no actual slavery," an "oppression akin to slavery" would emerge in the South if the federal government did not actively protect the rights (and especially the franchise) of its new citizens. A December 1865 letter to the newspaper from Samuel Childress, a freeman in Tennessee, confirmed Hamilton's fears. With former Confederates being allowed to keep their land, and former slaves being forced to work it, Childress wondered if it was in fact "the intention of the Government to drive us to our worst enemies to ask for work," and lamented that it "would seem that it was regarded as a greater crime to be black than to be a rebel." Such a state of affairs unsettled any faith in the United States as a protector of God's chosen people, and in his letter Childress returned to a rhetoric of black chosenness that would have been very familiar to the readers of antebellum black newspapers. "If this is the ethics which is to prevail," he concluded, "then we have more judgments in store for the nation."[11]

So while many prominent black leaders and black newspapers turned toward the United States and away from black chosenness, the radical vision of an insurgent chosen nation raining down "judgments" upon the United States continued to appeal to those battling the new forms of black bondage that appeared almost immediately after the Emancipation Proclamation. Those who confronted "oppression akin to slavery" in their daily lives, as soldiers in a Union Army camp in South Carolina or laborers in fields owned by a former Confederate in Tennessee, immediately understood that involuntary servitude could take many forms. Indeed, the Thirteenth Amendment to the U.S. Constitution offered a telling caveat when it abolished slavery and involuntary servitude "except as punishment for crime."[12] This was a chilling exception for black

Americans subject to laws passed and enforced by a state or federal government that, as Samuel Childress feared, considered it "a greater crime to be black than to be a rebel."[13]

Yet black chosenness offered hope even as the United States betrayed and criminalized its black inhabitants, reminding black Americans that their chosen status had nothing to do with U.S. citizenship. At the same time, though, antebellum biblical typologies that cast the United States as Egypt or Babylon seemed less applicable to a power that officially opposed racial slavery. Rather, the many trials that confronted black Americans after the Civil War harkened back to a different epoch in biblical history. Perhaps, as the soldier-correspondent E. W. D. had suggested, the postemancipation United States was not a modern incarnation of any ancient city or civilization, but represented instead that painful space between slavery and liberation, akin to the desert that the Israelites faced after they crossed the Red Sea. The United States had become, in other words, the wilderness. And just as the Israelites wandered for decades before they arrived at the land of milk and honey, the journey of black Americans to freedom would be neither quick nor easy. But as God's chosen nation, they could rest assured that they would eventually reach the end of the wilderness, and cross into the Promised Land.

# Notes

### Introduction. The Records of Black Chosenness

1. *Proceedings of the National Convention of Colored People, and Their Friends, Held in Troy, N.Y., on the 6th, 7th, 8th and 9th October, 1847* (Troy, N.Y.: J. C. Kneeland, 1847), 13.
2. Ibid., 7.
3. Ibid., 6.
4. Ibid., 7.
5. Ibid., 6.
6. James McCune Smith, George B. Wilson, and William H. Topp, "Report of the Committee on a National Press," in *Proceedings of the National Convention*, 18.
7. Ibid., 20.
8. Absalom Jones and Richard Allen, "A Narrative of the Proceedings of the Black People during the Late Awful Calamity in Philadelphia," in *Pamphlets of Protest: An Anthology of Early African-American Protest Literature, 1790–1860*, ed. Richard Newman, Patrick Rael, and Philip Lapsansky (New York: Routledge, 2001), 42.
9. Daniel Coker, "A Dialogue between a Virginian and an African Minister," in *Pamphlets of Protest: An Anthology of Early African-American Protest Literature, 1790–1860*, ed. Richard Newman, Patrick Rael, and Philip Lapsansky (New York: Routledge, 2001), 64.
10. William Miller, *A Sermon on the Abolition of the Slave Trade: Delivered in the African Church, New-York, on the First of January, 1810* (New York: John C. Totten, 1810), 3.
11. Ibid., 14.
12. Absalom Jones, *A Thanksgiving Sermon, Preached January 1, 1808, in St. Thomas's, or the African Episcopal, Church, Philadelphia: On Account of the Abolition of the African Slave Trade, on That Day, by the Congress of the United States* (Philadelphia: Fry and Kammerer, 1808), 17.
13. Ibid., 18–19.
14. John Winthrop, "A Model of Christian Charity," in *God's New Israel: Religious Interpretation of American Destiny*, ed. Conrad Cherry, rev. and updated ed. (Chapel Hill: University of North Caolina Press, 1998), 40; Jonathan Edwards, "The Latter-Day Glory Is Probably to Begin in America," in Cherry, *God's New Israel*, 54.

15. Ibid., 55; original emphasis.

16. Ezra Stiles, "The United States Elevated to Glory and Honour," in *God's New Israel: Religious Interpretations of American Destiny*, ed. Conrad Cherry, rev. and updated ed. (Chapel Hill: University of North Carolina Press, 1998), 83; Samuel Langdon, "The Republic of the Israelites an Example to the American States," in *God's New Israel: Religious Interpretations of American Destiny*, ed. Conrad Cherry, rev. and updated ed. (Chapel Hill: University of North Carolina Press, 1998), 99.

17. Thomas Jefferson, "First Inaugural Address," in *God's New Israel: Religious Interpretations of American Destiny*, ed. Conrad Cherry, rev. and updated ed. (Chapel Hill: University of North Carolina Press, 1998), 107.

18. American Studies scholars in the twentieth century repeatedly took up the question of American chosenness, with particular attention to how chosenness supported and justified American exceptionalism. See especially the work of Perry Miller. For a sampling of other foundational works, see Sacvan Bercovitch, *The American Jeremiad* (Madison: University of Wisconsin Press, 1978); and Ernest Lee Tuveson, *Redeemer Nation: The Idea of America's Millennial Role* (Chicago: University of Chicago Press, 1968). For more recent treatments see Carolyn A. Haynes, *Divine Destiny: Gender and Race in Nineteenth-Century Protestantism* (Jackson: University Press of Mississippi, 1998); and George Shulman, *American Prophecy: Race and Redemption in American Political Culture* (Minneapolis: University of Minnesota Press, 2008). For work focusing on, and critical of, U.S.-centered versions of American exceptionalism see especially Donald E. Pease, *The New American Exceptionalism* (Minneapolis: University of Minnesota Press, 2009).

19. Martin Delany, "Political Destiny of the Colored Race on the American Continent," in *Pamphlets of Protest: An Anthology of Early African-American Protest Literature, 1790–1860*, ed. Richard Newman, Patrick Rael, and Philip Lapsansky (New York: Routledge, 2001), 234.

20. For work that recovers in black American literature and culture the critical place of the biblical typology between black Americans in the United States and the Israelites in Egypt, see especially Eddie S. Glaude Jr., *Exodus! Religions, Race, and Nation in Early Nineteenth-Century Black America* (Chicago: University of Chicago Press, 2000); and Albert J. Raboteau, "African-Americans, Exodus, and the American Israel," in *African-American Christianity: Essays in History*, ed. Paul Johnson (Berkeley: University of California Press, 1994), 1–17.

21. Maria W. Stewart, "Productions," in *Pamphlets of Protest: An Anthology of Early African-American Protest Literature, 1790–1860*, ed. Richard Newman, Patrick Rael, and Philip Lapsansky (New York: Routledge, 2001), 127.

22. Delany, "Political Destiny of the Colored Race," 234.

23. T. Morris Chester, "Negro Self-Respect and Pride of Race," in *Pamphlets of Protest: An Anthology of Early African-American Protest Literature, 1790–1860*, ed. Richard Newman, Patrick Rael, and Philip Lapsansky (New York: Routledge, 2001), 310.

24. Eric Gardner, *Unexpected Places: Relocating Nineteenth-Century African American Literature* (Jackson: University Press of Mississippi, 2009), 10; original emphasis.

25. Alexander Mackay, *The Western World; Or, Travels in the United States in 1846–47*, vol. 3 (London: Richard Bentley, 1850), 3:241.

26. *Proceedings of the State Convention of the Colored Freemen of Pennsylvania, Held in Pittsburgh, on the 23d, 24th and 25th of August, 1841, for the Purpose of Considering Their Condition, and the Means of Its Improvement* (Pittsburgh: Matthew M. Grant, 1841), 13.

27. For this line of scholarship see especially Benedict Anderson, *Imagined Communities: Reflections on the Origin and Spread of Nationalism*, rev. ed. (London: Verso, 2006). Uncovering the uneven ways in which print creates, or fails to create, national community, Trish Loughran offers a crucial revision of Anderson's theory in *The Republic in Print: Print Culture in the Age of U.S. Nation Building, 1770–1870* (New York: Columbia University Press, 2007). Loughran's work, though, concentrates on print culture in relation to nation-state formation.

28. *Proceedings of the State Convention*, 13.

29. Samuel Cornish, "Why We Should Have a Paper," *Colored American*, March 4, 1837; Thomas Hamilton, "Our Paper," *Weekly Anglo-African*, July 23, 1859, original emphasis.

30. David Ruggles, "Introductory Remarks," *Mirror of Liberty* 1, no. 1 (August 1838): 1.

31. Anderson, *Imagined Communities*, 33n54.

32. Out of the seventeen essays contained in the volume *Early African American Print Culture*, for example, only Eric Gardner's chapter pays any sustained attention to black newspapers. See Eric Gardner, "Early African American Print Culture and the American West," in *Early African American Print Culture*, ed. Lara Langer Cohen and Jordan Alexander Stein (Philadelphia: University of Pennsylvania Press, 2012), 75–92.

33. See Robert A. Gross and Mary Kelly, eds., *An Extensive Republic: Print, Culture, and Society in the New Nation, 1790–1840* (Chapel Hill: University of North Carolina Press, 2010), 389–421; Scott E. Casper, Jeffrey D. Groves, Stephen W. Nissenbaum, and Michael Winship, eds., *The Industrial Book 1840–1880* (Chapel Hill: University of North Carolina Press, 2007), 224–78.

34. Jeannine DeLombard, "African American Cultures of Print," in *The Industrial Book 1840–1880*, ed. Scott E. Casper, Jeffrey D. Groves, Stephen W. Nissenbaum, and Michael Winship (Chapel Hill: University of North Carolina Press, 2007), 360–73.

35. See Frances Smith Foster, "A Narrative of the Interesting Origins and (Somewhat) Surprising Developments of African-American Print Culture," *American Literary History* 17, no. 4 (2005): 714–40; John Ernest, *Liberation Historiography: African American Writers and the Challenge of History, 1794–1861* (Chapel Hill: University of North Carolina Press, 2004); Elizabeth McHenry, *Forgotten Readers: Recovering the Lost History of African American Literary Societies* (Durham, N.C.: Duke University Press, 2002).

36. Foster, "Narrative of the Interesting Origins," 715.

37. See esp. Joycelyn Moody, *Sentimental Confessions: Spiritual Narratives of Nineteenth-Century African American Women* (Athens: University of Georgia Press, 2001); P. Gabrielle Foreman, *Activist Sentiments: Reading Black Women in the Nineteenth Century* (Urbana: University of Illinois Press, 2009); Carla L. Peterson, "Doers of the

Word": *African-American Women Speakers and Writers in the North (1830–1880)* (New Brunswick, N.J.: Rutgers University Press, 1995).

38. *Proceedings of the State Convention*, 8.

39. James Boardman, *America, and the Americans* (London: Longman, Rees, Orme, Brown, Green, & Longman, 1833), 75.

40. David Ruggles, "Our Reading Room," *Mirror of Liberty* 1, no. 1 (August 1838), 9.

41. For work that impressively recovers the readership of an individual newspaper, while also foregrounding the difficulty of such endeavors, see Eric Gardner, "Remembered (Black) Readers: Subscribers to the *Christian Recorder*, 1864–1865," *American Literary History* 23, no. 2 (2011): 229–59.

42. Anderson, *Imagined Communities*, 34.

43. Frederick Douglass, *Narrative of the Life of Frederick Douglass, An American Slave* (Boston: Anti-Slavery Office, 1845), 37.

44. Boardman, *America, and the Americans*, 76–77.

45. *Ibid.*, 77.

46. Douglass, *Narrative of the Life*, 41–42.

47. Mattie J. Jackson, *The Story of Mattie J. Jackson; Her Parentage—Experience of Eighteen Years in Slavery—Incidents during the War—Her Escape from Slavery. A True Story. Written and Arranged by Dr. L. S. Thompson (Formerly Mrs. Schuyler), as Given by Mattie* (Lawrence, Mass.: Printed at the Sentinel Office, 1866), 10. For an elegant reading of Jackson's narrative in the context of black reading, see Heather Andrea Williams, *Self-Taught: African American Education in Slavery and Freedom* (Chapel Hill: University of North Carolina Press, 2005), 10–11.

48. Jackson, *Story of Mattie J. Jackson*, 11.

49. Harriet Jacobs, *Incidents in the Life of a Slave Girl* (Boston: Published for the Author, 1861), 69–70.

50. Jacobs, *Incidents*, 70.

51. I have decided not to attempt a comprehensive account of the early black press. For a work that does offer a more wide-ranging account of the nineteenth-century black press see Irvine Garland Penn's pioneering *The Afro-American Press and Its Editors* (Springfield, Mass.: Willey & Company, 1891), which remains an essential resource. For helpful accounts of the early black press that offer broad overviews of many of the papers I have focused on in this study see also Martin E. Dann, *The Black Press, 1827–1890: The Quest for National Identity* (New York: G. P. Putnam's Sons, 1971); Frankie Hutton, *The Early Black Press in America, 1827 to 1860* (Westport, Conn.: Greenwood, 1993).

52. For work on black newspapers produced outside of the northeastern corridor, see esp. Gardner, *Unexpected Places*.

53. Carla Peterson provides an invaluable account of an elite black New York society that includes many of the same figures who edited and wrote for black newspapers in the city, and my understanding of the class contestations of black New York relies heavily upon her work. Elizabeth McHenry's work on black literary societies in New York City provides an excellent example of a study of black New York that focuses upon

institutions, while Elizabeth Lorang and R. J. Weir's reconstruction of the world surrounding the production of the *Weekly Anglo-African* superbly situates a specific instance of black print within the broader context of New York City. See Carla Peterson, *Black Gotham: A Family History of African Americans in Nineteenth-Century New York City* (New Haven: Yale University Press, 2011); McHenry, *Forgotten Readers*; Elizabeth Lorang and R. J. Weir, "'Will Not These Days be by Thy Poets Sung': Poems of the *Anglo-African* and *National Anti-Slavery Standard*, 1863–1864," *Scholarly Editing* 34 (2013), scholarlyediting.org.

54. My understanding of the porous boundaries between the sacred and the secular in the black press is indebted to Frances Smith Foster's pathbreaking work on Afro-Protestant print culture. See especially Foster, "Narrative of the Interesting Origins"; and Frances Smith Foster and Chanta Haywood, "Christian Recordings: Afro-Protestantism, Its Press, and the Production of African-American Literature," *Religion and Literature* 27, no. 1 (Spring 1995): 15–33. While reading a variety of black print materials, including multiple black newspapers, Foster often focuses her analysis on church-based publications like the *Christian Recorder*. For a work on the importance of religion in early African American literature more broadly, see Joanna Brooks, *American Lazarus: Religion and the Rise of African-American and Native American Literatures* (New York: Oxford University Press, 2003).

55. See, e.g., Candy Gunther Brown, *The Word in the World: Evangelical Writing, Publishing, and Reading in America, 1789–1880* (Chapel Hill: University of North Carolina Press, 2004); and David Paul Nord, *Faith in Reading: Religious Publishing and the Birth of Mass Media in America* (New York: Oxford University Press, 2004). While excellent studies of early religious printing, both books largely ignore the African American religious print cultures that overlapped with yet stood apart from the efforts of white Evangelical organizations.

## Chapter 1. Acting Chosen

1. For an excellent study of Cornish's early life and work see Christopher Allison, "Floating on the Stream of Prejudice: The Making of the Religious Activism of Samuel Cornish" (MA thesis, Yale University, 2010), 23–30.

2. For details on the meeting at Boston Crummel's home, see Jacqueline Bacon, *Freedom's Journal: The First African-American Newspaper* (New York: Lexington Books, 2007), 38–41; Irvine Garland Penn, *The Afro-American Press and Its Editors* (Springfield, Mass.: Willey & Company, 1891), 28. For more on John Brown Russwurm see Winston James, *The Struggles of John Brown Russwurm: The Life and Writings of a Pan-Africanist Pioneer, 1799–1851* (New York: New York University Press, 2010), 5–25.

3. See Erica L. Ball, *To Live an Antislavery Life: Personal Politics and the Antebellum Black Middle Class* (Athens: University of Georgia Press, 2012), 10–36. Ball's work recovers the ways in which the antebellum black middle class connected the everyday practice of propriety to the broader struggle for black freedom and equality in the United States.

4. Samuel Cornish and John Brown Russwurm, "To Our Patrons," *Freedom's Journal*, March 16, 1827.

5. For more on the *Freedom's Journal*'s readership see Bacon, *Freedom's Journal*, 51–52. For more on the rise of the white newspaper in early America see Frank Luther Mott, *American Journalism: A History, 1690–1960*, 3rd ed. (New York: Macmillan, 1962), 167–208; Carol Sue Humphrey, *The Press of the Young Republic, 1783–1833* (Westport, Conn.: Greenwood, 1996), 113–32.

6. V., "Walker's Appeal, No. 2," *Liberator*, May 14, 1831.

7. For more on New York City's white elite see Edwin G. Burrows and Mike Wallace, *Gotham: A History of New York City to 1898* (New York: Oxford University Press, 1999), 452–72.

8. For a seminal account of white working-class formation in New York City see Sean Wilentz, *Chants Democratic: New York City and the Rise of the American Working Class, 1788–1850*, 20th anniversary ed. (New York: Oxford University Press, 2004).

9. See Carla Peterson, *Black Gotham: A Family History of African Americans in Nineteenth-Century New York City* (New Haven: Yale University Press, 2011), 35–62; Carla Peterson, "Black Life in Freedom: Creating an Elite Culture," in *Slavery in New York*, ed. Ira Berlin and Leslie M. Harris (New York: New Press, 2005), 181–214.

10. Cornish and Russwurm, "To Our Patrons."

11. Ibid.

12. "Memoirs of Capt. Paul Cuffee," *Freedom's Journal*, March 16, 1827.

13. Cornish and Russwurm, "To Our Patrons."

14. "B. F. Hughes' School," *Freedom's Journal*, March 16, 1827.

15. Samuel Cornish and John Brown Russwurm, "Prospectus," *Freedom's Journal*, March 16, 1827. *Freedom's Journal* represents an early and powerful example of how an oppressed people attempted to craft a positive identity by changing how they recognized themselves. In doing so, the paper engaged in what scholars such as Charles Taylor have termed a "politics of recognition." Taylor argues that the drive for proper recognition emanates from the thesis that "our identity is partly shaped by recognition or its absence, often by the *mis*recognition of others, and so a person or group of people can suffer real damage, real distortion, if the people or society around them mirror back to them a confining or demeaning or contemptible picture of themselves." Yet, as Nancy Fraser has argued, the struggle for proper recognition contains within it serious pitfalls. Key among these is the tendency by those fighting against oppression to reify their own group identity. Fraser contends that by "[s]tressing the need to elaborate and display an authentic, self-affirming and self-generated collective identity," a politics of recognition "puts moral pressure on individual members to conform to a given group culture." Most damning, Fraser argues that those fighting a battle for proper recognition risk replicating that which they are battling against, as "the identity model serves as a vehicle for misrecognition: in reifying group identity, it ends by obscuring the politics of cultural identification, the struggles *within* the group for authority—and the power—to represent it." By insisting that its readers adopt specific values and behaviors, *Freedom's Journal* moved in this direction. See Charles Taylor, "The Politics of Recognition," in

*Multiculturalism: Examining the Politics of Recognition*, ed. Amy Gutmann (Princeton: Princeton University Press, 1994), 25; Nancy Fraser, "Rethinking Recognition," *New Left Review* 3 (May-June 2000): 112.

16. See Proverbs 14:34 (KJV). The full verse reads, "Righteousness exalteth a nation: but sin is a reproach to any people."

17. Samuel Cornish and John Brown Russwurm, Untitled Editorial, *Freedom's Journal*, March 23, 1827.

18. Ibid.

19. Philanthropos, "Education, No. II," *Freedom's Journal*, April 6, 1827.

20. Philanthropos, "Education, No. III," *Freedom's Journal*, April 13, 1827, original emphasis.

21. "What Shall I Eat?" *Freedom's Journal*, August 3, 1827.

22. See, for example, Ned, "Don't Carry Your Head Too High," *Freedom's Journal*, April 20, 1827; J., "The Two Graves," *Freedom's Journal*, May 25, 1827.

23. See the advertisement for Nicolas Pierson's Mead Garden, *Freedom's Journal*, August 17, 1827.

24. For a detailed discussion of gradual emancipation in New York see David N. Gellman, *Emancipating New York: The Politics of Slavery and Freedom 1777–1827* (Baton Rouge: Louisiana State University Press, 2006).

25. "Abolition of Slavery," *Freedom's Journal*, April 20, 1827.

26. "Meeting of the People of Colour," *Freedom's Journal*, April 27, 1827.

27. Pinkster, originally a Dutch religious holiday, was appropriated by free and enslaved black men and women in the Northeast and remained an occasion for black celebrations into the early nineteenth century. For work focused on black public performances in the North see Mitch Kachun, *Festivals of Freedom: Memory and Meaning in African American Celebrations, 1808–1915* (Boston: University of Massachusetts Press, 2003), 16–53; Leslie M. Harris, *In the Shadow of Slavery: African Americans in New York City, 1626–1863* (Chicago: University of Chicago Press, 2003), 96–133; David Waldstreicher, *In the Midst of Perpetual Fetes: The Making of American Nationalism, 1776–1820* (Chapel Hill: University of North Carolina Press, 1997), 294–348; Shane White, "'It Was a Proud Day': African Americans, Festivals, and Parades in the North, 1741–1834," *Journal of American History* 81, no. 1 (June 1994): 13–50.

28. Duke Bernard of Saxe-Weimar Eisenach, *Travels through North America, during the Years 1825 and 1826*, vol. 1 (Philadelphia: Carey, Lea & Carey, 1828), 1:133.

29. Untitled Notice, *Freedom's Journal*, March 30, 1827.

30. Untitled, *New-York Evening Post*, March 22, 1825.

31. For more on white Fourth of July celebrations as sites of class conflict see Simon P. Newman, *Parades and the Politics of the Street: Festive Culture in the Early American Republic* (Philadelphia: University of Pennsylvania Press, 1997), 83–119.

32. James Boardman, *America, and the Americans* (London: Longman, Rees, Orme, Brown, Green, & Longman, 1833), 306–7.

33. Untitled Notice, *Freedom's Journal*, June 22, 1827.

34. Mordechai Noah, "Emancipation of Slaves," *Freedom's Journal*, June 29, 1827.

35. For more on Noah's history of antiblack editorials, see Bacon, *Freedom's Journal*, 38–41.

36. Samuel Cornish and John Brown Russwurm, Untitled Editorial, *Freedom's Journal*, June 29, 1827, original emphasis.

37. Libertinus, "For the Freedom's Journal," *Freedom's Journal*, June 29, 1827.

38. R., "For the Freedom's Journal," *Freedom's Journal*, June 29, 1827.

39. "Extract from the Minutes of a Large and Respectable Meeting of the People of Colour, Held in the Mutual Relief-Hall, April 23d, 1827," *Freedom's Journal*, June 29, 1827.

40. Salem Dutcher Jr., "Extract from an ORATION, Delivered in Albany, before the Municipal Authorities, July 4th, 1827," *Freedom's Journal*, July 20, 1827, original emphasis.

41. For an account of a southern celebration, see "For the Freedom's Journal," *Freedom's Journal*, July 13, 1827.

42. Untitled Notice, *Freedom's Journal*, July 13, 1827.

43. "Cooperstown," *Freedom's Journal*, July 13, 1827.

44. Samuel Cornish and John Brown Russwurm, "Abolition of Slavery," *Freedom's Journal*, July 6, 1827.

45. I have pieced together this admittedly speculative vision of the parade from *Freedom's Journal*'s description as well as from two remembrances from James McCune Smith. In 1855, Smith recalled an earlier parade led by Hardenburgh, and ten years later wrote an account of the 1827 procession, which he witnessed as a teenager. See Samuel Cornish, Untitled Notice, *Freedom's Journal*, July 13, 1827; James McCune Smith, "From Our New York Correspondent," *Frederick Douglass' Paper*, February 16, 1855; James McCune Smith, "Sketch of the Life and Labors of Rev. Henry Highland Garnet," in *A Memorial Discourse; By Rev. Henry Highland Garnet, Delivered in the Hall of the House of Representatives, Washington, D.C., on Sabbath, February 12, 1865* (Philadelphia: Joseph M. Wilson, 1865).

46. Cornish, Untitled Notice, *Freedom's Journal*, July 13, 1827.

47. Samuel Cornish, "Propriety of Conduct," *Freedom's Journal*, July 13, 1827.

48. Samuel Cornish, "Propriety of Conduct, Part II," *Freedom's Journal*, July 20, 1827.

49. Samuel Cornish, "To the Patrons and Friends of 'Freedom's Journal,'" *Freedom's Journal*, September 14, 1827.

50. John Brown Russwurm, "To Our Patrons," *Freedom's Journal*, March 28, 1829.

51. John Brown Russwurm, "Liberia," *Freedom's Journal*, February 14, 1829.

52. For selections of Russwurm's writings for the Liberia *Herald* see James, *Struggles*, 218–30.

53. "Minutes and Proceedings of the Second Annual Convention, for the Improvement of the Free People of Color In These United States, Held by Adjournments in the City of Philadelphia, From the 4th to the 13th of June Inclusive, 1832," in *Minutes of the Proceedings of the National Negro Conventions, 1830–1864*, ed. Howard Holman Bell (New York: Arno Press and New York Times, 1969), 27.

54. "Minutes and Proceedings," 36.

55. David Walker, *David Walker's Appeal to the Coloured Citizens of the World*, ed. Peter P. Hinks (University Park: Pennsylvania State University Press, 2000), 30.

56. Ibid., 17.
57. Ibid., 32, original emphasis.
58. Libertinus, "For the Freedom's Journal," *Freedom's Journal*, June 29, 1827.

*Chapter 2. Prophecies for a Chosen Nation*

1. James and Lois Horton have observed that between 1834 and 1838 alone the antislavery press reported on 160 instances of anti-abolitionist or antiblack violence. See James Oliver Horton and Lois E. Horton, *In Hope of Liberty: Culture, Community, and Protest among Northern Free Blacks, 1700–1860* (New York: Oxford University Press, 1997), 239. For more on the 1834 riots in New York City see Edwin G. Burrows and Mike Wallace, *Gotham: A History of New York City to 1898* (New York: Oxford University Press, 1999), 556–62. On worsening conditions for black New Yorkers in general see Graham Russell Hodges, *Root and Branch: African Americans in New York and East Jersey, 1613–1863* (Chapel Hill: University of North Carolina Press, 1999), 232–35.

2. For more on Bell's early years see Carla Peterson, *Black Gotham: A Family History of African Americans in Nineteenth-Century New York City* (New Haven: Yale University Press, 2011), 68–78; and Philip M. Montesano, "Philip Alexander Bell," in *African American Lives*, ed. Henry Louis Gates Jr. and Evelyn Brooks Higginbotham (New York: Oxford University Press, 2004), 69–71. For his work on the New Haven school see "Minutes and Proceedings of the Second Annual Convention, for the Improvement of the Free People of Color in These United States, Held by Adjournments in the City of Philadelphia, From the 4th to the 13th of June Inclusive, 1832," in *Minutes of the Proceedings of the National Negro Conventions, 1830–1864*, ed. Howard Holman Bell (New York: Arno Press and New York Times, 1969), 23–24.

3. See M[onroe] N. Work, "The Life of Charles B. Ray," *Journal of Negro History* 4, no. 4 (October 1919): 361–71.

4. "Agents for This Paper," *Colored American*, June 26, 1841.

5. [Samuel Cornish], "Our Second Year," *Colored American*, January 13, 1838.

6. From January to May 1839, the *Colored American* listed Samuel Cornish and James McCune Smith as coeditors. The two men's names drop off the masthead on the June 1, 1839 edition, which lists no editors but Charles Ray, Philip Bell, and Stephen Gloucester as "Proprietors." By August 1839 the masthead listed only "Charles B. Ray & Co." as proprietors.

7. Unlike in the final issue of *Freedom's Journal*, where Russwurm announced the cessation of the newspaper, Ray nowhere announces that the December 25, 1841 issue will be the *Colored American*'s last issue. It is possible that the paper continued into January 1842, but those issues have not been recovered.

8. Lyman Beecher, "A Plea for the West," in *God's New Israel: Religious Interpretations of American Destiny*, ed. Conrad Cherry, rev. and updated ed. (Chapel Hill: University of North Carolina Press, 1998), 123.

9. C[harles] B. Ray, "Our Next Volume," *Colored American*, December 30, 1837.

10. [Samuel Cornish], "Age of Reform," *Colored American*, March 11, 1837.

11. For treatments of millennialism within the context of the antebellum United States, see esp. Ruth Alden Doan, *The Miller Heresy, Millennialism, and American Culture* (Philadelphia: Temple University Press, 1987), 6–30; and Daniel Walker Howe, *What Hath God Wrought: The Transformation of America, 1815–1848* (New York: Oxford University Press, 2007), 285–327. For broader studies of millennial rhetoric and its uses in and beyond the United States see Stephen D. O'Leary, *Arguing the Apocalypse: A Theory of Millennial Rhetoric* (New York: Oxford University Press, 1994); and Daniel Wojcik, *The End of the World as We Know It: Faith, Fatalism, and Apocalypse in America* (New York: New York University Press, 1997), 21–36. Cautioning scholars against establishing too stark a division between the different strains of American millennialism, James Moorhead has pointed to the significant overlap between pre- and postmillennialist thought and practice in the United States. See James H. Moorhead, "Between Progress and Apocalypse: A Reassessment of Millennialism in American Religious Thought, 1800–1880," *Journal of American History* 71, no. 3 (December 1984): 524–42.

12. [Samuel Cornish], "Why We Should Have a Paper," *Colored American*, March 4, 1837.

13. See, e.g., the "Prejudice in the Church" columns for March 11, 1837; March 18, 1837; April 1, 1837; October 3, 1837; October 28, 1837; December 9, 1837; February 17, 1838.

14. [Samuel Cornish], "Prejudice in the Church, No. III," *Colored American*, April 1, 1837.

15. For more on Himes's cagey use of print and visual cultures to spread the Millerite message, see David Morgan, *Protestants and Pictures: Religion, Visual Culture, and the Age of American Mass Production* (New York: Oxford University Press, 1999), 24–39; David T. Arthur, "Joshua V. Himes and the Cause of Adventism," in *The Disappointed: Millerism and Millennarianism in the Nineteenth Century*, ed. Ronald L. Numbers and Jonathan M. Butler (Bloomington: Indiana University Press, 1987), 36–58.

16. Samuel Cornish, "Prejudice in the Church," *Colored American*, March 11, 1837, original emphases. Cornish paraphrases Isaiah 58:1 (KJV).

17. For discussions of the American jeremiad in general see Sacvan Bercovitch, *The American Jeremiad* (Madison: University of Wisconsin Press, 1978); Perry Miller, *The New England Mind: From Colony to Province* (Cambridge: Belknap Press of Harvard University Press, 1953), 27–39; Andrew Murphy, *Prodigal Nation* (New York: Oxford University Press, 2009); and George Shulman, *American Prophecy: Race and Redemption in American Political Culture* (Minneapolis: University of Minnesota Press, 2008). For work that deals specifically with the black American jeremiad see Valerie C. Cooper, *Word, Like Fire: Maria Stewart, the Bible, and the Rights of African Americans* (Charlottesville: University of Virginia Press, 2011), 164–71; Willie J. Harrell Jr., *Origins of the African American Jeremiad: The Rhetorical Strategies of Social Protest and Activism, 1760–1861* (Jefferson, N.C.: McFarland, 2011); David Howard-Pitney, *The Afro-American Jeremiad: Appeals for Justice in America* (Philadelphia: Temple University Press, 1990); and Wilson Jeremiah Moses, *Black Messiahs and Uncle Toms: Social and Literary Manipulations of a Religious Myth* (University Park: Pennsylvania State University Press, 1982).

18. [Samuel Cornish], "Title of This Journal," *Colored American*, March 4, 1837, original emphases.

19. [Samuel Cornish], "On the Right of Colored People to Vote," *Colored American*, March 4, 1837, original emphasis. See also [Samuel Cornish], "Right of Suffrage," *Colored American*, March 4, 1837.

20. There is a vast amount of literature on the link between whiteness and American national identity. For particularly good discussions of this formation in the antebellum period see David R. Roediger, *The Wages of Whiteness: Race and the Making of the American Working Class*, rev. ed. (New York: Verso, 1999); and Alexander Saxton, *The Rise and Fall of the White Republic: Class Politics and Mass Culture in Nineteenth-Century America*, rev. ed. (New York: Verso, 2003).

21. See [Charles B. Ray], "Fellow Citizens of New York," *Colored American*, June 13, 1840; and [Charles B. Ray], "The Convention," *Colored American*, June 27, 1840.

22. "Convention of the Colored Inhabitants of the State of New York," *Colored American*, September 12, 1840.

23. [Charles B. Ray], "To the Polls," *Colored American*, October 31, 1840.

24. Robert Sears, "A Brief Description of the United States of America, Carefully Compiled by Robert Sears," *Weekly Advocate*, January 7, 1837, original emphasis.

25. Sears's notion of a nation that predates the state anticipates the work of Anthony Smith and Adrian Hastings, and clashes with the "modernity thesis" of scholars such as Ernest Gellner and Eric Hobsbawm, who argue that nationalism, or the desire for political statehood, creates nations. See Ernest Gellner, *Nations and Nationalism*, 2nd ed. (Ithaca: Cornell University Press, 2006); Adrian Hastings, *The Construction of Nationhood: Ethnicity, Religion and Nationalism* (Cambridge: Cambridge University Press, 1997); E. J. Hobsbawm, *Nations and Nationalism since 1780: Programme, Myth, Reality*, 2nd ed. (Cambridge: Cambridge University Press, 1990); and Anthony D. Smith, *The Antiquity of Nations* (Cambridge: Polity, 2004).

26. R[obert] S[ears], "Our Government," *Colored American*, November 4, 1837.

27. "United States Census, 1850," index and images, FamilySearch (https://family search.org/pal:/MM9.1.1/MCTW-RJH, accessed June 8, 2012); Robert Sears in household of Robert Sears, New York City, ward 4, New York, New York, United States. For more on Sears, see William Hunt, *The American Biographical Sketch Book* (New York: Cornish, Lamport, 1848), 62–66. According to Hunt, the entry on Sears is drawn from a longer sketch written by George Lippard.

28. [Philip Bell], "View of the Capitol at Washington," *Weekly Advocate*, January 14, 1837, original emphasis.

29. "Obituary Notes," *Publisher's Weekly*, 41, no. 9 (February 27, 1892): 368.

30. For more on illustrations in antebellum white newspapers see Joshua Brown, *Beyond the Lines: Pictorial Reporting, Everyday Life, and the Crisis of the Gilded Age in America* (Berkeley: University of California Press, 2002), 7–31. Brown's otherwise excellent study of newspaper illustrations in the nineteenth century makes little mention of black newspapers except to place them within a tradition of alternative media that did not have the means to include illustrations. "It would not be until the twentieth century,

for example," Brown writes, "that labor, immigrant, suffrage, and African American papers could afford to include illustrations (or, at least, more than the occasional cartoon)." See Brown, *Beyond the Lines*, 6. To be sure, the *Colored American* (like most white newspapers of its day) did not have the financial capability to maintain a staff of engravers. But the presence of numerous large-scale illustrations in the *Colored American*'s pages demonstrates how relationships between and among newspaper workers could provide papers with otherwise unavailable material.

31. *Proceedings of the National Convention of Colored People, and Their Friends, Held in Troy, N.Y., on the 6th, 7th, 8th, and 9th October, 1847* (Troy, N.Y.: Steam Press of J. C. Kneeland and Co., 1847), 19.

32. For the *Colored American*'s "Seven Churches of Asia" series see the paper's issues for June 19, 1841; June 26, 1841; July 3, 1841; July 10, 1841; July 17, 1841; July 31, 1841; August 7, 1841.

33. The Seven Churches, though, never appeared in *Pictorial Illustrations in the Bible*. Instead, Sears included the series in his *Pictorial Sunday Book*. See Robert Sears, *The Pictorial Sunday Book* (New York: Robert Sears, 1846), 436–49. In his book, Sears returns the Churches to their original order.

34. As one contemporary argued, "the epistles to the Asiatic churches" described "seven distinct periods of the world, each of which is to be ascertained by references to the actual ecclesiastical history of the corresponding items." See "Biblical Illustrations, No. 4," New York *Observer and Chronicle*, June 22, 1833. See also Doan, *Miller Heresy*, 6. By the end of the 1830s, accounts of the Seven Churches had become quite popular with American readers, with a variety of books printing accounts from travelers visiting their sites as well as scriptural commentary from clergy. The interest in books on the Seven Churches of Asia seems to have begun in Britain, with works such as Francis V. J. Arundell's *A Visit to the Seven Churches of Asia* (1828), Thomas Milner's *History of the Seven Churches of Asia* (1832), and Charles MacFarlane's *The Seven Apocalyptic Churches* (1832), which contained a number of illustrations from the artist Thomas Knox. In the United States, the interest in the Seven Churches increased in the late 1830s, with books such as *Constantinople and the Scenery of the Seven Churches of Asia Minor Illustrated* (1839), with illustrations by Thomas Allom and commentary from Robert Walsh; and Henry Blunt's *A Practical Exposition of the Epistle to the Seven Churches of Asia* (1839). MacFarlane's book would be especially important to Robert Sears, who reproduced Knox's images for his own publications.

35. [Charles B. Ray], "This Country Our Only Home," *Colored American*, May 9, 1840, original emphasis.

36. The *Colored American*'s editorial operations moved out of Sears's print shop at 2 Frankfort Street in June 1838, and the paper established its offices at 161 Duane Street. Sears remained listed as the paper's printer until January 1839, after which his name was dropped from the masthead. It was not until May of that year, though, that the phrase "Printed and Published every Saturday, by the Proprietors," appeared on the masthead. In March 1840 Charles Ray moved the paper's offices to the third floor of 9 Spruce Street, where they would remain through 1841. Though more work needs to be done

to conclusively establish the connection, it is possible that J. H. Tobitt printed the *Colored American* after Ray moved the paper's offices. Tobitt, a white printer who also had his offices at 9 Spruce Street, would in 1844 print a report from a New York State black convention coauthored by Ray, as well as the 1848 pamphlet that included David Walker's *Appeal* and Henry Highland Garnet's "Address to the Slaves of the United States of America."

37. "Cheapest Publications in the World," *Colored American*, May 2, 1840, original emphasis.

38. For more on the antebellum American interest in the Holy Land see John Davis, *The Landscape of Belief: Encountering the Holy Land in Nineteenth-Century American Art and Culture* (Princeton: Princeton University Press, 1996); Bruce A. Harvey, *American Geographics: U.S. National Narratives and the Representation of the Non-European World, 1830–1865* (Stanford: Stanford University Press, 2001), 97–149; Hilton Obenzinger, *American Palestine: Melville, Twain, and the Holy Land Mania* (Princeton: Princeton University Press, 1999); Molly Robey, "Sacred Geographies: Religion and Race in Women's Holy Land Writings," *American Literature* 80, no. 3 (September 2008): 471–500; Brian Yothers, *The Romance of the Holy Land in American Travel Writing, 1790–1876* (Burlington, Vt.: Ashgate, 2007).

39. I have been able to locate most, though not all, of the sources Ray used for "Sacred Geography and Antiquities." For his series' basic architecture, the editor turned to the *Critica Biblica*, a four-volume set of biblical commentaries that included a section on "Sacred Geography." *Critica Biblica* provides the basic information on Assyria's boundaries, climate, rivers, etc., in parts I, III, and IV, as well the section on "Asia" that introduces the series. See "Sacred Geography," in *Critica Biblica*, vol. 1 (London: William Booth, 1824), 13–21; 61–69; 115–17. For the section on Chaldea in the first installment, as well as pieces of the Assyria discussion in the third, Ray turned to the *Family Magazine*. See "History," in *The Family Magazine, or General Abstract of Useful Knowledge*, vol. 2 (New York: Redfield & Lindsay, 1835), 33–34. The second installment comes entirely from "Babylon," in *The Christian's Penny Magazine*, vol. 2 (London: Charles Wood and Son, 1833), 129–31. The section on Nineveh in the third installment reprints Stephen H. Tying, *The Bible Companion* (Philadelphia: Edward C. Mielke, 1833), 93–96. The fifth installment copies J. H. C., "Fall of Babylon," *Saturday Magazine* 6, no. 173 (March 14, 1835): 98–99. Of course, all of these publications may have reprinted their contributions from other sources, from which Ray may also have been drawing his materials. The above citations, though, should provide a starting point for scholars interested in exploring antebellum religious cultures of print.

40. "Sacred Geography and Antiquities, No. II," *Colored American*, May 9, 1840. See also Jeremiah 51:35–36.

41. "Sacred Geography and Antiquities, No. IV," *Colored American*, June 13, 1840. For the biblical quote, see Zephaniah 2:13.

42. The sections on the general histories of Chaldea and Assyria can be incredibly dry. For example, one installment on Assyria opens with a calculation of the empire's "situation and extent": "Length 345 miles, between 33 deg. and 41 min. north latitude.

Breadth 297 miles, between 43 deg. and 49 deg. east longitude." See "Sacred Geography and Antiquities, Number III," *Colored American*, June 6, 1840.

43. "Sacred Geography and Antiquities, Number IV."

44. The Nineveh image originally appeared in an eighteenth-century "geographical dictionary," and Sears included a copy of it in his *Pictorial Illustrations of the Bible*. See *A New Geographical Dictionary*, vol. 2 (London: J. Coote, 1760), unpaginated; Robert Sears, *Two Hundred Pictorial Illustrations of the Bible*, 4th ed. (New York: Robert Sears, 1841), 18. The Babylon piece copies a well-known engraving from the English artist John Martin. Martin had originally become famous for his paintings, but by the 1830s had turned his attention to mezzotint engravings. Early in the decade, he produced and published a series of cuts based upon biblical scenes. The *Colored American* reproduced his 1831 piece, *Destruction of Babylon*. See Michael J. Campbell, *John Martin: Visionary Printmaker* (York: Campbell Fine Art, 1992); and William Feaver, *The Art of John Martin* (Oxford: Clarendon Press, 1975). Martin's cut would not appear in any of Sears's books, but found its way into the British *Saturday Magazine*, where it accompanied the article that also appears in the fifth installment of "Sacred Geography and Antiquities." See J. H. C., "Fall of Babylon."

45. "Sacred Geography and Antiquities, Number V," *Colored American*, June 20, 1840.

46. The *Colored American*'s emphasis on the sudden arrival of God's judgment echoed the convictions of black American writers and activists such as Maria Stewart. As Valerie C. Cooper writes, Stewart possessed a "broader prophetic understanding that God would, both soon and suddenly, intervene in history to right the wrongs being committed against black slaves and, by extension, against all black people." See Cooper, *Word, Like Fire*, 3.

47. See Ellwood C. Parry III, *The Art of Thomas Cole: Ambition and Imagination* (Newark: University of Delaware Press, 1988), 131–87.

48. For a discussion of Cole's American allusions see Angela Miller, *The Empire of the Eye: Landscape Representation and American Cultural Politics, 1825–1875* (Ithaca: Cornell University Press, 1993), 21–39. For his references to biblical cities see Davis, *Landscape of Belief*, 24.

49. For more on this practice in white households see Georgia Barnhill, "Transformations in Pictorial Printing," in *An Extensive Republic: Print, Culture, and Society in the New Nation, 1790–1840*, ed. Robert A. Gross and Mary Kelley (Chapel Hill: University of North Carolina Press, 2010), 422–40; Brown, *Beyond the Lines*, 9–14; and Cynthia Patterson, *Art for the Middle Classes: America's Illustrated Magazines of the 1840s* (Jackson: University Press of Mississippi, 2010).

50. For more on Indian removal in general during the 1830s see Howe, *What Hath God Wrought*, 411–23. Christina Snyder provides an especially nuanced account of the complex relationship between black Americans and the Seminole tribes. See Snyder, *Slavery in Indian Country: The Changing Face of Captivity in Early America* (Cambridge, Mass.: Harvard University Press, 2010), 213–43. For more on the basic contours of the Second Seminole War see James W. Covington, *The Seminoles of Florida* (Gainesville: University Press of Florida, 1993), 72–109; John Missall and Mary Lou Missall,

*The Seminole Wars: America's Longest Indian Conflict* (Gainesville: University Press of Florida, 2004), 94–202; Bruce Edward Twyman, *The Black Seminole Legacy and North American Politics, 1693–1845* (Washington, D.C.: Howard University Press, 1999), 115–43.

51. Joshua Giddings, "Speech of Mr. Giddings, of Ohio, Delivered in the House of Representatives, February 9, 1841, Upon the Proposition to Appropriate 'One Hundred Thousand Dollars for the Removal, &c., of Such of the Seminole Chiefs and Warriors as May Surrender for Emigration,'" *Colored American*, April 3, 1841, original emphasis. Giddings's speech appeared on the *Colored American*'s front page without interruption from March 27, 1841 to April 24, 1841.

52. Joshua Giddings, "Speech of Mr. Giddings," *Colored American*, March 27, 1841. Snyder argues that Native and Black Seminoles remained for the most part separate and only very rarely intermarried. See Snyder, *Slavery in Indian Country*, 233. Regardless of its accuracy, though, Giddings's claim provided the *Colored American* with a rhetorical way to connect black Americans and American Indians.

53. [Charles B. Ray], "Florida Indians," *Colored American*, April 24, 1841. For more of Ray's writings on the Second Seminole War see [Charles B. Ray], "Another Indian Skirmish," *Colored American*, March 27, 1841; [Charles B. Ray], "Florida Again," *Colored American*, May 1, 1841.

54. Walter Scott, *The Lay of the Last Minstrel, A Poem* (London: Longman, Hurst, Rees, and Orne, 1805), 161.

55. H. S. Dale, "Love of Country," *Colored American*, July 25, 1840.

56. Alexander W. Bradford, *American Antiquities and Researches into the Origin and History of the Red Race* (New York: Dayton and Saxton, 1841).

57. "Ancient Inhabitants of America," *Colored American*, December 4, 1841.

58. "History of the Red Race," *Colored American*, December 4, 1841.

59. "Ancient Inhabitants of America."

60. Ibid.

61. For more on Stephens's Central American journey see R. Tripp Evans, *Romancing the Maya: Mexican Antiquity in the American Imagination, 1820–1915* (Austin: University of Texas Press, 2004), 44–87; Harvey, *American Geographics*, 150–71.

62. Evans, *Romancing the Maya*, 49. In addition to his artistic contributions, Catherwood serves as something of a Sancho Panza to Stephens's Don Quixote, often serving as the butt of the narrative's jokes while questioning his companions' more ludicrous schemes.

63. "American Antiquities," *Colored American*, August 14, 1841. See also "American Antiquities," *Colored American*, June 12, 1841. This earlier piece reprints a review of a lecture delivered by Catherwood.

64. "American Antiquities," *Colored American*, August 14, 1841.

65. Ibid. Stephens's plans for the museum were shattered when Frederick Catherwood's New York Panorama burned to the ground. Stephens had been storing the artifacts he had acquired in that space while he searched for a more permanent location.

66. "American Antiquities," *Colored American*, August 14, 1841.

67. Indeed, though beyond the scope of this chapter, the nuanced ways in which

Stephens's entire *Incidents in Central America* engages with antebellum American imperialism deserve extended attention. The Copan episode alone frames such imperialism as a combination of performance, economics, and anxiety. For example, in order to gain access to Copan in the first place Stephens decides to purchase the entire city. Hoping to achieve the best price, Stephens visits the local landowner dressed in the uniform of an American diplomat. The performance works, and he succeeds in buying the city for the price of fifty dollars. See Stephens, *Incidents of Travel in Central America*, 117-28.

*Chapter 3. Revolutionary Chosenness*

1. Frederick Douglass, *Life and Times of Frederick Douglass*, in *The Frederick Douglass Papers*, series 2, vol. 3, ed. John R. McKivigan (New Haven: Yale University Press, 2012), 159. For more on Douglass's time in New York City see William S. McFeely, *Frederick Douglass* (New York: Norton, 1991), 71.

2. See Graham Russell Gao Hodges, *David Ruggles: A Radical Black Abolitionist and the Underground Railroad in New York City* (Chapel Hill: University of North Carolina Press, 2010).

3. For more on Douglass's European sojourn see McFeely, *Frederick Douglass*, 119-45; and Alan J. Rice and Martin Crawford, "Triumphant Exile: Frederick Douglass in Britain, 1845-1847," in *Liberating Sojourn: Frederick Douglass and Transatlantic Reform*, ed. Alan J. Rice & Martin Crawford (Athens: University of George Press, 1999), 1-14. For work that situates black American abolitionists in general, and Frederick Douglass in particular, within a larger Atlantic context see R. J. M. Blackett, *Building an Antislavery Wall: Black Americans in the Atlantic Abolitionist Movement, 1830-1860* (Baton Rouge: Louisiana State University Press, 1993); Paul Gilroy, *The Black Atlantic: Modernity and Double Consciousness* (Cambridge, Mass.: Harvard University Press, 1993); and Fionnghuala Sweeney, *Frederick Douglass and the Atlantic World* (Liverpool: Liverpool University Press, 2007).

4. Frederick Douglass, *My Bondage and My Freedom*, in *The Frederick Douglass Papers*, series 2, vol. 2, ed. John W. Blassingame, John R. McKivigan, and Peter P. Hinks (New Haven: Yale University Press, 2003), 226; 227.

5. For a general overview of the 1848 revolutions see Mike Rapport, *1848: Year of Revolution* (New York: Basic Books, 2009); Heinz-Gerhard Haupt and Dieter Langewiesche, "The European Revolution of 1848: Its Political and Social Reforms, Its Politics of Nationalism, and Its Short- and Long-Term Consequences," in *Europe in 1848: Revolution and Reform*, ed. Dieter Dowe, Heinz-Gerhard Haupt, Dieter Langewiesche, and Jonathan Sperber, trans. David Higgins (New York: Berghahn Books, 2001), 1-24; Jonathan Sperber, *The European Revolutions, 1848-1851*, 2nd ed. (New York: Cambridge University Press, 2004). For a specific account of the French uprisings see Pierre Leveque, "The Revolutionary Crisis of 1848-1851 in France: Origins and Course of Events," in *Europe in 1848: Revolution and Reform*, ed. Dieter Dowe et al., trans. David Higgins (New York: Berghahn Books, 2001), 213-22.

6. Quoted in Timothy Mason Roberts, *Distant Revolutions: 1848 and the Challenge*

to *American Exceptionalism* (Charlottesville: University of Virginia Press, 2009), 58. The U.S. ambassador to France adopted a similarly patronizing tone when he congratulated the French provisional government on its commitment to republican institutions: "Under similar institutions the United States have enjoyed 70 years of increasing prosperity with a government of stability, and if the Union gives to others the choice of government, without interference, it naturally feels gratified in seeing another nation, under similar institutions, assuring themselves the benefits of social order and public liberty." See the New York *Tribune*, March 28, 1848.

7. "French Sympathy Meeting," *North Star*, May 12, 1848.

8. In 1844, Samuel Morse successfully demonstrated his electric telegraph by transmitting the Whig nominations for president and vice president from Baltimore to Washington, D.C. Almost immediately, telegraph poles began popping up across the country. The wires initially carried stock prices between commercial centers, but newspaper editors soon saw the value of near-instantaneous news reports. By 1850, 12,000 miles of telegraph wires crisscrossed the United States, and that number nearly doubled in the next three years. See Daniel Walker Howe, *What Hath God Wrought: The Transformation of America, 1815-1848* (New York: Oxford University Press, 2007), 690-98; Paul Starr, *The Creation of the Media: Political Origins of Modern Communications* (New York: Basic Books, 2004), 153-77.

9. [Frederick Douglass], "France," *North Star*, April 28, 1848.

10. For more on Martin Delany's role as coeditor see Robert S. Levine, *Martin Delany, Frederick Douglass, and the Politics of Representative Identity* (Chapel Hill: University of North Carolina Press, 1997), 18-57. For more on William C. Nell see Dorothy Porter Wesley and Constance Porter Uzelac, "William Cooper Nell, 1816-1874," in *William Cooper Nell: Nineteenth-Century African American Abolitionist, Historian, Integrationist: Selected Writings from 1832-1874*, ed. Dorothy Porter Wesley and Constance Porter Uzelac (Baltimore: Black Classic Press, 2002), 5-60.

11. During his time in Rochester, Dick met and married Eliza Griffiths, sister of Julia Griffiths. The two moved to Toronto in 1850, and settled in New Zealand in 1861. Dick's 1895 obituary inflates his role at the *North Star*, claiming that after the printer completed his apprenticeship in London "he crossed the Atlantic Ocean to America, where he was introduced to Mr. W. Lloyd Garrison, through whose influence he was enabled to start an anti-slavery paper at Rochester." The obituary makes no mention of Douglass. See Untitled Notices, *Otago Daily Times*, April 8, 1895. See also McFeely, *Frederick Douglass*, 152-53. Douglass also asked his friend Joseph Barker to move from England to the United States and assist him with his paper, but Barker evidently declined. See "Frederick Douglass to Joseph Barker," in *The Frederick Douglass Papers*, series 3, *Correspondence*, vol. 1, *1842-1852*, ed. John R. McKivigan (New Haven: Yale University Press, 2009), 265.

12. During the spring and summer of 1848, Douglass frequently left Rochester to fulfill speaking engagements. In one letter to the paper's readers, he admitted that, while away, he had little energy to compose pieces for the paper. "One feels little like sitting down at the close of an exciting meeting, in the midst of warm friends of the

cause, anxious to exchange opinions," he explained, "and write an editorial article." But Douglass promised readers that "our publisher and printer [are] doing the best they can" and "will leave little cause for complaint on the part of our readers during our absence." See Frederick Douglass, Untitled Letter, *North Star*, March 31, 1848.

13. See Frederick Douglass and Martin Delany, "Ledger No. 1," Frederick Douglass Papers, Library of Congress, Manuscript Division. This ledger offers an indispensable window into the financial operations of the paper, as well as the makeup of its readership. The record does, however, present some difficulties when attempting to provide precise figures. For example, multiple subscriber names and exchange papers have been crossed out. One cannot be certain whether this means that the *North Star*'s editors unsuccessfully solicited subscriptions and exchanges, or that existing arrangements were later canceled. Moreover, there is no clear indication of when certain entries were made. For more on the paper's readership, as well as the importance of the ledger, see McFeely, *Frederick Douglass*, 151–53.

14. [Frederick Douglass], "American Prejudice," *North Star*, January 21, 1848, my emphasis.

15. For more on the relationship between antebellum Americans and Great Britain see Elisa Tamarkin, *Anglophilia: Deference, Devotion, and Antebellum America* (Chicago: University of Chicago Press, 2008).

16. For more on the "environment" of the newspaper, see Kevin G. Barnhurst and John Nerone, *The Form of News: A History* (New York: Guilford Press, 2001), 6.

17. See Benedict Anderson, *Imagined Communities: Reflections on the Origin and Spread of Nationalism*, rev. ed. (London: Verso, 2006), 63.

18. In revealing the gap in time between the occurrence of an event and its appearance in print, the *North Star* illustrates Trish Loughran's observation that early American print cultures not only created a sense of unity in space and time but also "worked in many cases to register the failures of such simultaneity." See Trish Loughran, *The Republic in Print: Print Culture in the Age of U.S. Nation Building, 1770–1870* (New York: Columbia University Press, 2007), 12.

19. [Frederick Douglass], "France," *North Star*, March 24, 1848.

20. "The Slave Abduction Excitement," New York *Herald*, April 24, 1848. For a detailed account of the *Pearl* affair see Josephine F. Pacheco, *The Pearl: A Failed Slave Escape on the Potomac* (Chapel Hill: University of North Carolina Press, 2005).

21. [Frederick Douglass], "France," *North Star*, April 28, 1848.

22. Henry Highland Garnet, "The Model Republic," *North Star*, April 28, 1848.

23. W[illiam] C. N[ell], "The Morning Dawns," *North Star*, May 5, 1848. Harriet Beecher Stowe makes a similar claim about the genesis of the *Pearl* escape plan. See Harriet Beecher Stowe, *A Key to Uncle Tom's Cabin* (1853; Port Washington: Kennikat Press, 1968), 157–58. As Pacheco demonstrates, pro-French speeches from congressmen had, in fact, little to do with the escape attempt aboard the *Pearl*, whose details had been meticulously planned.

24. See Pacheco, *The Pearl*, 70.

25. Garnet, "The Model Republic." Garnet's argument here echoes that of his 1843 "Address to the Slaves of the United States of America." Garnet had the speech republished,

as an appendix of sorts to a new edition of David Walker's *Appeal to the Coloured Citizens of the World*, in April of 1848. See Henry Highland Garnet, *Walker's Appeal, with a Brief Sketch of His Life. By Henry Highland Garnet. And Also Garnet's Address to the Slaves of the United States of America* (New York: J. H. Tobitt, 1848).

26. *Proceedings of the National Convention of Colored People, and Their Friends, Held in Troy, N.Y., on the 6th, 7th, 8th, and 9th October, 1847* (Troy, N.Y.: Steam Press of J. C. Kneeland and Co., 1847), 31.

27. Ibid., 13.

28. Ibid., 17.

29. Henry Highland Garnet, *Walker's Appeal*, 23; 94. In the pamphlet, Garnet dates the preface to his address April 15, 1848, which suggests that the pamphlet was published in the midst of the *North Star*'s coverage of the 1848 revolutions.

30. For more on emancipation in France's Caribbean colonies in 1848 see Lawrence C. Jennings, *French Anti-Slavery: The Movement for the Abolition of Slavery in France, 1802–1848* (New York: Cambridge University Press, 2000), 282–83.

31. "Martinique and Guadaloupe," *North Star*, June 30, 1848, original emphasis.

32. Ibid.

33. "Insurrection in Cuba," *North Star*, July 7, 1848.

34. [Frederick Douglass], "What of the Night?" *North Star*, May 5, 1848, original emphasis.

35. See, e.g., John S. Slingerland, "The Recaptured Fugitives," *North Star*, May 12, 1848, reprinted from the Albany *Evening Journal*; "Slaveholding Justice," *North Star*, May 26, 1848, reprinted from the Cleveland *True Democrat*; "Visit to the Prison," *North Star*, May 26, 1848, reprinted from the Boston *Courier*; "The Captured Slaves," *North Star*, June 2, 1848, reprinted from the Haverhill *Gazette*.

36. "The Prisoners," *North Star*, May 12, 1848. The notice appears again in the May 26 issue.

37. [Frederick Douglass], "The Captain and Crew of the Schooner Pearl," *North Star*, May 5, 1848.

38. I use the term "English" rather than "British" intentionally. As Douglass knew from his own travels, and perhaps especially through his relationship with the radically anti-institutional Scot John Dick, the emphasis placed on reserve and faith in institutional reform by the English in London did not necessarily extend to other parts of Great Britain.

39. The New York *Herald*'s coverage exemplifies this practice. The New York *Tribune*, by contrast, had its own correspondent, the German radical Henry Börnstein, reporting directly from Paris. For the *Tribune*'s coverage of the 1848 revolutions see Adam-Max Tuchinsky, "'The Bourgeoisie Will Fall and Fall Forever': The *New-York Tribune*, the 1848 French Revolution, and the American Social Democratic Discourse," *Journal of American History* (September 2005): 470–97.

40. "Taxation in England," *North Star*, March 24, 1848.

41. R. S. D., Untitled letter, *North Star*, April 7, 1848.

42. Jonathan Carr, "Address, of the Inhabitants of Carlisle, England, in Public Meeting Assembled, to Their Brethren in France," *North Star*, April 21, 1848.

43. "Taxation in England."

44. R. S. D., Untitled letter, *North Star*, April 7, 1848.

45. Douglass Jerrold, "Paris As It Is," *North Star*, April 21, 1848.

46. London *Times* reporter quoted in John Saville, *1848: The British State and the Chartist movement* (Cambridge: Cambridge University Press, 1987), 89.

47. R .S. D., "State of Europe," *North Star*, May 5, 1848.

48. Ibid. For more on the Chartist movement in general see Malcolm Chase, *Chartism: A New History* (Manchester: Manchester University Press, 2007); Gareth Stedman Jones, *Languages of Class: Studies in English Working Class History, 1832–1982* (Cambridge: Cambridge University Press, 1983), 90–178; and Dorothy Thompson, *The Chartists* (London: Temple Smith, 1984). For more on the context and aftermath of the April 10 meeting in particular see Saville, *1848*.

49. [Frederick Douglass], "Chartists of England," May 5, 1848.

50. For more on Douglass's connections to the Chartists see Richard Bradbury, "Frederick Douglass and the Chartists," in *Liberating Sojourn: Frederick Douglass and Transatlantic Reform*, ed. Alan J. Rice and Martin Crawford (Athens: University of Georgia Press, 1999), 169–86.

51. [Frederick Douglass], "Fugitive Slaves from Washington," *North Star*, April 28, 1848.

52. [Frederick Douglass], "The Riot in Washington," *North Star*, May 5, 1848.

53. [Gamiel Bailey], "Disturbance," *North Star*, April 28, 1848.

54. "The Senate.—April 20," *North Star*, May 12, 1848.

55. Garnet, "Model Republic."

56. [Frederick Douglass], "What Are the Colored People Doing for Themselves," *North Star*, July 14, 1848.

57. Ibid., original emphasis.

58. Ibid.

59. Great Britain passed an act for gradual emancipation in the West Indies in 1834, but black Americans in the United States largely refrained from celebrating the event until the removal of the apprenticeship system and declaration of immediate emancipation in 1838. For more on First of August celebrations see Mitch Kachun, *Festivals of Freedom: Memory and Meaning in African American Emancipation Celebrations* (Amherst: University of Massachusetts Press, 2003), 54–96.

60. [Frederick Douglass], "First of August Celebration," *North Star*, August 4, 1848.

61. "First of August," *North Star*, August 11, 1848; "The Celebration of August 1st," *North Star*, August 11, 1848.

62. [Frederick Douglass], "Frederick Douglass' Address," *North Star*, August 4, 1848.

*Chapter 4. The Limits of Black Chosenness*

1. M[artin] R. D[elany], Untitled Letter, *North Star*, February 16, 1849. Throughout this chapter I refer to Mary Ann Shadd by her maiden name, rather than by her married name Shadd Cary. In doing so I follow her own usage for most of the period covered

here, as well as references made to her by others. I do, however, use the name Shadd Cary in the rare instances where I cite a piece she explicitly signed with that name, such as the "Plastering" article that serves as the epigraph to this chapter.

2. J. B. Y., "Miss Shadd's Pamphlet," *North Star*, June 8, 1849.

3. M[ary] A[nn] Shadd, Untitled Letter, *North Star*, March 23, 1849.

4. "Mary Ann Shadd Cary to George Whipple, 27 November 1851," in *The Black Abolitionist Papers*, vol. 2: *Canada, 1830–1865*, ed. C. Peter Ripley (Chapel Hill: University of North Carolina Press, 1986), 184. See also Jane Rhodes, *Mary Ann Shadd Cary: The Black Press and Protest in the Nineteenth Century* (Bloomington: Indiana University Press, 1998), 25–26.

5. *Proceedings of the Colored National Convention, Held in Franklin Hall, Sixth Street, Below Arch, Philadelphia, October 16th, 17th, and 18th, 1855* (Salem, N.J.: Printed at the National Standard Office, 1856), 10.

6. Jane Rhodes's biography of Mary Ann Shadd Cary is an invaluable resource for those interested not only in Shadd and black newspapers but also in the importance of gender in nineteenth-century black activism. For more on Shadd's antebellum activities in particular see Rhodes, *Mary Ann Shadd Cary*, 1–41. See also Carla L. Peterson, *"Doers of the Word": African-American Women Speakers and Writers in the North (1830–1880)* (New Brunswick, N.J.: Rutgers University Press, 1995), 89–118; Carol B. Conaway, "Mary Ann Shadd Cary: A Visionary of the Black Press," in *Black Women's Intellectual Traditions: Speaking Their Minds*, ed. Kristin Waters and Carol B. Conaway (Burlington: University of Vermont Press, 2007), 216–45; Kathy L. Glass, *Courting Communities: Black Female Nationalism and "Syncre-Nationalism" in the Nineteenth-Century North* (New York: Routledge, 2006), 57–75; Shirley J. Yee, "Finding a Place: Mary Ann Shadd Cary and the Dilemmas of Black Migration to Canada, 1850–1870," *Frontiers: A Journal of Women Studies* 18, no. 3 (1997): 1–16.

7. For more on black settlement and life in Canada before the American Civil War see Jason Silverman, *Unwelcome Guests: Canada West's Response to American Fugitive Slaves, 1800–1865* (New York: Associated Faculty Press, 1985), 1–79; Robin Winks, *The Blacks in Canada: A History*, 2nd ed. (Montreal: McGill-Queen's University Press, 1997), 142–232.

8. For the American Anti-Slavery Society's population estimate see Benjamin Drew, *The Refugee: Narratives of Fugitive Slaves in Canada* (1856; Toronto: Dundurn Press, 2008), 27. In his autobiography, Samuel Ward estimated the black population at Canada in the 1850s at between 35,000 and 40,000. See Samuel Ringgold Ward, *Autobiography of a Fugitive Negro* (1855; New York: Arno Press, 1968), 154. For a detailed study of black life in Chatham see Heike Paul, "Out of Chatham: Abolitionism on the Canadian Frontier," *Atlantic Studies* 8, no. 2 (2011): 165–88.

9. Quoted in Silverman, *Unwelcome* Guests, 106.

10. Ward, *Autobiography*, 144.

11. See Roger W. Hite, "Voice of a Fugitive: Henry Bibb and Ante-Bellum Black Separatism," *Journal of Black Studies* 4, no. 3 (March, 1974): 269–84; Rhodes, *Mary Ann Shadd Cary*, 35.

12. [Frederick Douglass], Untitled Notice, *Frederick Douglass' Paper*, June 24, 1852.

13. Rhodes, *Mary Ann Shadd Cary*, 57.

14. Henry Bibb, "17th, Anniversary of West India Emancipation," *Voice of the Fugitive*, August 12, 1852.

15. Quoted in Rhodes, *Mary Ann Shadd Cary*, 72.

16. "Voice of the Colored People of Sandwich, C.W.," *Frederick Douglass' Paper*, April 8, 1853.

17. Rhodes, *Mary Ann Shadd Cary*, 81.

18. Ibid., 83.

19. William S. McFeely, *Frederick Douglass* (New York: W. W. Norton, 1991), 166; Rhodes, *Mary Ann Shadd Cary*, 82–84.

20. Silverman, *Unwelcome Guests*, 113; "Henry Bibb Is Dead," *Frederick Douglass's Paper*, August 11, 1854.

21. Rhodes, *Mary Ann Shadd Cary*, 83–84.

22. [Mary Ann Shadd], "Number Two," *Provincial Freeman*, March 25, 1854.

23. [Mary Ann Shadd], "To All Whom It May Concern," *Provincial Freeman*, October 28, 1854, original emphasis.

24. S., "The Dodgers," *Provincial Freeman*, November 3, 1855.

25. Mary A. Shadd, *A Plea for Emigration; Or, Notes of Canada West*, ed. Richard Almonte (Toronto: Mercury Press, 1998), 45.

26. Shadd, *Notes of Canada West*, 46.

27. Ward, *Autobiography*, 155.

28. Mary Jane Robinson, "Letter From Canada," *Provincial Freeman*, January 13, 1855.

29. Samuel Cartwright, "Diseases and Peculiarities of the Negro Race," *De Bow's Southern and Western Review* 11, no. 3 (1851): 331–36.

30. "Things As They Are in America: Canada West to Michigan," *Provincial Freeman*, October 28, 1854.

31. "Condition of Canada, as Compared with the United States, &c.," *Provincial Freeman*, April 21, 1855.

32. "Progress of Canada West," *Provincial Freeman*, January 13, 1856.

33. "Canadian Prosperity," *Provincial Freeman*, May 19, 1855, original emphasis.

34. E. R. Johnson, "Visit to Canada," *Provincial Freeman*, January 13, 1855.

35. "Fugitive Slaves in Canada," *Provincial Freeman*, November 24, 1855.

36. Quoted in Drew, *Refugee*, 119; 248.

37. Quoted in Drew, *Refugee*, 230.

38. Ibid.

39. D., "About Canada," *Provincial Freeman*, April 22, 1854.

40. Quoted in Drew, *Refugee*, 256.

41. Ward, *Autobiography*, 207.

42. For more on the arguments surrounding black emigration within and among black communities see Floyd J. Miller's seminal work *The Search for a Black Nationality: Black Emigration and Colonization 1787–1863* (Urbana: University of Illinois Press, 1975), 134–69.

43. Not all of the issues of the newspaper in which the letters from Whitfield and Watkins appeared remain extant, but the entire exchange was collected in Frederick Douglass, W. J. Watkins, and J. M. Whitfield, *Arguments, Pro and Con, on the Call for a National Emigration Convention, to be Held in Cleveland, Ohio, August, 1854* (Detroit: M. T. Newsom, 1854).

44. Douglass, Watkins, and Whitfield, *Arguments, Pro and Con*, 22, original emphasis.

45. Ibid., 30, original emphasis.

46. Ibid.

47. See Samuel Matthews, "John Isom Gaines: The Architect of Black Public Education," in *Queen City Heritage: Journal of the Cincinnati Historical Society* 45, no. 1 (1987): 41–47.

48. J. I. Gaines, "Emigration," *Provincial Freeman*, January 10, 1855.

49. I have been unable to conclusively link the Samuel A. S. Lowery who wrote to the *Provincial Freeman* to any Samuel Lowery in the historical record.

50. Samuel A. S. Lowery, "Gaines on Submission, or an Anti-Emigrationist Reviewed," *Provincial Freeman*, February 17, 1855.

51. J. I. Gaines, "Emigration No. V," *Provincial Freeman*, April 7, 1855.

52. Gaines, "Emigration No. V."

53. Samuel A. S. Lowery, "Gaines on Submission, or an Anti-Emigrationist Reviewed, No. II," *Provincial Freeman*, March 17, 1855, original emphasis.

54. Lowery, "Gaines on Submission, No. II," my emphasis.

55. Ibid.

56. M[ary] A[nn] S[hadd], "The Emigration Convention," *Provincial Freeman*, July 5, 1856, original emphasis.

57. Ibid.

58. See J. M. Bumsted, "The Consolidation of British North America, 1783–1860," in *Canada and the British Empire*, ed. Phillip Buckner (New York: Oxford University Press, 2008), 43–65.

59. Shadd, *A Plea for Emigration*, 94, original emphasis.

60. Ibid., 92.

61. M[ary] A[nn] S[hadd] C[ary], "Obstacles to the Progress of Colored Canadians," *Provincial Freeman*, January 31, 1857.

62. M[ary] A[nn] S[hadd] C[ary], "Things Most Needed," *Provincial Freeman*, April 25, 1857.

63. Ibid.

64. H. F[ord] D[ouglass], "The Duties of Colored Men in Canada," *Provincial Freeman*, March 28, 1857, original emphasis.

65. Martin Delany, "Political Destiny of the Colored Race on the American Continent," in *Pamphlets of Protest: An Anthology of Early African-American Protest Literature, 1790–1860*, ed. Richard Newman, Patrick Rael, and Philip Lapsansky (New York: Routledge, 2001), 230.

66. See J. M. Bumsted, *The Peoples of Canada: A Pre-Confederation History* (Toronto: Oxford University Press, 1992), 285.

67. Ibid., 316–37.

68. H. F[ord] D[ouglass], "Let My People Go That They May Serve Me," *Provincial Freeman*, April 11, 1857.

69. Quoted in Winks, *Blacks in Canada*, 149.

70. Dwight L. Dumond, ed., *Letters of James Gillespie Birney, 1831–1857* (New York: D. Appleton-Century, 1938), 395.

71. H. F[ord] D[ouglass], "God Made the Country—Man Made the Town," *Provincial Freeman*, April 11, 1857.

72. "Colonel Prince and the Colored People," *Provincial Freeman*, July 4, 1857, original emphasis.

73. Indeed, in 1861 Prince would lose to a Reform opponent, and black votes would prove decisive in his defeat. See Winks, *Blacks in Canada*, 214–15.

74. "Our Colored Neighbours," *Provincial Freeman*, July 4, 1857.

75. M[ary] A[nn] S[hadd] C[ary], "The Indignation Meeting, Col. Prince &c.," *Provincial Freeman*, July 4, 1857, original emphasis.

76. Ibid., original emphasis.

77. M[ary] A[nn] S[hadd] C[ary], "Purely Local—What Shall We Do? &c.," *Provincial Freeman*, July 11, 1857.

78. My phrasing here reworks the subtitle of Stuart Hall's seminal essay, "The Problem of Ideology: Marxism without Guarantees," in *Stuart Hall: Critical Dialogues in Cultural Studies*, ed. David Morley and Kuan-Hsing Chen (New York: Routledge, 1996): 26–46. Hall explores the implications of his insights in this essay for questions of racial identity in "New Ethnicities," in *Stuart Hall: Critical Dialogues in Cultural Studies*, ed. David Morley and Kuan-Hsing Chen (New York: Routledge, 1996): 442–49.

79. [Frederick Douglass], "Canada—Liberia—H. Ford Douglass—*Provincial Freeman*—Mary A. Shadd," *Frederick Douglass' Paper*, July 4, 1856, original emphasis.

80. Ibid.

81. Ibid.

82. Douglass, Watkins, and Whitfield, *Arguments, Pro and Con*, 10, original emphasis.

83. Delany, "Political Destiny," 230, original emphasis.

84. Ibid.

85. M[ary] A[nn] S[hadd] Cary, "Plastering, &c.," *Provincial Freeman*, July 19, 1856.

*Chapter 5. Joining the Chosen Army*

1. David Walker, *David Walker's Appeal to the Coloured Citizens of the World*, ed. Peter P. Hinks (University Park: Pennsylvania State University Press, 2000), 5.

2. "Letter from Rev. J. W. Loguen," *Weekly Anglo-African*, August 31, 1861.

3. "Letter from H. H. Garnet," *Weekly Anglo-African*, October 19, 1861.

4. [Frederick Douglass], "Nemesis," *Douglass' Monthly* 3, no. 12 (May 1861): 450, original emphasis. For more on Douglass's reading of the war in apocalyptic terms see David W. Blight, *Frederick Douglass' Civil War: Keeping Faith in Jubilee* (Baton Rouge: Louisiana State University Press, 1989), 101–21.

5. "Letter from Rev. J. W. Loguen."
6. G[eorge] E. S[tephens], Untitled Letter, *Weekly Anglo-African*, December 14, 1861.
7. "Auditor," Untitled Letter, *Freedom's Journal*, July 13, 1827. For Hamilton's oration see William Hamilton, "Extract from an ORATION, *Delivered in the African Zion Church, in the City of New-York, on the Fourth of July, 1827, in Commemoration of the ABOLITION of DOMESTIC SLAVERY, in this State*," *Freedom's Journal*, October 12, 1827.
8. Untitled Notice, *Colored American*, July 1, 1837.
9. For more on the Hamiltons see Debra Jackson, "'A Cultural Stronghold': The *Anglo-African* Newspaper and the Black Community of New York," *New York History* (Summer 2004): 331–57; Debra Jackson, "A Black Journalist in Civil War Virginia: Robert Hamilton and the 'Anglo-African,'" *Virginia Magazine of History and Biography* 116, no. 1 (2008): 42–72.
10. For more on the *Anglo-African Magazine* see Ivy G. Wilson, "The Brief Wondrous Life of the *Anglo-African Magazine*: Or, Antebellum African American Editorial Practice and Its Afterlives," in *Publishing Blackness: Textual Constructions of Race since 1850*, ed. George Hutchinson and John K. Young (Ann Arbor: University of Michigan Press, 2013), 18–38.
11. [Thomas Hamilton], "Apology," *Anglo-African Magazine* 1, no. 1 (January 1859): 2.
12. Ethiop [William J. Wilson], "Afric-American Picture Gallery," *Anglo-African Magazine* 1, no. 2 (February 1859): 53.
13. Ibid., 54.
14. [Thomas Hamilton], "Our Paper," *Weekly Anglo-African*, July 23, 1859, original emphasis.
15. Ibid.
16. "New Subscribers," *Weekly Anglo-African*, March 4, 1865.
17. For more on the circulation of black newspapers in black Union regiments see Keith P. Wilson, *Campfires of Freedom: The Camp Life of Black Soldiers during the Civil War* (Kent, Ohio: Kent State University Press, 2002), 74–77. The *Weekly Anglo-African* also made its way onto the ships of the Union Navy, where black sailors had been serving since the war's inception. See William B. Gould IV, *Diary of a Contraband: The Civil War Passage of a Black Sailor* (Stanford: Stanford University Press, 2002), 179. I focus in particular on the letters of black soldiers to black newspapers in the Conclusion.
18. [Thomas Hamilton], "Our Paper," original emphasis.
19. "Thomas Hamilton to John Jay, 27 May 1859," in C. Peter Ripley, ed., *The Black Abolitionist Papers*, vol. 5, *The United States, 1859–1865* (Chapel Hill: University of North Carolina Press, 1992), 26.
20. See Elizabeth Lorang and R. J. Weir, "Introduction," "'Will Not These Days be by Thy Poets Sung': Poems of the *Anglo-African* and *National Anti-Slavery Standard*, 1863–1864," ed. Elizabeth Lorang and R. J. Weir, *Scholarly Editing* 34 (2013), scholarly editing.org.
21. For more on Gould's life and service in the Union Navy see Gould, *Diary of a Contraband*, 1–72. During his 1864 stay in New York City, Gould recorded visits to the *Weekly Anglo-African*'s offices on April 5 (180–81), April 11 (181), May 7 (186), May 11

(187), and May 14 (188). For more on the implications of Gould's diary for black literacy as well as his engagement with black newspapers see Christopher Hager, *Word by Word: Emancipation and the Act of Writing* (Cambridge, Mass.: Harvard University Press, 2013), 119–34.

22. Untitled Advertisements, *Weekly Anglo-African*, August 17, 1861.

23. Thomas Hamilton certainly played a major role in the paper's daily operations from 1863 on, when Robert embarked on extended tours of the Union-occupied South. See Jackson, "A Black Journalist in Civil War Virginia."

24. For more on the location of the *Weekly Anglo-African*'s offices, as well as a detailed discussion of the paper's place in a broader New York City print culture, see Lorang and Weir, "Introduction."

25. "The Union Forever," New York *Times*, April 21, 1861.

26. "A Significant Fact," New York *Times*, April 21, 1861.

27. See Edwin G. Burrows and Mike Wallace, *Gotham: A History of New York City to 1898* (New York: Oxford University Press, 1999), 868–72.

28. [Frederick Douglass], "Black Regiments Proposed," *Douglass' Monthly* (May 1861): 452.

29. [Frederick Douglass], "How to End the War," *Douglass' Monthly* (May 1861): 451, original emphasis.

30. Frederick Douglass, "To Rev. Samuel J. May," in *The Life and Writings of Frederick Douglass*, vol. 3, ed. Philip S. Foner (New York: International Publishers, 1952), 3:159.

31. Unsigned, "Let Us Drill!" *Weekly Anglo-African*, October 5, 1861.

32. Ibid.

33. Rec in Cur, "We Should Not Drill," *Weekly Anglo-African*, October 12, 1861. "Rec in Cur," the pseudonym of this author, is the Latin legalistic phrase "recognized in court."

34. C. Peter Ripley has included part of this debate in his *Black Abolitionist Papers*, hypothesizing that "R. H. V." (the signature line for the letters) is "most likely Robert H. Vandyne, a New York City correspondent and financial contributor to the [Weekly] Anglo-African." See Ripley, *Black Abolitionist Papers*, 5:117. Alfred M. Green, a militant black abolitionist from Philadelphia, had served thirty days in jail in 1860 for attempting to rescue a fugitive slave from recapture. In April 1861 he, along with black abolitionist Thomas Bowers, attempted to form two black regiments in Philadelphia. For more on Green see Benjamin Quarles, *Black Abolitionists* (New York: Oxford University Press, 1969), 214–15.

35. R[obert] H. V[andyne], "Formation of Colored Regiments," *Weekly Anglo-African*, September 28, 1861.

36. Alfred M. Green, "Colored Regiments," *Weekly Anglo-African*, October 19, 1861.

37. R[obert] H. V[andyne], "Formation of Colored Regiments," *Weekly Anglo-African*, October 26, 1861.

38. Alfred M. Green, "Colored Regiments," *Weekly Anglo-African*, October 26, 1861.

39. Exodus 14:13 (KJV).

40. 2 Chronicles 20:17.

41. 2 Chronicles 20:21.

42. 2 Chronicles 20:22.

43. [Robert Hamilton], "Blake: or the Huts of America," *Weekly Anglo-African*, November 16, 1861.

44. *Freedom's Journal* serialized the short story "Theresa; A Haytien Tale" from January 18, 1828 to February 15, 1828. To cite only a few other examples, *Frederick Douglass's Paper* published Douglass's own novella, *The Heroic Slave*, in 1853, as well as the entirety of Charles Dickens's mammoth *Bleak House*. The *Weekly Anglo-African* published multiple novels in serial form, including William Wells Brown's *Miralda* (a revision of his earlier *Clotel*). See Frances Smith Foster, "How Do You Solve a Problem Like Theresa?" *African American Review* 40, no. 4 (Winter 2006): 631–45; and Daniel Hack, "Close Reading at a Distance: The African Americanization of *Bleak House*," *Critical Inquiry* 34, no. 4 (Summer 2008): 729–53.

45. [Robert Hamilton], "Blake: or the Huts of America," *Weekly Anglo-African*, November 16, 1861.

46. Introducing the novel's initial 1859 serialization in the *Anglo-African Magazine*, editor Thomas Hamilton claimed that the work had been "written in two parts, so as to make two volumes in one, con[t]aining some 80 Chapters and about 600 pages." Given this notice and the extant novel's abrupt conclusion after only seventy-four chapters, editor Floyd Miller reasoned in his 1970 edition of the text that the "complete novel contains perhaps six chapters that have not yet been uncovered." The May 1862 issues of the *Weekly Anglo-African*, where the novel's conclusion would have likely appeared, remain unrecovered. See [Thomas Hamilton], "Blake: Or The Huts Of America," in *Anglo-African Magazine*, vol. 1, *1859* (New York: Arno, 1968), 1:20; Martin Delany, *Blake; Or, the Huts of America*, ed. Floyd J. Miller (Boston: Beacon, 1970), ix. For more on the novel's composition and publication history see Robert S. Levine, *Martin Delany, Frederick Douglass, and the Politics of Representative Identity* (Chapel Hill: University of North Carolina Press, 1997), 177–223.

47. For other readings of *Blake* within the contexts of its periodical publication see Katy Chiles, "Within and without Raced Nations: Intratextuality, Martin Delany, and *Blake; or the Huts of America*," *American Literature* 80, no. 2 (June 2008): 323–52; Jean Lee Cole, "Theresa and Blake: Mobility and Resistance in Antebellum African American Serialized Fiction," *Callaloo* 34, no. 1 (Winter 2011): 158–75; and Patricia Okker, *Social Stories: The Magazine Novel in Nineteenth-Century America* (Charlottesville: University of Virginia Press, 2003).

48. [Robert Hamilton], "Blake: or the Huts of America."

49. Rebecca Biggio reads *Blake*'s slave conspiracy, and the ambiguity of its intended outcome, as potentially more threatening than a clearly imagined uprising. See Rebecca Skidmore Biggio, "The Specter of Conspiracy in Martin Delany's *Blake*," *African American Review* 42, nos. 3–4 (Fall/Winter 2008): 439–54.

50. Martin Delany, "Blake; Or, the Huts of America," *Weekly Anglo-African*, November 23, 1861.

51. Martin Delany, "Blake; Or, the Huts of America," *Weekly Anglo-African*, December 14, 1861.

52. Martin Delany, *The Condition, Elevation, Emigration, and Destiny of the Colored People of the United States: Politically Considered* (Philadelphia: Published by the Author, 1852), 37–38.

53. Delany, *Condition*, 38, original emphasis.

54. "'Have We A War Policy?'" *Weekly Anglo-African*, April 27, 1861. This editorial was printed just after George Lawrence purchased the paper, but before he transformed it into a pro-emigration organ and changed its name to the *Pine and Palm*. It is thus possible that Thomas Hamilton composed the piece.

55. "'Have We A War Policy?'" original emphasis.

56. Ibid.

57. See George E. Stephens, *A Voice of Thunder: The Civil War Letters of George E. Stephens*, ed. Donald Yaconove (Urbana: University of Illinois Press, 1997). For another reading of *Blake* in the context of Stephens's reports see Cole.

58. G[eorge] E. S[tephens], "Army Correspondence," *Weekly Anglo-African*, December 7, 1861.

59. G[eorge] E. S[tephens], "Army Correspondence," *Weekly Anglo-African*, February 8, 1862.

60. G[eorge] E. S[tephens], "Army Correspondence," *Weekly Anglo-African*, January 18, 1862.

61. Martin Delany, "Blake; Or, the Huts of America," *Weekly Anglo-African*, January 18, 1862.

62. [Robert Hamilton], "The Present—and Its Duties," *Weekly Anglo-African*, January 17, 1863.

63. G[eorge] E. S[tephens], "The Copperheads and the Enlistment of Colored Men," *Weekly Anglo-African*, April 11, 1863.

64. [Robert Hamilton], "None but Brave Officers for Black Troops," *Weekly Anglo-African*, June 20, 1863.

65. For a concise history of black soldiers in the Civil War see John David Smith, "Let Us All be Grateful That We Have Colored Troops That Will Fight," in *Black Soldiers in Blue: African American Troops in the Civil War Era*, ed. John David Smith (Chapel Hill: University of North Carolina Press, 2002), 1–77. For more on the experience of black soldiers at the front see Wilson, *Campfires of Freedom*. For work focused on black soldiers from New York in particular see William Seraile, *New York's Black Regiments during the Civil War* (New York: Routledge, 2001).

66. "New Subscribers," *Weekly Anglo-African*, April 8, 1865.

67. [Robert Hamilton], "Our Paper for Colored Soldiers," February 18, 1865.

68. [Hamilton], "The Present—and Its Duties."

69. [Frederick Douglass], "The Work of the Future," *Douglass' Monthly* (November 1862): 737.

## Conclusion. The Ends of Black Chosenness

1. E. W. D., "Army Correspondence," *Christian Recorder*, June 25, 1854.

2. For more on the pay gap between black and white soldiers, and especially black responses to it, see Keith P. Wilson, *Campfires of Freedom: The Camp Life of Black Soldiers during the Civil War* (Kent, Ohio: Kent State University Press, 2002), 44–48. For a selection of letters from black soldiers specifically addressing unequal pay see Edwin S. Redkey, ed., *A Grand Army of Black Men: Letters from African-American Soldiers in the Union Army, 1861–1865* (Cambridge: Cambridge University Press, 1992), 229–48.

3. E.W.D., "Army Correspondence."

4. Ibid.

5. For a broad overview of the *Christian Recorder* that pays particular attention to its postbellum era see Julius H. Bailey, *Race Patriotism: Protest and Print Culture in the AME Church* (Knoxville: University of Tennessee Press, 2012). For an in-depth account of the paper's earlier years see Eric Gardner, *Black Print Unbound: The Christian Recorder, African American Literature, and Periodical Culture* (New York: Oxford University Press, 2015). I am grateful to Eric Gardner for sharing sections of this work with me while it was still in manuscript form. Unfortunately, *Black Print Unbound*'s publication came too late in my own writing for me to take full advantage of its arguments regarding not only the *Recorder* but also black print culture more broadly. For important work situating the *Recorder* within African American literary studies see Frances Smith Foster and Chanta Haywood, "Christian Recordings: Afro-Protestantism, Its Press, and the Production of African-American Literature," *Religion and Literature* 27, no. 1 (Spring 1995): 15–33; Chanta Haywood, "Constructing Childhood: The 'Christian Recorder' and Literature for Black Children, 1854–1865," *African American Review* 36, no. 3 (Autumn 2002): 417–28; Mitch Kachun, "Interrogating the Silences: Julia C. Collins, 19th-Century Black Readers and Writers, and the 'Christian Recorder,'" *African American Review* 40, no. 4 (Winter 2006): 649–59; Elizabeth McHenry, *Forgotten Readers: Recovering the Lost History of African American Literary Societies* (Durham, N.C.: Duke University Press, 2002), 137–40.

6. H[enry] M[cNeal] T[urner], "Army Correspondence," *Christian Recorder*, December 7, 1864. For more on the *Christian Recorder* and black soldiers, with special attention to the connection between the newspaper and black literacy, see Christopher Hager, *Word by Word: Emancipation and the Act of Writing* (Cambridge, Mass.: Harvard University Press, 2013), 182–213. For more on Henry McNeal Turner's role as war correspondent see Jean Lee Cole, "Introduction," in *Freedom's Witness: The Civil War Correspondence of Henry McNeal Turner*, ed. Jean Lee Cole (Morgantown: West Virginia University Press, 2013), 1–32; Edwin S. Redkey, "Henry McNeal Turner: Black Chaplain in the Union Army," in *Black Soldiers in Blue: African American Troops in the Civil War Era*, ed. John David Smith (Chapel Hill: University of North Carolina Press, 2002), 336–60.

7. [Elisha Weaver], "The Pay of Colored Soldiers," *Christian Recorder*, December 26, 1863, original emphasis.

8. "Payment of Colored Troops," *Christian Recorder*, August 20, 1864. As Hager writes, "[i]t was as if the *Recorder*'s editors had read only the first few lines of Higginson's letter—'it is at length ruled that colored soldiers shall be paid the full pay of soldiers from the date of enlistment'—and willfully ignored the crucial caveat—'provided they were free on April 19th, 1861'—as well as everything else Higginson wrote." See Hager, *Word by Word*, 205.

9. J. H. Hall, "Letter from the 54th Massachusetts Regiment," *Christian Recorder*, August 27, 1864.

10. G[arland] H. White, "Letter from the Front," *Christian Recorder*, September 17, 1864. Hager too reads White's attack on the Massachusetts regiments as part of a larger intraracial struggle over the meaning of citizenship, though he does not address White's letter as part of a new and growing consensus within and among black communities that equated citizenship with loyalty to the United States. See Hager, *Word by Word*, 201–13.

11. Samuel Childress, Untitled Letter, *Weekly Anglo-African*, December 16, 1865.

12. U.S. Const., amend. XIII.

13. For an absolutely crucial analysis of how the United States' criminalization of blackness has authorized forms of racial slavery from the early Republic to the present see Michelle Alexander, *The New Jim Crow: Mass Incarceration in the Age of Colorblindness* (New York: New Press, 2010).

# Index

abolitionism: abolitionists visit Europe, 73; American Babylon and, 79–80, 84, 143, 148; discussion at 1847 National Convention of Colored People, 1; 1848 revolutions and, 79; interracial movement, 71; legal challenge to slavery, 84–85; use of violence and, 81–84

"Address to the Slaves of the United States of America" (Garnet), 82

"Afric-American Picture Gallery," 122–23

African Free School, 25, 42–43

Allen, Richard, 4

A.M.E. Church, 18; *Christian Recorder*, 143–46

*American Antiquities and Researches into the Origin and History of the Red Race* (Bradford), 66–67

American Indians, 46, 63–66; black Americans and, 69; removal, 64

*Anglo-African Magazine*, 122–24

*Appeal to the Coloured Citizens of the World* (D. Walker), 40–41

*Autobiography of a Fugitive Negro* (Ward), 100

Bailey, Gamaliel, 89–90

Beard, J. R., 124

Beecher, Lyman, 45–46

Bell, Philip: connections to *Freedom's Journal*, 43; Douglass and, 71–72; educational background, 42; Garrison's *Liberator* and, 43; promise of illustrations, 54. See also *Colored American*

"Best Means to Abolish Slavery and Caste in the United States" (F. Douglass), 82

Bibb, Henry: death of, 102; founds *Voice of the Fugitive*, 100–101; Shadd attacked by, 98; Shadd's relationship with, 100–101

Bibb, Mary, 100

Birney, James, 114

black Americans as Israelites, 4–6, 58–63, 111; from book of Exodus, 129–33; emancipation and, 143, 148; indigenous chosenness and, 63, 65; from second book of Chronicles, 129–33

black chosenness: America as Babylon, 133; American Indians and, 64; American national identity, 50–53, 57, 109, 111; American national identity transcending nation-state, 68–70; American national identity unlinked, 110; black exceptionalism and, 6; black liberation as global struggle, 74, 76,

black chosenness (*continued*)
79, 90, 137–39; before black press, 4; citizenship, postemancipation, and, 143, 146–48; citizenship and, 8–9, 140–41; Civil War, role in, 132–33; education leading to liberation, 27; Emancipation Proclamation and, 139–41; to gain white allies in abolition, 4–6; God's promise to his people, 60; indigenous chosenness, 63, 64, 65–66, 69–70; military action to gain black liberation, 135; propriety, 34–35, 38, 39, 91–94, 109, 127; propriety, postemancipation, 140; public gatherings and, 32; responsibilities of, 4–5, 22–23; transcending nation-state, 8–9; transnational liberation, 74; United States, relationship with, 146–48; white American exceptionalism and, 5. *See also* black Americans as Israelites

black military action: enlistment, 139–41; 54th Massachusetts regiment, 142–43; fight for U.S. government, 146; government pay for black soldiers, 142–43; propriety, 127–28; 21st U.S. Colored Infantry, 142; unequal pay, 144–47

black press: black activism and, 2; on black military activity, 126–33; call for propriety, 7–8, 10; call to action, 7–8; in Canada, 100; communities, 7, 11; as educational, 10; as history of black America, 122–23; interconnectedness of, 18, 19, 59, 97, 122–23, 159n30; interracial productions, 54–56; national black newspaper, debate on creation of, 1–2; opposing voices printed in, 81–84, 97, 106–10, 116–18, 144–46; readers, expectations for, 10; readership beyond subscribers, 11–14, 24–25, 77; religious nature of, 18; scholarship on, lack of, 9–10, 18; serialization of fiction in, 134–39; social activity/public reading rooms, 10–11; as vehicle for emancipation, 3; visual culture, 13, 54, 56, 60–63, 67, 125; white audience, 120. *See also specific editors and newspapers*

*Blake* (Delany), 134–39; plot, 134–35; significance of "stand still," 135–36; *Weekly Anglo-African* serialization, 134–39

Bradford, Alexander, 66–67
Brady, William, 75

Calhoun, John C., 89–90
Canada: black Canadians, 99–101 (*see also* Shadd, Mary Ann); black Canadians as British subjects, 112–15; black Canadians' economic progress, 105–6; part of British empire, 111–15; politics, 113–15; racial discrimination against black peoples, 100, 114–15
Carr, Jonathan, 86
Cartwright, Samuel, 104
Cary, Mary Ann Shadd. *See* Shadd, Mary Ann
Catherwood, Frederick, 67–70
Chartists, 87–88
Cheeves, George B., 124
Chester, T. Morris, 6
Childress, Samuel, 147
chosenness: America as God's chosen nation, 49–50, 52; God's promise to his chosen people, 61; jeremiads, 49–50. *See also* black chosenness; millennialism
*Christian Recorder*, 18, 143–46
Civil War: accounts in newspapers, 13; black soldiers, exclusion of, 126–33; as God's plan to free chosen people, 119
Coker, Daniel, 4
Cole, Thomas, 62–63
*Colored American*, 42–70; American Babylon and, 49, 58–63, 67–68, 70,

79–80, 90, 111; American Indians, coverage of, 63–66; biblical geography, 59–60, 67; black chosenness and American national identity, 57; black chosenness and millennialism, 46, 111; black elites, concerns of, 47; circulation, 44, 103; Cornish as editor, 44; on disenfranchisement, 51–52; established as *Weekly Advocate*, 43–44; illustrations, use of, 54, 56, 60–63, 67; indigenous chosenness, 50–53; interconnectedness of newspaper workers, 59; jeremiads, 58; millennialism and, 42–70, 47, 56–57, 58, 60–63, 66–70; name change from *Weekly Advocate*, 44; New York City roots, 46–47; offices, 160n36; paper's run, 44; prophetic publication, 48–50; Ray as editor, 44; reform through politics, 51–53, 58; Seminoles, support for, 64–66; on voting, 51–53; white readers, 48, 49–50, 58–59

Colored Conventions: 1832 Convention for the Improvement of the Free People of Color, 39–40; 1847 National Convention of Colored People, 1–3, 82; 1855 Colored National Convention, 97–98; emigration conventions, 107

Colored National Convention, 97–98

Committee of Thirteen, 122

Committee on a National Press report, 1, 2–3

*Condition, Elevation, and Destiny of the Colored People of the United States, The* (Delany), 107, 136

conduct manuals, 23

Copan, 67–70

Cornish, Samuel: biographical information, 20; black peoples as true Americans, 50; as *Colored American* editor, 39, 47–50; connections to other members of press, 19; and Douglass, 71; educational background, 27; as *Freedom's Journal* editor, 20–21; *Freedom's Journal* founded by, 20–21; *Freedom's Journal* left by, 38; ministerial training, 20; on newspaper's role, 7–8, 20–41; postmillennialism and, 47; recruited to newspaper, 20; *Rights of All* founded by, 39; at *Weekly Advocate*, 44; work with poor black Americans, 20. See also *Freedom's Journal*

*Course of Empire, The* (Cole), 62–63

Crummel, Boston, 20–21

Davis, Jefferson, 89

Delany, Martin: on black chosenness, 5–6; connections to other members of press, 19; on emigration, 113, 117; enlists in Union army, 141; at *North Star*, 77; Shadd, relationship with, 95, 98

—works of: *Blake*, 19, 134–39; *The Condition, Elevation, and Destiny of the Colored People of the United States*, 107, 136

*Destruction of Babylon, The* (Martin), 60–63

Dick, John, 77; biographical information, 102, 165n11; connections to other members of press, 19; *Provincial Freeman* and, 102

Douglass, Frederick: biographical information, 71; in British Isles, 73; on Civil War beginning, 119; connections to other members of press, 19; *Douglass' Monthly*, 119, 120; at 1847 National Convention of Colored People, 1, 82; emigration opposed by, 107; *Frederick Douglass' Paper*, 107, 116–18; international partners, 72–73; newspaper reading, account of, 11–13; on northern support of slavery, 93; as *North Star* editor, 2; Shadd supported by, 98; speaking engagements, 77; Union, private ambivalence about supporting, 127; on violence and black

Douglass, Frederick (*continued*)
liberation, 82, 83, 84. See also *North Star*
—works of: "Best Means to Abolish Slavery and Caste in the United States," 82; *My Bondage and My Freedom*, 73; *Narrative of the Life of Frederick Douglass, an American Slave, Written by Himself*, 73
Douglass, H. Ford, 103, 112–13, 113–14, 117
Downing, Thomas, 71–72
Drayton, Daniel, 80
*Dream, The, or The True History of Deacon Giles' Distillery* (Cheeves), 124
Drew, Benjamin, 110; *A North-Side View of Slavery; The Refugee*, 105–6

Edwards, Jonathan, 5
1848 revolutions, 74–76; American reactions to, 75; Douglass on, 75; emancipation in French Caribbean, 83; *North Star* coverage of, 76
Emancipation Proclamation, 120–21, 139, 146
emigration, 106–10, 117–18. See also *Provincial Freeman*; Shadd, Mary Ann
Erie Canal, 25
E. W. D. (member of 54th Massachusetts regiment), 142–44

54th Massachusetts regiment, 142–43, 145–46
First Colored Presbyterian Church of New York, 20, 71
Fourth of July celebration: anniversary celebration, 42; contested holiday, 31; public celebrations across nation, 35; public gathering, 36; white press response, 35–36
*Frederick Douglass' Paper*: debate with *Provincial Freeman*, 116–18; propriety, 116–17

*Freedom's Journal*: advertisements, 27, 29; alienation of readers, 96; black chosenness and propriety, 111; black gratitude for white benefactors, 30, 34, 35–36; circulation, 24, 103; colonization and, 38, 106; criticism for, 23; as educational institution, 27–29; first issue, 22; founding of, 20–21, 23; Fourth of July, preparation for, 23, 29; Fourth of July condemnation, 32, 33–35, 36–38; Fourth of July condemnation, black response to, 37–38; lack of support among New York black population, 38; legacy, 39–41; misrepresentations, countering of, 26–27; mission of, 22, 23, 26–29; mission of, failed, 38–39; Noah, response to, 33–34; offices, 22, 26; propriety, 8, 19, 22–23, 28, 37, 39–40, 91, 92, 93; on public celebrations, 29; racial solidarity necessary for liberation, 116; readership, 24; reflection of black middle class of New York City, 23, 25–26, 28–29, 39–40; run of, 23; slave access to newspaper, 24–25; subscription agents, 24; united black leaders, 23–24; Walker, influence on, 40; white readers, 23, 26–27, 31, 32; writers inspired by, 40
*Front View of and Idol at Copan* (Catherwood), 67–70
Fugitive Slave Act, 99, 108, 122

Gaines, John, 107–10
Garnet, Henry Highland: "Address to the Slaves of the United States of America," 82; on Civil War beginning, 119; at 1847 National Convention of Colored People, 2, 82; in *North Star*, 78, 81–82; on violence and emancipation, 81–83
Garrison, William Lloyd, 43, 72. See also *Liberator*

Giddings, Joshua, 64–65
Gould, William, 125
Great Britain: antitax riots, 87; emancipation, 92. *See also* Canada
Green, Alfred M., 129–33, 139

Hale, John Parker, 89–90
Hall, J. H., 145
Hamilton, Robert: biographical information, 121–22; at *Colored American*, 122; connections to other members of press, 19; *Turning the Tables on the Overseer*, 125; *Weekly Anglo-African*, relaunch of, 120. See also *Weekly Anglo-African*
Hamilton, Thomas: *Anglo-African Magazine*, founds, 122; biographical information, 121–22; book publisher, 124; at *Colored American*, 122; connections to other members of press, 19; newspaper, role of, 8; *Turning the Tables on the Overseer*, 125; *Weekly Anglo-African*, founds, 122. See also *Weekly Anglo-African*
Hamilton, William, 35–36; connections to other members of press, 19; *Freedom's Journal* connection with, 121–22; on public gatherings, 121–22
Hardenburgh, Samuel, 36
Higginson, Thomas Wentworth, 144–45
Himes, Joshua, 48
*Hints to the Colored People of the North* (M. A. Shadd), 95–97
Holland, Henry, 138
Hopper, Isaac, 71–72

immigrants, 66
imperialism, 69, 163n67
*Incidents of Travel in Central America, Chiapas, and Yucatan* (J. L. Stephens), 67

Jackson, Mattie, 13, 14; newspaper reading, account of, 11–12

Jacobs, Harriet, 13–14; newspaper reading, account of, 11–12
Jay, John, 124
Jefferson, Thomas, 5
Jones, Absalom, 4–5

King, William, 114

Lawrence, George, 176n54
*Liberator*, 24, 25, 43, 72, 101, 105
*Life of Toussaint L'Ouverture, The* (Beard), 124
Lincoln, Abraham, 13
Loguen, Jermain, 119–20
Lowery, Samuel, 107–10

Mackenzie, William Lyon, 114
Martin, John, 63, 67, 70; *The Destruction of Babylon*, 60–63
McArthur, Alexander, 103
millennialism, 44–46; abolitionism and, 47–50, 57; premillennialism versus postmillennialism, 47. See also *Colored American*
Miller, William, 4, 45, 48
*Mirror of Liberty*, 8, 11, 72
*Morning Chronicle*, 32–34
*My Bondage and My Freedom* (F. Douglass), 73

*Narrative of the Life of Frederick Douglass, an American Slave, Written by Himself* (F. Douglass), 73
nativism, 50
Nell, William C., 81; at *North Star*, 77
newspapers: decorations in homes, 63; role of, 76; simultaneity and, 78–79
New York (state): gradual emancipation law, 23, 29; gradual emancipation law parade, 29–35; property requirements for elections, 51–52

New York City: black middle class, 25–26, 71; economic possibilities, 25; 1834 riot, 42; labor unrest, 25

New York Evangelical Missionary Society of Young Men, 20

Noah, Mordechai, 32–34

*North-Side View of Slavery, A; The Refugee* (Drew), 105–6

*North Star*: black chosenness and American reform, 111; black liberation as global struggle, 80–82, 83–84, 85, 89–90, 91–94; British audience, 77–78, 85–86; British reform tradition and, 86–90; Chartists coverage, 87–88; circulation, 77; on Cuban insurrection, 83–84; 1848 revolutions, 73, 76, 78–79, 79–82, 86–90; on legal challenge to slavery, 85; local conditions, 91; *Pearl* coverage, 80–82, 84–85, 87, 88, 91; propriety, 74, 91–94; on public processions, 92–93; run of, 73; on slave insurrection, 93–94; spatial architecture, 78–79; transatlantic character, 73, 77; on violence and abolition, 81–82, 83, 88–90. *See also* Douglass, Frederick

*Notes of Canada West* (M. A. Shadd), 99, 104, 111

O'Connor, Feargus, 87

Paul, Nathaniel, 24, 30
Paul, Thomas, 21, 24
*Pearl*, 80–82, 89–90
*Pine and Palm*, 124
politics of recognition, 154n15
press: authority of, 14; distribution, 12, 14; ephemeral popularity, 12; expectations for readers, 14; freedom of, 89–90; importance in United States, 7; nationalism, creation of, 7, 8; oral tradition of, 14; unintended readers, 14–15. *See also* black press

Prince, John, 114–15
print culture, 11–12, 48, 71–72. *See also* black press

propriety: black chosenness and, 34–35, 38, 39, 91–94, 109, 111, 127, 140; black military action and, 127–28; black press and, 7–8, 10; in *Frederick Douglass' Paper*, 116–17; in *Freedom's Journal*, 8, 19, 22–23, 28, 37, 39–40, 91, 92, 93; in *North Star*, 74, 91–94; in *Provincial Freeman*, 110; in *Weekly Anglo-African*, 140

*Provincial Freeman*: America as new Babylon, 109–10; articles criticizing United States, 107–10; black chosenness, limits of, 98; black chosenness critiqued by, 8, 116–18; black chosenness unlinked from American identity, 111; black peoples as British subjects to ensure liberty, 111–15, 118; black power structures challenged by, 101–2; Canada praised by, 104–6; as Canadian, 103; circulation, 103; concerns of American annexation of Canada, 113–15; connection to *Notes of Canada West*, 104; emigration to Canada encouraged, 98, 104, 110; *Frederick Douglass' Paper*, debate with, 116–18; funding, 102, 103; identity, British over black, 98; legal protections for freedom in Canada, 106; moral and material conditions connected by, 104–6; office, 102; postmillennialism, 108–9; premillennialism, 109–10; Prince, response to, 114–15; production, 102; propriety, 110; rejection of racial solidarity as path to liberation, 116; run of, 102; on segregation, 112–13; *Voice of the Fugitive*, as response to, 101. *See also* Shadd, Mary Ann

public gatherings, 92–93; black civic life, central to, 31–32; black degradation

184   *Index*

before white audience, 129; black men drilling, 128; black middle-class concerns, 31–35, 39; black middle-class response to, 29–35; in support for Union, 125–26; whites' scorn for, 30. *See also* Fourth of July celebration

racial violence, 42
Ray, Charles B.: biographical information, 44; black American national identity, 57; as *Colored American* editor, 2, 44, 51
Refugee Home Society, 100–101
*Rights of All*, 44
R. S. D. (*North Star* correspondent), 86–87
Ruggles, David, 8, 11, 71–72
Russwurm, John Brown: biographical information, 21; disillusionment, 38; educational background, 27; founds newspaper in Liberia, 39; as *Freedom's Journal* editor, 21; *Freedom's Journal* founding, 21; *Freedom's Journal* left by, 38. See also *Freedom's Journal*

Sears, Robert: biographical information, 53; career, 53–54; on chosenness, 52–53; *Colored American*, continued influence at, 59–65; *Colored American*, role at, 53; illustrations, publications of, 53–54. See also *Colored American*
Second Great Awakening, 47
Seminoles, 64–66
Seven Churches of Asia, 56–57
Shadd, Isaac, 103
Shadd, Mary Ann, 95–118; Bibb, relationship with, 98, 100–101; biographical information, 98–99; connections to other members of press, 19; Cornish, relationship with, 97; Delany, relationship with, 98; Douglass, relationship with, 98; emigration to Canada, 97, 99; gendered experiences, 97–98; in *North Star*, 95–97; *Provincial Freeman* founded by,

97, 101; on public gatherings, 96; Ray, relationship with, 97; returns to United States, 141; suspicious of black race-based communal identity, 98. See also *Provincial Freeman*
—works of: *Hints to the Colored People of the North*, 95–97; *Notes of Canada West*, 99, 104, 111
slaves reading newspapers, 11–13, 24–25
Smith, James McCune, 1, 2, 42–43, 156n45
Stephens, George E., 120, 123, 137–38, 139
Stephens, John Lloyd, 67
Stewart, Maria, 6

Tappan, Arthur, 71–72
Tappan, Lewis, 71–72, 114
telegraphs, 76
*Temple of the Sun at Nineveh, The*, 60–63, 67–68
Thirteenth Amendment, 147–48
Tobitt, J. H., 160n36
Turner, Henry McNeal, 144
*Turning the Tables on the Overseer* (R. and T. Hamilton), 125
21st U.S. Colored Infantry, 142

Vandyne, Robert H., 129–33
Van Rensselaer, Thomas, 1, 2
*Voice of the Fugitive*, 101–2

Walker, David, 21, 24, 82–83, 119; *Appeal to the Coloured Citizens of the World*, 40–41
Walker, William, 142
Ward, Samuel Ringgold, 10, 103, 104, 106; *Autobiography of a Fugitive Negro*, 100
Watkins, William J., 107
Weaver, Elisha, 144
*Weekly Advocate*. See *Colored American*
*Weekly Anglo-African*, 119–41; advertisements, 125; black liberation through military action, 120–21, 127–33; on black military preparedness,

*Weekly Anglo-African* (*continued*) 136–39; circulation, 123; connects black readers across country, 123; criticisms for Union, 137–38; Delany's *Blake* serialization, 134–39; Emancipation Proclamation and Union fight for black liberation, 139; encourages readers to educate freedpeople, 121; endorses black military activity, 137, 139–40; fight for enslaved people, not government, 121; funding, 124; on government protection of rights, 147; newspaper as advocacy, 123; offices, 124–25; on postemancipation propriety, 140; racial unity for uplift, 140; relaunch by Robert Hamilton, 124; renamed *Pine and Palm*, 176n54; role of, 8; run of, 122; self-emancipation, accounts of, 138; shapes black response to war, 120–21, 129; sold to Lawrence and Redpath, 124; transnational cause, 124; in Union camps, 123–24, 139–40; in U.S. Navy ships, 173n17; as wartime newspaper, 120; white readers, 120

White, Garland H., 145–47
Whitfield, James M., 107, 117
Wilson, William J. ("Ethiop"), 122–23
Winthrop, John, 5
Wright, Theodore S., 71

Young, Henry, 138

www.ingramcontent.com/pod-product-compliance
Lightning Source LLC
Chambersburg PA
CBHW011745220426
43666CB00018B/2902